THE
100-YEAR
DECISION

Texas A&M and the SEC

R. Bowen Loftin
with Rusty Burson

First published by Dog Ear Publishing
4010 W. 86th Street, Ste H
Indianapolis, IN 46268
www.dogearpublishing.net

ISBN: 978-1-4575-3235-1

Library of Congress Control Number: has been applied for

This book is printed on acid-free paper.

Printed in the United States of America

Dedication

If you have ever observed me during a commencement ceremony at Texas A&M or at Mizzou, you may have noticed that I spend a little extra time with some of the graduates as their names are called and they cross the stage to shake my hand (or give me a "high five," fist bump, hug or something similar). I make sure that each student-athlete is known to me as his/her name is called. When they get to me, I take the extra time to tell them something like this: "You have been a student-athlete here. At a place like this, being a student and being an athlete are each full-time endeavors. I congratulate you both on receiving your diploma today and on the manner in which you represented our great university!" It is to these student-athletes—extraordinary men and women all—that I dedicate this book. The move of Texas A&M to the Southeastern Conference was for you. – R. Bowen Loftin

To my great friend, editor and Aggie mentor, Homer Jacobs, who left us way too soon. To my wife, Vannessa, and our three kids, Payton, Kyleigh and Summer, for allowing me to sit on the couch with a laptop and write—night after night after night—and never complaining about it. And to all the student-athletes I've had the privilege to work with through the years at Texas A&M. I've always cherished my association with Aggie athletics. (John 8:32) – Rusty Burson

Acknowledgements

Many individuals deserve my thanks and deep appreciation for their contributions, both to the move of Texas A&M University to the Southeastern Conference and to the writing of this book. First and foremost, my co-author—Rusty Burson—must be acknowledged for his writing skills, his patience and his perseverance. We spent many hours together as I told him the story. He then did the research to "fill in the blanks" and wrote drafts that I reviewed and edited. Without him, this book could not have been done.

To former Regent Jim Wilson and former TAMU Vice President Jason Cook, I give my heartfelt gratitude. Jim and I worked together countless hours for over two years. He kept me sane when our efforts seemed to be in vain. He took a lot of undeserved abuse from a lot of angry Aggies, but Jim never lost his focus on the goal. He is a true Aggie, through and through. To Jason, Texas A&M and I owe so much. He had the job of shaping our public image, especially in 2011. We both knew we were often "late to the gate" in 2010, and we learned from that experience. As we approached our second run at membership in the SEC, Jason plotted our marketing course and made sure that it was our message that was the first to go out.

To former Regent and Chair, Dr. Richard Box, and to Regent Jim Schwertner, I simply thank them for believing that Texas A&M belonged in the SEC and in doing all in their power to keep the system leadership supporting our efforts. Their counsel was always "spot on," and they were always there—on the phone or in the meetings providing stability and wisdom. Their friendship means the world to me. Regent Cliff Thomas became engaged in 2011 and was firm in his support of our goals. As the book records, I am thankful to Regent and former Chair Morris Foster for a specific piece of guidance in 2010 that kept our sights on the SEC.

A special note of thanks goes to Southeastern Conference Commissioner Mike Slive, a brilliant leader, a truly wise man and a wily negotiator. His vision for the SEC has built it into the premier athletic conference in the land. Our many, many 7:15 a.m. telephone conversations were critical throughout our journey, and his personal friendship is priceless.

There are many others who know who they are—too numerous to mention here—to whom my appreciation is also extended.

Finally, to Aggies everywhere who, like me, were convinced early on that the SEC was the right place for Texas A&M. Thanks and Gig 'em!

TABLE OF CONTENTS

CHAPTER 1

Fact Is Stranger Than Fiction

By nature, I'm an analytical, systematic, numbers-oriented person. That's just how my mind works. These reflective and methodical traits helped me pursue a bachelor's degree in physics from Texas A&M University and later earn masters and doctoral degrees from Rice University.

Throughout most of my professional career, I continued to follow along a scholarly, analytical path, serving as professor at various universities in fields such as physics, computer science, electrical and computer engineering, and industrial and systems engineering. At the University of Houston, I was the director of the National Aeronautics and Space Administration (NASA) Virtual Environments Research Institute. At Old Dominion University, I served as executive director of the Virginia Modeling, Analysis and Simulation Center. I've also served as a consultant to government agencies, as well as private and public corporations, in areas of modeling and simulation, advanced training technologies, and scientific/engineering data visualization. I read scholarly journals, and I've always genuinely enjoyed the pursuit of research in fields such as artificial intelligence and searching for solutions to multifaceted scientific issues by modeling and simulating complex processes.

In other words, nothing in my background—absolutely, positively nothing at all—would have led anyone who knew me as recently as 2009 to predict that I would one day author a first-person, athletics-focused book. They certainly would not have expected me to recount my involvement in developments that have reshaped the future makeup of major college athletics conferences. In the past, I've written or coauthored plenty of technical publications geared toward academia. But a sports book? By me? No way!

My students from the 1980s, 1990s, and early 2000s would have likely burst into laughter at the mere suggestion of something that would have struck them as so utterly preposterous. In the university setting, I've never been mistaken for being a jock, a coach, an athletics administrator, or even a "sports guy." I am fairly certain that the students I taught viewed me as the bow tie-wearing, bespectacled computer sciences/simulation specialist (or geek?), who probably spent most of his Saturday afternoons writing research papers, not watching football games. Quite frankly, that description has some truth in it. Throughout my teaching career, I was asked for my professional input or to share my research and discoveries at numerous conferences devoted to physics, engineering and computer science. But never in a million years would I have once envisioned anyone valuing my opinions or my analytical conclusions regarding athletics conferences.

Yet, fact is indeed sometimes stranger than fiction. And thanks to an unusual sequence of events that no one could have predicted, I was placed—provisionally, at first—in a position of presidential leadership at Texas A&M in 2009. Following another unforeseen chain of events, I subsequently came to lead the internal decision-making processes in 2010 and 2011 that would ultimately determine the future direction of Texas A&M athletics and its conference affiliation for (in my words) the next one hundred years or more. We made those decisions based entirely on the best interests of Texas A&M, but the domino effect of the choices we made on A&M's behalf in 2010 and 2011 have continued to reverberate from the Deep South to the Pacific Northwest, altering the national landscape of college athletics as we know it.

Much has happened as a result of the momentous choices facing Texas A&M during this pivotal time. Although my mind is accustomed to working with mathematical equations, the statistical odds against what actually transpired in 2011, 2012, 2013, and at the start of 2014 . . . well, quite frankly, I can't even begin to fathom the improbability of it all.

For me personally, the implausibility factor reached an all-time high and came full circle during the closing minutes of the Cotton Bowl on January 3, 2014, in Arlington, Texas. The University of Missouri's football team was wrapping up the SEC's tenth Cotton Bowl win in the last eleven years over a Big 12 opponent, and the Tigers would finish the year ranked in the top five of the final *Associated Press* poll. Mizzou, which had been picked near the bottom of the SEC standings in the

2013 preseason polls, was one of the nation's most surprising success stories. After plenty of naysayers claimed that Missouri had no business in the SEC, the Tigers had won the league's East Division title and had clearly proven that they belonged in the league of champions. I was privileged to attend the 2014 Cotton Bowl at AT&T Stadium almost one month to the day from when I was officially introduced as the new chancellor at Missouri, equivalent to president at Texas A&M, and I certainly took pride in the fact that the decisions we made on A&M's behalf in 2010 and 2011 had somewhat paralleled those made at Missouri, perhaps smoothing the way for the Tigers to become the fourteenth member of the SEC. During the closing minutes of Missouri's 41–31 victory over Oklahoma State, I was also struck by the similarity of Missouri's 2013 season with Texas A&M's 2012 season. In the words of the great baseball "philosopher" Yogi Berra, "it was like déjà vu all over again."

One year earlier, Texas A&M, led by then first-year head coach Kevin Sumlin and sensational quarterback Johnny Manziel, had also scored forty-one points en route to soundly defeating another Big 12 foe from the other side of the Red River in the Cotton Bowl. The Aggies trounced Oklahoma 41-13 to conclude a magical season in which A&M had captivated the country's attention as Manziel became the first freshman to win the Heisman Trophy, and A&M finished its first season in the powerful SEC ranked in the top five of the national polls for the first time since the mid-1950s. A&M was one of the great Cinderella stories in all of college football in 2012, just as Missouri would become in 2013. Imagine the odds against that scenario playing out when the two schools first joined the SEC.

Texas A&M and Missouri will forever be members of the SEC family. Both schools left an atmosphere of uncertainty and inequality in the Big 12 in favor of a far more stable environment in the SEC. I believe that both schools are significantly better off in the SEC than they ever were or could have been in the Big 12. Texas A&M and Missouri also bring tremendous value to their new conference in terms of revenue opportunities, part of the reason why, according to the official SEC website, the conference and ESPN signed a "landmark broadcast rights agreement" through 2034 for a multiplatform network; both schools are most certainly linked by the 100-year decisions Texas A&M

made in 2010 and 2011. From my perspective as the former president of Texas A&M and the current chancellor of Missouri, I am certain that joining the SEC was the best choice for both of these outstanding universities.

Unlike the Big 12 when A&M and Mizzou were members of that league, there is no revenue distribution hierarchy in the SEC. There are no favored few at the top or second-class citizens at the bottom. Instead, each member institution is valued, treated, and paid equally— what a concept! Being part of such a satisfying, mutually beneficial partnership would not have been possible for Texas A&M or for Missouri if different decisions had been made in 2010 and 2011. Though it was impossible to imagine at the time that Texas A&M's choices would also effect Missouri as well, that is exactly what happened. Perhaps it was all meant to be.

It's been said that "choices are the hinges of destiny," and I believe history will reflect that we at Texas A&M acted thoughtfully, proactively, strategically, judiciously, and bravely in ultimately making the move to the SEC. But we did not act antagonistically toward longtime rivals in our home state. We didn't draw a line in the sand, and we didn't set out to cause a national commotion or to break off regional rivalries that dated back more than a century.

Texas A&M was backed into a corner and responded to the circumstances at hand in the same calculated and courageous manner that has defined this University since its early days as a small, all-male, military school on the Brazos River. Long before A&M developed a prestigious academic reputation, the school was most known for producing valiant men who were willing to take a stand for what they believed to be right. In that same spirit and tradition, we acted in A&M's best interests.

The resulting decisions altered the country's college athletics landscape. That's not an exaggeration. Texas A&M was at the epicenter of the college athletics universe for a couple of years. These changes factored significantly in the chaotic conference realignment frenzy at that time and played a role in the state of Texas producing two consecutive Heisman Trophy winners.

Back in 2010, for example, the path that others would have chosen for us would have led Texas A&M to the Pac-10, just as the University of Texas had attempted clandestinely to arrange it. The ripple effect of that move, however, would have created the equivalent of a tsunami sweeping across college athletics. If Texas A&M would have merely accepted the Longhorns' 2010 plans, it would have paved the way for the Pac-10 to add Texas, Texas Tech, Colorado, Oklahoma, Oklahoma State, and A&M, becoming the "Pac-16." In all likelihood, the powers-that-be in the new league would have pushed to expedite the expansion details in order to begin play in time for the fall of 2011.

Think about the consequences. This would have gutted the Big 12 Conference, potentially leaving its remaining members scrambling to find another conference affiliation. It is quite possible that the expansion of the Pac-10 could have ushered in the four, sixteen-team, super-conference era, as the SEC, ACC, and Big Ten would have likely felt pressured to respond to the Pac-16's expansion into Middle America. In all likelihood, there would have been sixty-four schools in four power conferences. Dozens of other universities—from Syracuse to San Diego State, and from the University of Central Florida to Boise State—faced with fewer options for securing favorable arrangements, might have forever lost even the slightest possibility of playing on college football's biggest bowl stages.

With the demise of the Big 12 in the Lone Star State, Baylor might well have joined Conference USA, which would have seriously diminished the chances of Robert Griffin III ever generating enough national exposure to win the 2011 Heisman Trophy. If the Bears were no longer part of a major power conference, it could have been difficult for Baylor to convince donors and fans to invest in the new $260 million McLane Stadium, or to offer head football coach Art Briles a multimillion contract extension through the year 2023. Briles might have become the University of Texas head coach following Baylor's astounding run in 2013, in which the Bears won their first-ever outright Big 12 title and earned a spot in the Fiesta Bowl. All of this would have become much more likely if A&M had simply agreed to be part of the Pac-16 plan.

Elsewhere in Texas, Big East-bound Texas Christian University would have never joined a Big 12 that no longer existed, and the University of Texas probably would have attempted to circumvent the Pac-16's television agreements to deliver a yet-to-be-revealed Longhorn Network from Central Texas to Southern California.

From Texas A&M's perspective, however, the geography of the Pac-16 move looked problematic: Would Texas A&M recruiters and coaches be able to compete effectively in a conference with a center of gravity located so far to the west? Another concern was the cultural fit. Texas A&M has been ranked among America's most conservative universities by the *Princeton Review;* that is a simple fact of our demographics. Would our students, supporters, coaches, and teams really feel at home among schools like Cal Berkeley, Oregon, Colorado, and Washington, all ranked by the *Princeton Review* among the nation's most liberal universities?

All of that could have so easily happened if A&M officials had not made the decision to tap the brakes on the Longhorns' mass exodus plans, which had been orchestrated behind closed doors with Pac-10 commissioner Larry Scott. At first, I was somewhat blindsided by the Longhorns' audacity in playing the puppeteer role for so many other schools. As will become apparent in later chapters, UT officials had basically attempted to determine our future conference destination without even bothering to ask us for our opinion. In addition to charting A&M's future, Texas was also making groundbreaking decisions for numerous other universities, believing that all the other schools would merrily load up the westward-bound, burnt-orange bus and go along for the ride.

At Texas A&M, we were not content to blithely board the Bevo Express. If going west was truly in the best interest of Texas A&M, we would first need to consider all the options and consequences and then map out our own course. We would not, under any circumstances, relinquish control of our destiny to Texas or any other school. Nor would we act hastily or feebly.

As I will describe in much greater detail in ensuing chapters, our first major step in determining Texas A&M's future conference affiliation was to simply delay the Pac-16 stampede. We needed time to gather our thoughts and to determine which conference affiliation would be best for our long-term future. As university administrators and Board of Regents members, our duty was to take a team-oriented approach to assessing the pros and cons of staying in our existing conference or making a move. This was clearly a landmark decision that would affect generations of future Texas A&M student-athletes, coaches, students, and fans, and we believed it was imperative to take a big-picture, long-term approach.

We considered conference structures, the welfare of student-athletes as a result of frequent travel to different time zones, the overall revenue potential of the various leagues, the opportunity to increase national exposure, marketing, branding and licensing, academic prestige, traditional rivalries, the culture of conference members, and more. Our decision needed to be based on which conference provided Texas A&M with the best combination of "fit," benefits and opportunities over the course of a century, as opposed to continually grasping for short-term payoffs or feeling constrained by regional boundaries.

In other words, we took a look back at how the Big 12 Conference was originally formed in the mid-1990s . . . and vowed not to make those same glaring mistakes again. To a lesser degree, we also considered the breakup of the Southwest Conference, the reasons behind its demise, and how Texas A&M could have chosen a different conference direction—if not for the political pressures of the times—twenty years before we actually moved to the SEC. If ever philosopher and novelist George Santayana's admonition applied—"Those who cannot remember the past are condemned to repeat it"—it was now. External threats had forced A&M and Texas to merge with Baylor and Texas Tech and join the Big Eight to form the Big 12 in the mid-1990s. But giving into fear is a poor chisel with which to carve out tomorrow. We remembered, and we were determined not to be pressured again into an obligatory union.

This time, we acted more thoughtfully in our own best interests. We first decided, in 2010, that it was best to explore all of our options, including the possibility of moving to the SEC. This temporary delay almost certainly frustrated Texas officials, who'd hoped to avoid political pressures (from local, statewide, and national sources) with a quick exit. Our delay also saved the Big 12, although not entirely. Colorado went ahead with its move to the Pac-10 that year, and Nebraska left for the Big Ten.

We reached our tipping point of exasperation with Texas the following summer, when UT first announced the launch of the Longhorn Network, and explored—or, some might say, flaunted—how it might use that network to give itself recruiting advantages and distance itself financially even more from the rest of the Big 12. At that point, I reengaged SEC commissioner Mike Slive, whom I'd befriended the previous summer, and laid the groundwork for what I referred to later as a "100-year decision." In the summer of 2010, A&M students and former students expressed mixed emotions about whether we should stay in the Big 12, move to the Pac-16, or pursue membership in the SEC. In 2011, however, it was my sense that our fan and former student base had reached the consensus that we could no longer trust Texas in this arena, and that our best option was to go to the SEC. As Texas A&M's marketing expert Jason Cook likes to say, we needed a dragon to slay; Texas became that dragon, and membership in the SEC became the reward for boldly stepping out on our own.

It was a great move for Texas A&M, and one that the SEC readily embraced, until Baylor—a school that had faced tremendous uncertainty the year before until we at Texas A&M decided to stay in the Big 12—began threatening to sue anyone involved with our transition to the SEC. Baylor president Ken Starr, who'd once been at the center of the Bill Clinton-Monica Lewinsky investigation, alleged "tortious interference," a claim that was ultimately judged to have no merit. Fortunately, the legal threats did not stop but only delayed our move, and we all enjoyed a spectacular celebration on September 26, 2011, when we were officially introduced as the thirteenth member of the Southeastern Conference. Thanks to an aggressive marketing and brand awareness plan crafted and guided by Cook, we capitalized on the move by winning public relations battles in the media, strategically shaping our own messages, and taking the University brand to unprecedented new heights. Everything was going smoothly, except what was transpiring on the football field.

Our football team, under the direction of then–head coach Mike Sherman, was good enough in 2011 to take the lead against twelve of the thirteen opponents we played. Unfortunately, we displayed no killer instinct or staying power and blew double-digit leads in five of our six losses. The final straw came on Thanksgiving night before a capacity crowd of 88,645 at Kyle Field, when we lost to a mediocre University of Texas team on a last-second field goal that completely sucked the air out of Kyle Field. It also temporarily ended the 118-year rivalry, because then–Texas athletic director DeLoss Dodds stated publicly that he refused to play A&M anymore in any sport once we made the decision to go to the SEC.

Following the frustrating loss to Texas, we made the difficult decision to fire Sherman, who'd compiled a 25–25 record in four seasons as head coach at A&M. He was a good man and had done a really good job recruiting. But I and others did not believe he was the right coach to be leading us into the SEC. That conclusion should also have been evident to then–A&M director of athletics Bill Byrne. But Byrne maintained support for Sherman, and he was already angry that he had been largely kept out of the loop in our behind-the-scenes meetings regarding our plans to move to the SEC. Byrne had been heavily involved in our 2010 meetings and discussions, but it quickly became obvious to me that there were too many leaks in A&M Athletics. We determined that it was in Texas A&M's best interest to not share sensitive information with Byrne—a decision that I assumed would anger him. In the end, the way Sherman was fired was a complete disaster, and should never have happened. It was certainly not handled in the manner we had planned.

Nevertheless, we knew the firing was a necessity. Texas A&M needed a new coach with new energy and a different mindset for its start in our new conference. Kevin Sumlin, then the head coach at the University of Houston, was the perfect fit for A&M in the same way the Aggies were a perfect fit for the SEC. Sumlin exuded tremendous confidence; he was an offensive innovator; he was a fantastic recruiter; and he was obviously a true college coach. Sherman, who'd spent many years in the NFL, seemed to have difficulty adjusting to the college game. To me, during games, he appeared mostly stoic, detached, and rigid: an offensive coordinator at heart, much more than a head coach. I believed that he expected players to run plays exactly as he had designed and would not tolerate improvisation on the run, especially from his quarterback.

If Sherman had not been fired, Sumlin would have likely left the University of Houston instead to fill the opening at Arizona State, and Heisman Trophy winner Johnny Manziel (if he started at all) may have instead played receiver at A&M or possibly served as a backup quarterback to Jameill Showers, who was the more pure, drop-back pocket passer that Sherman clearly coveted for his traditional, pro-style offense. In other words, if Sherman had not been fired, there may have been no 2012 Heisman Trophy winner at A&M, no 2013 Cotton Bowl, no top-five finish, and no monumental upset at Alabama.

In addition to the 20–6 record the Aggies produced during Manziel's two seasons as quarterback, the excitement Johnny generated played a role in determining the magnitude of the $450 million redevelopment of Kyle Field. A&M officials were already committed to making upgrades to Kyle Field. But Sumlin's golden touch, Manziel's fabulous feats, and an 11–2 season in 2012 helped lead to making the scope of the project the most comprehensive redevelopment in the history of college athletics.

Manziel may have had the most positive impact of any player in the history of Texas A&M. Following the conclusion of the 2013 season, Dat Nguyen, who belongs on the Mount Rushmore of Aggie football, called Manziel the greatest Aggie ever to wear the maroon and white uniform. And if he's not the greatest player in college football history—even after just two mesmerizing seasons—he is certainly one of the most exciting and captivating. As longtime columnist and radio talk-show host Randy Galloway wrote in the *Fort Worth Star-Telegram* on January 4, 2014, after Manziel's spectacular performance in the 2013 Chick-fil-A Bowl: "For starters, he put Texas A&M on the national map, which also includes the SEC map. Johnny did it in that conference, not the weaker Big 12. Better yet for the Aggies, that map now shows College Station with a bigger dot than, oh, say, Austin. First time ever for that to happen."

Imagine what a shame it would have been for Texas A&M and all college football fans if Manziel had never played quarterback for the Aggies. If Manziel had not broken new ground in becoming the first freshman to win the Heisman Trophy in 2012, one might wonder whether Jameis Winston would have won it as a freshman in 2013. Imagine how different the college athletics universe would be today if A&M had joined Texas, Texas Tech, Oklahoma, Oklahoma State, and Colorado in the Pac-16. How different would things be for Baylor, TCU, Kansas State, Kansas, and so many other schools?

Now, more than ever before, I am convinced that we made the right decision for Texas A&M by choosing not to go to the Pac-10 in 2010. We made the right decision by joining the SEC in 2011. And we made the right personnel decisions in 2012. British Prime Minister

Benjamin Disraeli once said that the secret of success in life is for a man to be ready for his opportunity when it comes. This is the story of how we seized opportunities and positioned Texas A&M for long-term success, which also positively affected many other universities. More than that, though, this is a story that epitomizes the power of choices. In life, we first make decisions. Then our decisions make us. This is the story of how we made the decisions that will impact college athletics for many years to come.

CHAPTER 2

The Dysfunctional Dozen

On April 24, 2013, CBSSportsline.com posted an interesting timeline detailing the chaos of conference realignment, beginning in the summer of 2005 when Boston College finalized its move to the ACC and concluding with the fifteen members of the Atlantic Coast Conference agreeing to a grant of rights (GOR) on April 22, 2013. Along with the comprehensive timeline, CBSSportsline.com boldly predicted that the ACC's actions—announced in conjunction with the Bowl Championship Series (BCS) commissioners' official unveiling of the College Football Playoff—would put an end to the realignment madness as we know it for the foreseeable future. Essentially, the GOR means that if ACC members leave for another league, their TV rights, along with tens of millions of dollars, will not follow the individual schools. Those rights will be retained by the ACC.

"So schools don't leave," wrote CBSSportline.com senior college football columnist Dennis Dodd. "It hasn't happened in the Big Ten since members agreed to a grant of rights in 1988. The Big 12—after a couple of contentious years—is good with a GOR until the end of its TV deal in 2025. The Pac-12 has one. The only BCS league that doesn't have one is the SEC. And you've got to be crazy to leave the SEC . . ."

I have no idea if conference shuffling has truly come to an end now that there are five highly-branded power conferences (SEC, ACC, Pac-12, Big Ten, and Big 12), and I certainly would not be willing to make a similar prediction. But I completely concur with the last part of Dodd's statement regarding the SEC. No school has left the Southeastern Conference since Tulane in 1966. And now that Texas A&M and Missouri are members of the SEC, I believe both schools intend to plant roots deeply and stay there for generations to come. For numerous reasons, both schools are ideal fits in the SEC . . . after leaving less than ideal circumstances in the Big 12.

Upon becoming the twenty-fourth president of Texas A&M, I could not possibly have envisioned the twists and turns, highs and lows, senses of deception and elation, and promises and threats that Texas A&M would encounter over the course of the next three years. Nor did I have the background, at the time, to recognize that the decisions we were making regarding Texas A&M's future conference destination were actually pondered by school officials twenty years earlier.

The reality is that, while CBSSportsline.com compiled a terrific timeline about the modern era of schools changing conferences, the roots of realignment can be traced back to the late 1970s and the creation of the College Football Association (CFA), and to the early 1980s when the University of Oklahoma and the University of Georgia first sued the NCAA over control of their television rights. In 1977, the CFA was formed as an alliance of sixty-four schools from the major conferences and a handful of independents. Then in 1979, the CFA, through its executive director Chuck Neinas, began to negotiate a TV contract with NBC for its members. But the NCAA, which had an existing and exclusive contract at that time with ABC, quickly intervened, threatening to place all universities that participated in the CFA contract on probation in football and other sports, as well.

From 1940—the date of the first televised college football game—until the United States Supreme Court ruled in June 1984 in favor of the schools, the NCAA maintained an absolute stranglehold on the TV market, controlling the rights of its member institutions. Until that time, only one network (ABC from 1965 to 1981) broadcast college football games, and since the NCAA monopolized the TV inventory of all of its schools, member institutions were all paid equally . . . and rather poorly. The amount of payment was determined by the NCAA's television program director. For example, in an incident that was later documented in the Supreme Court's decision, Number 1 USC defeated Number 2 Oklahoma on September 26, 1981, in a game that appeared on two hundred television stations in a regional broadcast. During that same weekend, ABC also televised The Citadel-Appalachian State game that appeared on four stations. Yet, all four teams received the same amount of money for appearing on TV. Ultimately, the Supreme Court's decision in the summer of 1984 that the NCAA's plan violated the Sherman and Clayton Antitrust

Acts opened the door for individual schools to begin negotiating their own television rights. College football games began appearing on multiple networks, including ESPN, soon thereafter.

The timing of that decision was great for Texas A&M, which played a huge role in ESPN's early increase in popularity the following year. In 1985, Jackie Sherrill's Aggies finished the year with four impressive wins to earn the school's first outright Southwest Conference championship and first Cotton Bowl bid in eighteen years. Three of those games were at home against fellow contenders SMU, Arkansas, and Texas. All three were at night, and all three were broadcast from Kyle Field on ESPN, a network which had not initially attracted many viewers for its college football broadcasts in 1984 and early in 1985. Those Saturday night games at Kyle Field, however, generated impressive primetime ratings, and both ESPN and A&M benefited tremendously moving forward from the 1985 "November to remember."

The Southwest Conference as a whole, on the other hand, was a big loser in the deregulated days of the mid- and late-1980s, even though it had once shone brightly on the national stage. In the 1930s, SMU, TCU, and Texas A&M each won national titles. The postwar 1940s gave Southwest Conference fans heroes like SMU's Doak Walker and Kyle Rote, Texas' Bobby Layne and Rice's James "Froggy" Williams, captain of the Owls' 1949 SWC title team. The early 1950s produced celebrated names like Yale Lary of A&M, Dicky Maegle of Rice, and Raymond Berry of SMU, while the late 1950s produced players such as Jim Swink of TCU and John David Crow of A&M, who were coached by legends like Abe Martin and Bear Bryant. From 1963 to 1970, Darrell Royal's Texas teams won three national titles, and All-Americans like Jerry Sisemore (Texas), Roosevelt Leaks (Texas), Louie Kelcher (SMU), Pat Thomas (A&M), Ed Simonini (A&M), Wilson Whitley (Houston), Tommy Kramer (Rice), Robert Jackson (A&M), Tony Franklin (A&M), Gary Green (Baylor), Earl Campbell (Texas), Johnnie Johnson (Texas), Emanuel Tolbert (SMU), Steve McMichael (Texas), and Mike Singletary (Baylor) filled the star-studded rosters.

"It would be hard to exaggerate the excitement that the first kiss of autumn generated at all levels of Texas society," wrote Gary Cartwright in a 1995 *Sports Illustrated* article bidding adieu to the SWC.

"As early as 1934 the air was literally filled with Southwest Conference football, thanks to the Humble Radio Network, the nation's first broadcast network. You couldn't visit a drugstore or barbershop or even walk along a sidewalk without hearing the roar of the crowd and the boom of the marching bands at Kyle Field or the Cotton Bowl—or the voice of Humble's master of word pictures, Kern Tips. . . . You didn't have to be college-educated to have a favorite team. Service stations operated by Humble Oil & Refining Company, which also owned the radio network, gave out pennant-shaped window decals, each with the colors and name of a conference school. Bank presidents with degrees from SMU and pipefitters who hadn't finished third grade displayed their choices on the rear windows of their cars. Millions of Texans from Beaumont to Laredo to Amarillo never saw a game but lived and died from Saturday to Saturday with the Frogs, Mustangs, Bears, Longhorns, Aggies, Owls, Hogs—and later the Red Raiders and Cougars. In our division of loyalty we discovered unity: Everyone loved the Southwest Conference."

Then along came the 1980s and the disbanding of the brotherhood. Prior to 1984, when the NCAA had the market cornered on TV rights, the SWC and other leagues didn't need to market or sell themselves. Every league, from the Pac-10 to the Big Ten and from the SEC to the SWC, received the same amount of television money, so it didn't matter how regionalized one conference was compared to another, or how many major television markets were located within the footprint of the league. In the aftermath of the 1984 Supreme Court decision, however, the dynamics for conference marketability and generating revenues changed dramatically.

Among all major conferences, the SWC—with eight schools located within the Lone Star State and only Arkansas positioned outside of its boundaries—was clearly the nation's most regionalized league. And that was only one of several major issues eroding the SWC. Private schools like TCU, SMU, and Rice—all located in major metropolitan areas—had rarely been highly competitive in the 1960s and 1970s, a time period when professional sports teams in the Dallas and Houston markets began winning sports fans who had once attended SWC games in those locations. As the bottom of the SWC became less and less competitive, marquee matchups and attendance figures began to dwindle across the league. In 1978, the nine SWC schools averaged 45,182 fans per game. In 1986, less than a decade later, those same schools attracted an average of 37,862 fans per game (a decrease of 7,320 fans per game). In comparison, the SEC averaged 63,070 fans per home game in 1986, while the Big Ten averaged 65,686.

The small, private schools were often responsible for the weakest crowds. In November 1984, Baylor played at Rice before an announced crowd of 11,125, while co-champion SMU played Arkansas in a marquee matchup in Dallas that attracted only 28,712. Larger schools like A&M also played before plenty of empty seats. On November 24, 1984, A&M played Number 17 TCU at Kyle Field before an announced crowd of only 38,209.

Even winning big did not necessarily cure the apathy epidemic. SMU made a dramatic turnaround in the early- and mid-1980s, going 10-1 in 1981 and rising to as high as Number 2 in the final national polls following the Mustangs' unbeaten (11-0-1) 1982 season. But an 8-1 SMU team finished the 1981 home schedule against Texas Tech before a crowd of just 24,410.

While SMU's on-the-field success did not consistently generate big crowds, it did generate big penalties and problems, as the school was placed on NCAA probation for two years for violating recruiting rules in 1981. In 1985, SMU received three more years of NCAA probation, and in 1987, the Mustangs were handed the harshest punishment—before or since—in what became known as the "death penalty." Texas A&M also came under intense media and investigative scrutiny during the Sherrill era because of NCAA violations, and by the end of the 1980s, six of the nine SWC schools had been penalized at some level by the NCAA. The negative national publicity from the probation scandals, along with the in-state backstabbing, further weakened the product on the field, as more and more of the top Texas high school players chose to leave the SWC for other leagues in other states.

"By the late 1980s, the retention rate by the SWC of the state's top 100 prospects, as identified by the *Dallas Morning News*, dwindled to sixty percent," wrote Ivan Maisel, who has worked as a college football columnist or beat writer for the *Dallas Morning News, Newsday, Sports Illustrated*, and ESPN.com. "The better the player, the more likely he would be to leave. From 1980 to 1984, of the eighteen

All-Americans who listed Texas cities or towns as their homes, twelve (66.7 percent) attended SWC schools. In the next five-year period, (1985–89), seventeen Texas residents won All-America recognition. Only five (29.4 percent) played in the SWC. Tim Brown, the Notre Dame wide receiver who won the 1987 Heisman Trophy, grew up in Dallas and attended Woodrow Wilson High. Brown narrowed his choice to SMU and Notre Dame. On the day before the signing date, Brown claimed, SMU recruiters made promises that would have broken NCAA rules. He went to Notre Dame, where he spearheaded the Fighting Irish's resurgence under head coach Lou Holtz. Other Texans who achieved greatness elsewhere included quarterback Ty Detmer of Brigham Young, tailback Thurman Thomas of Oklahoma State, linebackers Brian Bosworth of Oklahoma and Alfred Williams of Colorado, and center Jake Young of Nebraska."

As the SWC's image continued to decline, another event expedited the league's demise. While the CFA didn't officially cease to exist until June 30, 1997, it began to unravel in 1990 when Notre Dame and NBC agreed to an exclusive contract that paid the Irish $7.6 million a year, an outlandishly lucrative figure at the time. Penn State, another high-profile and successful independent football program, joined the Big Ten early in 1990, and in August 1990, the University of Arkansas's Board of Trustees voted to end the school's seventy-six-year association with the Southwest Conference and accept an invitation to join the Southeastern Conference. Arkansas's departure ultimately doomed the SWC, but first it truly kick-started the first full-scale wave of major conference realignment. A month after Arkansas made its announcement, South Carolina followed the Razorbacks to the SEC. Florida State then joined the ACC, and the Big East, which had been only a basketball conglomerate throughout the 1980s, embraced football and added Miami, Rutgers, West Virginia, Virginia Tech, and Temple in 1991.

As the college athletics landscape shifted, it became apparent that conferences that could deliver the largest number of viewers on any given Saturday would also receive the majority of television dollars. Members of those conferences would also receive the most national exposure, which would help schools attract more high-profile recruits. The SWC, with eight schools all located within Texas and only six percent national television viewership at the time, did not have a promising long-term future in its weakened status. After Arkansas accepted the invitation from the SEC, predictions were immediately made that this was merely the beginning of the SWC's downfall. In a July 31, 1990, article in the *Chicago Tribune*, for example, reporter Ed Sherman wrote: "There's strong speculation that Arkansas's defection opens the door for Texas and Texas A&M to follow suit. The SEC covets the large television markets in Texas, and both schools are said to be wary of staying in the SWC now that Arkansas is gone. Neither school would comment on the situation."

While neither school was offering public commentary, officials at both universities were exploring their options and creating contacts in other leagues. Roughly a week after the newspapers reported that the SEC might be a destination for the Aggies and Longhorns, the now-defunct *Dallas Times-Herald* ran a story claiming that A&M and Texas had more interest in joining the Pac-10, which was also interested in expanding. According to the *Times-Herald*, the Aggies and Longhorns were looking to join quickly, "before the issue of their departure becomes a political issue in the state Legislature." But the paper quoted state Sen. John Montford, D-Lubbock, saying: "The Legislature is not going to turn a deaf ear to [an attempted departure]." The *Times-Herald* also cited the financial advantages of leaving the SWC. According to their story, Pac-10 schools were paid an average $1.25 million each in 1989 from bowl, NCAA Tournament, and television revenues. In comparison, SWC schools earned an average of $700,000 each from bowl, NCAA Tournament, and television revenues. The newspaper reported that A&M and Texas were also particularly interested in the Pac-10 because of the academic fit, as many Pac-10 schools are research universities. "Do not understate the national trend for academics, compliance and accreditation," a Pac-10 athletic director, who requested anonymity, told the *Times-Herald*.

Like so many other newspaper reports during those chaotic summer days, there was probably at least some truth in the *Times-Herald* story. But the media-generated stories were changing and the situation was evolving so rapidly that it was difficult to determine fact from fiction. In early August 1990, Gene Wojciechowski of the *Los Angeles Times* wrote that Miami, Florida State, South Carolina, Texas, and

Texas A&M were all under serious consideration as potential SEC members. On August 17, though, the *Houston Post* reported that A&M and Texas appeared to be leaning toward the Pac-10 and that the University of Houston would likely be approached about SEC membership if the Aggies and Longhorns went to the west. Frank Broyles, the athletic director at Arkansas from 1974–2007, later told Kevin Sherrington of the *Dallas Morning News* that the rumors regarding a possible union between the Pac-10 and A&M and Texas were major factors in the Razorbacks' efforts to join the SEC. "We were worried about Texas and Texas A&M pulling out and leaving us for the Pac-10," Broyles said. "Where would we have been if they'd done that? What kind of athletic prestige could we [the SWC] have without those two?"

Meanwhile, on another front, SWC commissioner Fred Jacoby still had hopes of somehow—against all odds—salvaging the league. On August 20, 1990, the *Orlando Sun-Sentinel* reported that University of Miami athletic director Sam Jankovich had met with Jacoby about the possibility of the Hurricanes joining the SWC. Four days later, the *Associated Press* produced a story stating that the presidents of A&M and Texas had announced that their schools would remain in the SWC, temporarily ending speculation that the league was heading for a breakup. A statement from presidents William H. Mobley of Texas A&M and William H. Cunningham of Texas was issued, they said, because speculation regarding the situation had reached "excessive proportions." Remember, this was long before the days of Internet chat rooms or Twitter, so "excessive proportions" was only in relation to the abundance of mostly "sourced" media reports that were being generated across the state and country.

It wasn't until years later that the full truths of those times were actually disclosed. In an interview with Texas A&M's *12th Man Magazine*, R. C. Slocum, who'd replaced Jackie Sherrill as A&M head coach prior to the 1989 season, recalled attending the American Football Coaches Association meeting in the winter of 1990, where realignment talk built to a crescendo in the backrooms and hotel hallways. No one at the meeting had a clear picture of exactly what the future held for college athletics, but many coaches and administrators anticipated seismic shakeups.

"I came back to College Station and met with John David Crow, the athletic director at the time, and I told him I thought we needed to really explore our options," Slocum recalled. "John David also had heard through athletic director friends that changes were being considered in conference alignments. From there, John David and I met with Dr. Mobley, Billy Clayton, the Speaker of the Texas House of Representatives (from 1975 to 1983) and a member of our Board of Regents, and Ross Margraves, the Chairman of the Board of Regents. We all agreed that the SWC was unraveling. We didn't want to break it up, but we knew we needed to explore our options. At that time, it was rumored Texas was most interested in the Pac-10. We decided within our little group that the SEC was a better fit for us culturally. We didn't have formal talks, but I was friends with (former SEC Commissioner) Roy Kramer, and the subject came up casually. I was totally for it."

So was Crow, who confirmed in an interview for this book that he was also concerned about Texas moving to the Pac-10. He was hearing numerous rumors—from the sublime to the ridiculous—including one that involved Texas Tech being targeted by the Pac-10. After hearing that rumor and reading about so many others, Crow laid the groundwork for Texas A&M's possible entry into the SEC. At the time, any potential newcomer to the SEC first needed one of the existing member institutions to be its expansion sponsor. Crow, originally from Springhill, La., a small community in Webster Parish along the Louisiana-Arkansas state line, returned to his roots to locate the sponsor.

"I knew Joe Dean [the athletic director at LSU from 1987 to 2000] pretty well," Crow said. "I called Joe and asked him about the possibility of us joining the SEC if something happened to break up the Southwest Conference once and for all. Joe said he would be glad to be the person to nominate, push, and sponsor us for membership in the SEC. But he mentioned to me, 'John, it would be very difficult for y'all to get into the SEC alone. You need to find another school as a partner to come in with A&M.' Right off the bat, I mentioned the University of Houston. He said, 'Well, that's not what we are really looking for. Y'all already have the Houston market from a TV standpoint. We need another school with something more to offer. How about Oklahoma?' I told him that I had been thinking about SWC schools, but that I would do what I could to get OU to join us if the SWC broke up. But I then reminded him that we were only talking about a scenario if

Texas—and maybe Tech, too—left for the Pac-10. We were not trying to take the lead in breaking up the SWC, but we were ready to pull the trigger if necessary. I had coached in the SEC (as an assistant at Alabama), and I was very familiar with the SEC. I felt all along that if we were going to go anywhere, the SEC was our best fit. If that didn't work out, going to the Big Eight would be the next best fit for us."

Neither Slocum nor Crow recalled anyone associated with A&M being particularly intrigued with the Pac-10. But it appears that the Longhorns did have wandering eyes toward the west . . . long before they attempted to lead a mass exodus in that direction in 2010. In a 1997 story by former *San Antonio Express-News* investigative reporter Russell Gold, various University of Texas officials acknowledged they had strong interest in joining the Pac-10, beginning in the late 1980s. But Arkansas beat Texas to the punch in leaving the SWC. Following the Razorbacks' announcement in the summer of 1990, along with the rumor-rampant chaos that ensued, the presidents of A&M and Texas felt compelled—and pressed by legislators threatening funding cuts if the Aggies and Horns abandoned the SWC—to calm the stormy waters by announcing that the two largest state schools were not leaving any of their Lone Star State brethren behind.

Crow recalls there was initially some legitimate hope that the SWC could survive some other way. After the Mobley/Cunningham coauthored statement, Crow said one thought was to attempt to form some type of television-based, nonconference rivalry between the eight remaining SWC schools and the members of the Big Eight. "I did not see Arkansas's departure coming," Crow said. "But to me, it was a natural fit because of where they were located. It made sense when you stepped back and looked at it. Plus, Frank Broyles, who was heavily involved in the announcing of televised college football games at that time, understood how TV affected revenues better than most. But after Arkansas left and the rumors were flying, we all knew something was going to happen. In fact, the athletic directors of the SWC and the SWC commissioner went to Oklahoma City to meet with the athletic directors of the Big Eight. At first, we were trying to figure out with them a way for us to schedule games against each other—not form a new conference—but schedule so that we could both be more favorable to the television markets in both regions."

Nothing ever came from those meetings, primarily because the Big Eight schools apparently didn't see much of a benefit. Jacoby, the SWC commissioner from 1982 to 1993, had already tried unsuccessfully to lure Miami into the SWC, and he could tell immediately that the Big Eight schools did not want to discuss a full merger with the SWC or even a TV-friendly alliance. "I went over scheduling, marketing, negotiations of TV," Jacoby told Maisel in the 1995 *Athlon's Big Eight* magazine. "When I got through, they looked at me like, 'What the hell are you talking about?'"

Jacoby initially pushed the presidents of the SWC to pursue every possible expansion plan. Tulane made a pitch to the league, but in spite of Jacoby's urging, the SWC presidents and athletic directors didn't believe the private school could actually deliver the New Orleans TV market. Jacoby also suggested adding Memphis and Louisville to strengthen the league's basketball presence. But no one wanted to make a move only for basketball. As Jacoby encountered continued expansion resistance, he did what he could to keep the ship afloat.

"I failed," Jacoby told Maisel. "I spent more time trying to hold it together and trying to make changes than working on expansion."

In all likelihood, the SWC wasn't truly salvageable. Attendance continued to dwindle outside of College Station and Austin. In 1990, for example, the University of Houston went 10-1 behind the league's Offensive Player of the Year, David Klingler. But the Cougars only averaged 29,934 fans per game inside the 62,439-seat Astrodome. The conference's beleaguered reputation also hurt the strongest teams, especially after the Razorbacks began competing in the SEC in 1992. Texas A&M went 12-0 overall and 7-0 in the SWC in 1992, but the Aggies entered the Cotton Bowl with a Number 4 national ranking (behind unbeaten Alabama and Miami and once-beaten Florida State) and with no chance of winning the national title. That became a moot point when Number 5 Notre Dame manhandled A&M in the Cotton Bowl 28-3 on New Year's Day 1993, but it was apparent that under normal circumstances, the SWC's damaged reputation would prevent any of its member schools from being seriously considered as a national title contender.

That expedited a sense of urgency that A&M and UT officials had to find new homes. The Longhorns continued to look to the west. New president Robert Berdahl was impressed by the fact that seven of the ten schools in the Pac-10 were members of the Association of American Universities (AAU), a group comprising the nation's top research universities. Berdahl, who ironically left UT in 1997 to become the chancellor at Cal-Berkeley, told Mark Wangrin of the *San Antonio Express-News* in a 2005 story: "Texas wanted desperately the academic patina that the Pac-10 yielded. To be associated with UCLA, Stanford and Cal in academics was very desirable."

Apparently, the Pac-10 in the early 1990s did not yet have someone like Larry Scott, who in 2010 helped sell the existing members of the league on the benefits of expanding into Texas. As such, the Longhorns were not extended an invitation to join the Pac-10. Berdahl and others at UT then turned their attention to the Big Ten, where ten conference members belonged to the AAU. But after adding Penn State in 1990, Big Ten officials had placed a four-year freeze on expansion. Berdahl told Wangrin that the Longhorns briefly considered the SEC, but UT officials believed admissions standards to SEC schools were too lenient. "We were quite interested in raising academic standards," Berdahl said. "The Southeastern Conference had absolutely no interest in that."

A&M did not agree with Berdahl's assessment. Prior to the 1992 A&M-LSU football game in Baton Rouge, Crow and Ross Margraves met for lunch with Joe Dean and LSU System president Dr. Allen A. Copping. Both parties expressed continued interest in A&M becoming a part of the SEC. Then, following the NCAA Convention in Dallas in January 1993, Dean told reporters he believed UT was headed north, to either the Big Eight or Big Ten, while A&M was the most logical addition to the SEC. That sentiment continued into August 1993 when Margraves flew to LSU for his son's graduation, meeting with LSU chancellor William Davis to discuss A&M's potential future in the SEC. Margraves later said he favored a move.

Despite all the mutual interest, the relationship was never consummated. Crow says A&M administrators were particularly worried about a backlash from state legislators if the Aggies left on their own. Many of A&M's high-ranking athletic department leaders at the time were convinced that the SEC would have been a great fit for the Aggies. But there were so many threats—publicly and behind the scenes— being heaped toward A&M System and University leaders by lawmakers and elected officials with degrees from other SWC schools. "Austin had gotten heavily involved," Crow said. "And when I say 'Austin' I don't mean the University of Texas; I mean politicians." The University of Texas wasn't interested in going with A&M to the SEC, and the league backed off from expanding further.

But at the end of 1993, another TV-related development finally instigated the breakup of the SWC. The TV-rights marketplace changed significantly at the end of 1993, when Fox outbid CBS for the rights to televise National Football Conference games in the NFL. CBS suddenly had money to spend on its sports programming, and by February 1994, the network had negotiated a five-year, $90 million contract with the SEC and a $60 million deal over five years with the Big East. During the same month, the Atlantic Coast Conference signed separate agreements with ABC, ESPN, and Jefferson-Pilot that brought the league more than $80 million over five years.

"We would have much preferred for the CFA to have stayed together as one bargaining unit," ACC commissioner Gene Corrigan said after the three leagues had signed different deals in February 1994. "But these circumstances allowed us the opportunity to find our value in the open marketplace."

Following the SEC, Big East, and ACC deals that broke up the CFA coalition, the Big Eight and SWC agreed to negotiate a TV deal together. Initially, it was reported that the Big Eight and SWC had been offered a $60 million television deal by ABC that would jump to $70 million if the leagues merged. Because the leagues were negotiating together, it was assumed by many in the media that a merger was imminent. Even many insiders were convinced during the early negotiations that all sixteen schools from both conferences would be included in some sort of alliance, even if the two leagues didn't merge and instead formed a championship game between the winners of each conference.

"I feel TCU will be a major player regardless," former TCU athletic director Frank Windegger told the *Associated Press* on February 15, 1994. "There are lots of rumors, but I know our commitment is to being a major program, so I'm not worried."

He should have been worried. One day later, the negotiations at the Dallas/Fort Worth Airport Hyatt hit a major snag, as Berdahl announced that—unlike previously—all the stars were aligned in terms of Texas' desire to move to the Pac-10 and that he was quite content to leave the floundering SWC. Berdahl cited A&M's probation problems as an example of the SWC's inability to police its own. Just a few days after the Aggies lost to Notre Dame 24-21 in the 1994 Cotton Bowl, the NCAA announced that A&M had been banned from appearing on TV or playing in a bowl game for the 1994 season. Nine A&M players were found to have received nearly $18,000 in unearned wages from 1990 to 1992 as a result of their employment at apartment complexes operated by Warren A. Gilbert Jr., a Dallas developer. Gilbert was the president of the 12th Man Foundation, the fundraising organization of Texas A&M athletics, when the infractions occurred.

Meanwhile Berdahl had major questions about the Big Eight's acceptance of Proposition 48 students, freshmen who failed to meet the NCAA minimum academic standards for athletic eligibility. One senior UT official told the *Dallas Morning News* that Texas would have an offer to join the Pac-10 "as fast as a fax machine works."

My guess is that the Big Eight schools probably didn't appreciate Berdahl and the Longhorns looking down their collective noses toward the league's academic requirements. Certainly A&M officials had no hesitancy about renewing their inquiries with the SEC. And the rest of the SWC schools, who were extremely hopeful entering the negotiations, likely began to realize that Texas had no real allegiance to any of its Lone Star State neighbors.

As A&M officials again reached out to the SEC and Big Eight executives pondered the bleak possibilities of attempting to negotiate a television deal without adding schools that would deliver the Dallas, Houston, and San Antonio TV markets, Lone Star State legislators and politicians went to work on behalf of their respective alma maters. David Sibley, then a Republican state senator from Waco with a high-ranking position on the powerful Senate Finance Committee, was a Baylor graduate who began rallying BU alumni with political clout. He didn't need to look far. Ann Richards, then the governor of Texas, was a Baylor graduate and Bob Bullock, the lieutenant governor at the time, had an undergraduate degree from Texas Tech and a law degree from

Baylor. Sibley threatened to cut state funding for UT and A&M if they bolted on their own.

Meanwhile, Texas Tech president Robert Lawless called his legislators into action. Robert Junell, who would eventually become chairman of the House Appropriations Committee, Speaker of the House Pete Laney and John Montford, president pro tempore of the Senate, sprung into action on the Red Raiders' behalf. Junell sternly laid out a potential scenario to Berdahl. "As I recall," Berdahl told Wangrin of the *San Antonio Express-News* in 2005, "it wasn't a very veiled threat to cut budgets if Tech was left behind."

Bullock, who died in 1999, was reported to be the actual ring leader of rallying the Baylor and Tech movers and shakers into action. He called Bernard Rappaport, a Waco businessman then serving on the UT Board of Regents, and Rappaport informed Bullock that things had changed in the days following Berdahl's February 16 statements at the DFW Airport Hyatt, where he indicated UT's intention to leave for the Pac-10, infuriating others at the meeting. First, the Pac-10 really did want Texas, but the league needed another school for expansion, and Pac-10 officials weren't interested in Texas Tech or any other existing SWC schools, with the possible exception of A&M. But Aggie officials did not believe such a move was in their best interest. A&M, too, encountered a similar situation with the SEC, which was highly interested in taking the Aggies but had no interest in any other SWC school aside from the University of Texas, which did not want to be part of the SEC. And the Big Eight officials realized, reluctantly, that they needed A&M *and* Texas to broker a big TV deal before any financial windows closed. Partly out of necessity and partly by default, A&M and Texas were invited to join the Big Eight, and the Aggies and Longhorns accepted.

Rappaport explained all that to Bullock, and on February 20, 1994, Bullock began rounding up his troops. He called a meeting in an Austin office that included Cunningham, Sibley, Montford, Mobley (who had, by then, become the A&M System's chancellor), A&M interim president Dean Gage, and House Speaker and A&M regent Bill Clayton. At that meeting, Bullock did not mince words. He was prepared to use every political weapon to buy Baylor and Tech a spot into the Big Eight. That included threats and promises. For his part,

Clayton was still reluctant about signing off on A&M's entry into the Big Eight, believing it would be best to hold out for another partner to join the SEC.

"It just so happened that A&M needed two votes from the Texas Higher Education Coordinating Board, which governs construction projects at state colleges, to proceed with the construction of its $33.4 million basketball and convocation facility, which became Reed Arena," Wangrin wrote in his 2005 story. "'Don't worry about it,' Bullock told Clayton. 'I'll get them for you tomorrow.' On February 24, 1994, just four days after Bullock's round of emergency phone calls, the Big Eight officially absorbed UT, A&M, Baylor, and Tech, and a new league was formed, using a name the Big Eight had curiously trademarked years earlier: The Big 12. That Capitol intrigue ended a revolt that had been in the works since the late 1980s, when UT and A&M officials first considered leaving the SWC."

On March 10, 1994, the Big 12 signed a five-year, $100 million deal with ABC and Liberty Sports to carry the league's football games. So that's how the Big 12 became one big, happy family . . . with threats, promises, and a forced marriage. Of course, officials of the new league were quickly saddled with multiple issues. Virtually every one of those issues created controversy.

The Big Eight schools didn't see the Big 12 as a "new" league. They still viewed it as their conference, and it appeared that they believed they were accepting A&M and Texas into their league for TV purposes and were doing a favor for Tech and Baylor to appease legislators. But A&M and Texas officials proudly believed they brought the new conference the television clout to play with the big boys of the Big Ten, Pac-10, SEC, and ACC.

The Big Eight schools—particularly Nebraska—bristled publicly when the league's headquarters were located in Dallas, not Kansas City. More resentment was created when Steve Hatchell, who'd been the commissioner of the SWC in its dying days, was announced as the Big 12's first commissioner, another decision driven by Texas schools. But apparently, the bigger issues for Nebraska, which won the national championship in football in 1994 and 1995, were entrance requirements and a championship game. Nebraska officials had stated publicly that they did not want a title game and wanted to keep the same, lenient entrance requirements the Big Eight had maintained for many years, despite Berdahl and UT's push for higher entrance requirements.

In the summer of 1995, the Big 12's presidents, reflecting on the revenue and media exposure that come from the SEC title game which began in 1992, voted 11-1 to play a Big 12 championship game. Several months later, the league's school presidents agreed to allow each Big 12 school to award two male and two female partial qualifiers athletic scholarships each season. When Nebraska officials pleaded to delay implementation, league presidents again voted 11-1 to put the rules into effect immediately. Even before the league had ever played a game, controversy brewed and Nebraska stewed. The Big 12 was a shotgun wedding and a dysfunctional mess from day one.

CHAPTER 3

Out of the Hurricane's Path, but into the Storm

During a February 2010 interview with *Time* magazine, then–United States Secretary of Defense Robert Gates, who had previously held roles as deputy assistant to the president for National Security Affairs and director of the Central Intelligence Agency, told reporter Elizabeth Rubin that his current job as the leader of the most powerful military in the free world wasn't actually as stressful as his previous one as president of Texas A&M University. The reporter thought he was joking. He was not. Gates was comfortable making tough decisions, and he will forever be remembered fondly at A&M for his push to add 440 new faculty positions, as well as overseeing increases in minority enrollment and numerous construction projects on campus during his presidency (2002–06). But what he has said in several interviews was that he never envisioned the pressure—internally, externally, and continually—that the Texas A&M president feels in regard to Aggie athletics, particularly football.

"I always used to tell people that Texas A&M football caused me more stress than any job I've ever had," Gates told *Time*. "And they always thought I was exaggerating, but I wasn't. I asked my wife one time, 'Why [do you think I feel that way]?' And she said, 'Because you have no control.' Here [within the Department of Defense], I have a little control."

Gates made those comments on February 5, 2010. One week later, I was officially named as the twenty-fourth president of Texas A&M. By then, I already knew exactly what Gates was referring to in regard to athletics-related stress, as I had first served as interim president beginning on June 15, 2009. We did not need to make any major conference realignment decisions during my time as interim president, and there were not any major personnel moves required in the hiring of athletics coaches or administrators either. But early in my tenure as interim president, I did call our athletic director into my office in an uncomfortable meeting regarding finances. I attempted to establish a chain of command that did not seem to have been enforced previously, and it was clear to me that he resented this.

In the ensuing years, some of the moves we made on the Aggies' behalf probably angered plenty of other high-ranking officials from A&M and other schools. Fortunately, I'd been raised and trained at home to do the right thing, even if it meant confronting someone.

When I was growing up in the 1950s and 1960s as an only child in a small town just southeast of College Station, money was always a challenge. My father spent over forty years working for the highway department (now the Texas Department of Transportation or TxDOT), mostly as a dragline operator. He was well-respected, but since he had only finished sixth grade in a one-room schoolhouse before he started working, he was never considered "management material." While he was able to read, write, and perform basic arithmetic, his lack of education was a little embarrassing to me as a kid, especially since my dream was to become a college professor, but, as I became older, I began to appreciate how intelligent he really was.

The lack of money was also a major concern as I began planning to attend college. From a fairly early age, I knew my parents simply could not afford to pay my way to a four-year university of my choice. My mother, who grew up on a cotton and peanut farm northwest of College Station (near Cameron), worked part-time in sales for JC Penney and as a checker at a grocery store. She was twelve years younger than my father and a go-getter with tremendous energy, enthusiasm, and zest for life, known throughout the community for doing things efficiently and effectively.

It really wasn't until my early twenties that I began to appreciate that many of the character traits that my parents had instilled in me were far more valuable than anything money could buy. In particular, I credit my father, who was a perceptive student of people, for helping me identify and rely on key figures in our leadership team—university officials like marketing and communications professional Jason Cook and trusted former Board of Regents member Jim Wilson—whose opinions, counsel and strategies would be so vital in determining the best course of action for Texas A&M. The conference realignment decisions we made were a total team effort, but my parents had prepared me to make difficult decisions that were the responsibility of the president of a major university.

My father and his brother ran cattle together, and my uncle was also a cotton farmer. I labored in those fields as a kid and a teenager—and "labor" is the proper word—sweating and toiling in the heat and humidity of the Texas summers. Those many hours of manual labor, along with the influence of some of my high school teachers, played a significant role in shaping my career goal to become a college professor. No one in my family had ever attended college, but by the time I turned sixteen, I knew that a future in the higher education teaching field was much more appealing than a lifetime in the cotton field.

I worked hard in high school, and when I applied to Texas A&M, the University of Texas at Austin, and Rice, I was accepted by all three universities. Texas A&M felt like home to me because I had been on campus often over the years, but my decision to attend A&M had much more to do with monetary issues. After I received three acceptance letters, I received a second letter from A&M, informing me that I was eligible to receive a physics scholarship that would essentially provide me with a full ride. Additionally, the A&M department of physics would provide me a job working up to twenty hours per week. It was the ultimate no-brainer decision on my part, and I arrived as a student at Texas A&M in June 1967 with plenty of incentive and just enough fear to push myself to succeed.

I took as many hours as possible every semester and worked as diligently as I could within the department of physics. I also knew that since I wanted to be a professor, I needed to make outstanding grades so I would be accepted into postgraduate programs at another quality school. Consequently, I didn't have much spare time and didn't notice much beyond the realm of physics. I did, however, take note of what was happening on campus as it related to the 1967 Texas A&M football team. It would have been impossible not to notice.

I was certainly not a sports fanatic when I arrived at A&M, and at 5 foot 8, I was destined never to be recruited to play any sport by a major college. Yet as a freshman student at Texas A&M, I witnessed firsthand how an outstanding football team can unite a college campus and generate a tremendous sense of pride and camaraderie unlike anything else. The Aggies' success in 1967 was my first lesson in the effect of a powerful athletics program on the current and former students of a university. Unfortunately, during the following two years, I also witnessed how a disappointing football program can negatively affect morale on campus. Unbeknownst to me at the time, this proved to be a valuable lesson that figured into my decisions decades later as president of A&M.

After Paul "Bear" Bryant left Texas A&M for Alabama following the 1957 season because, as he said, "Mama called," the fortunes of Aggie football took a nosedive. A&M endured nine consecutive losing seasons from 1958 to 1966, and the 1967 season also began dismally as the Aggies lost their first four games. A&M played well in close losses to SMU (20-17), Purdue (24-20), LSU (17-6), and Florida State (19-18). Nevertheless, the Aggies couldn't find any solace or satisfaction in close calls. A&M needed something big to happen to turn things around in order to salvage a season that was quickly slipping away. That's what happened on October 14, 1967, in Lubbock. Texas Tech led 24-21 with less than a minute remaining in the game, but A&M moved the ball to the Tech forty-three and faced fourth-and-fifteen with eleven seconds left. Quarterback Edd Hargett then tossed the ball in the direction of Bob Long, who outleapt three Tech defenders to make a sensational catch at the Red Raiders' fifteen with three seconds left.

Just before the center snapped the ball to Hargett on the next and final play, one of Tech's defenders jumped offsides, so Hargett knew he had a free play. He rolled out and noticed Tech had his receivers blanketed. He looked back to his right and saw that Larry Stegent had just one defender on him. Hargett tucked it and ran, as Stegent made a great block that allowed the quarterback to scramble into the end zone for the game-winning score with no time left. That dramatic victory turned the season around, as A&M then rolled past TCU, Baylor, Arkansas, and Rice, and went into the Texas game with a chance to win the SWC and earn a berth in the Cotton Bowl.

While the football team was winning games, the mood of the entire campus shifted and improved. You could feel the excitement building across the campus with each win. The students smiled more, the band played a little louder, staff members had more life in their step, the professors seemed to possess more energy, and the entire campus somehow appeared to be more radiant.

Prior to the 1967 season, construction had just been completed on the middle third of the second deck at Kyle Field. That's where my seat was for home games, and where I probably received the worst sunburn of my life. But at the time it was worth it, and I learned my lesson. I returned regularly to Kyle Field as momentum built toward the Thanksgiving Day showdown against the Longhorns. If we beat Texas, we'd go to the Cotton Bowl for the first time since New Year's Day 1943. But if we lost, it was home for the holidays yet again.

Early in the fourth quarter, the Longhorns pieced together a complete drive for the first time, and with 11:11 left in the game, UT quarterback Bill Bradley scored on a two-yard run to give the Horns a 7-3 lead. Plenty of time still remained, but the record-setting Kyle Field crowd of 49,200 spectators grew eerily quiet after the Texas touchdown, squirming in their seats as a cloud of uncertainty filled the otherwise clear skies. A&M had dominated most of the game statistically, but with just one impressive drive, Texas took the lead and A&M fans took a trip back in time, reliving haunting memories involving the Longhorns. A&M had not beaten Texas at Kyle Field since 1951, and it had been eleven years since A&M had beaten Texas anywhere. The football program and A&M fans needed this win in the worst way.

Eleven years of frustration was put to rest—ironically—just eleven seconds after Texas took the lead. Following the kickoff and a first-down incomplete pass, the Aggies faced second-and-ten from their own twenty. The next play was designed for a short pass to tight end Tom Buckman—the same play the Aggies had run one series earlier. But on the earlier play, Bob Long had noticed that Texas safety Pat Harkins was cheating up, looking for the tight end and leaving the deeper route open. Harkins intercepted Hargett earlier in the day, and the Aggies' signal caller listened with great interest as Long described to him how Texas' secondary was playing.

"Bob said the (defensive back) was coming up," Hargett recalled. "The safety would come up to cheat toward that inside guy, and Bob was able to get in behind them. I just laid it up there for Bob."

Long caught the ball at around the Texas forty-five and outraced the Longhorns' defenders into the end zone to give the Aggies a 10-7 lead. That's the way it stayed, as A&M won the game and went on to the Cotton Bowl, where the Aggies beat Bear Bryant and Alabama, 20-16 to finish the season with a seven-game winning streak. With a 6-1 conference record, A&M also became the first team in SWC history to lose its first four games and still win the league crown. Like practically everyone else on the A&M campus, I was captivated by the turnaround of the team.

The entire student body eagerly anticipated the 1968 season, hoping for more of the same magic. Unfortunately, it was not meant to be, as A&M sputtered to a 3-7 record in 1968 and an identical record in 1969. The excitement that permeated Aggieland in 1967 disappeared in 1968 and beyond, and I didn't spend as much time attending games following my freshman year.

I received a high number in the draft lottery and did not serve in the Vietnam War. Instead, I finished my degree in three years, graduating from A&M in the spring of 1970, shortly after the death of Aggie President James Earl Rudder. I started my graduate work at Rice the following fall, where I earned my master's in 1973 and my PhD in 1974. I also met my wife, Karin, who was a student at the University of Texas Graduate School of Biomedical Sciences. I finished up my doctorate in physics in the summer of 1974 and accepted a postdoctoral research appointment at Rice to "tee" me up for my intended academic career. When we discovered Karin was pregnant with our first child, I ramped up my job search and ended up landing what amounted to a full-time job with part-time wages at the University of Houston downtown campus, which was brand new at that time. I taught five classes in the spring of 1976, and that was the starting point of my career as a professor.

Then the main UH campus hired me in the second half of the summer of 1976 to teach a class in astronomy, and I was later called by the Texas A&M at Galveston branch campus, where I received my first tenure-track job. This meant commuting from Houston for a year until the University of Houston-Downtown offered me a position that paid $3,000 more than I had been making in Galveston. I stayed at the University of Houston for the next twenty-three years, ultimately becoming chair of the department of computer science at the main campus and director of the NASA Virtual Environments Research Institute. I then joined Old Dominion University in Norfolk, Virginia, as professor of electrical and computer engineering and professor of computer science in 2000. A few years later, in 2004, I had a telephone conversation with an old acquaintance at the Texas A&M at Galveston branch campus who urged me to apply for an opening, and I returned to Texas in 2005 as a vice president of Texas A&M University and chief executive officer of Texas A&M University at Galveston.

I never considered it at the time, but returning to run the Galveston campus—with 400 faculty and staff members and roughly 1,800 students—served as a great preparation to oversee the flagship institution of the A&M System in College Station. In Galveston, I received a crash course in managing people and fundraising, and I learned on the run how to handle some extremely difficult situations.

In June 2008, for example, we dealt with a tragedy when the thirty-eight-foot *Cynthia Woods* sailboat (carrying six people, including four students from the Houston area) capsized in the Gulf of Mexico. Five crew members were rescued, but fifty-three-year-old Roger Stone, who worked at the University of Texas Medical Branch at Galveston and had been hired by Texas A&M to serve as a safety officer on the *Cynthia Woods*, died after helping two students escape from below decks seconds after the boat capsized. In the aftermath of that tragedy, I first worked with Jason Cook, who was then the vice president of marketing and communications at the College Station campus. Even then, I could tell that Jason was masterful in his marketing and public relations savvy. We developed a friendship, and I had complete trust in his abilities, his opinions, and his marketing strategies. Jason would later play a monumental role in shaping the message of Texas A&M's move to the SEC.

While the capsized sailboat incident was heartbreaking, a more devastating event was yet to come. On September 13, 2008, Hurricane Ike made US landfall at Galveston at 2:10 a.m., blasting the coastal community in what was later confirmed as the costliest hurricane ever to hit Texas. Eighty percent of Galveston's homes and businesses were damaged by Ike. Ten days after the storm hit, Texas A&M at Galveston's students, faculty and administrators—including myself—resumed classes and operations 150 miles away in College Station. Those were extremely difficult circumstances, but those times also provided me with a great opportunity to grow as a leader, and it allowed me to make even more connections in College Station.

Overall, my entire four years at A&M at Galveston provided remarkable training for me in running what I referred to as a "mini

Texas A&M." My career until 2005 had only been in the academic chain of command. But in Galveston, I was placed in a role where I was responsible for student affairs, physical plant issues, fundraising, dealing with the legislature, handling hardships from a leadership role, and practically everything else I would encounter as the president of Texas A&M . . . except for working with a major college athletic department. Making mistakes in Galveston wasn't as visible as making them in College Station, and I learned a tremendous amount about management. After the challenges of 2008, things seemed to be going smoothly in Galveston entering the summer of 2009. Karin and I were happy and not looking to make a move.

But all was not well in the office of the president in College Station. Late in the fall of 2006, Robert Gates had stepped down as president of A&M to replace Donald Rumsfeld as US Secretary of Defense. After some tension in the selection process for a new A&M president, the Board of Regents chose Elsa Murano, then the dean of the College of Agriculture and Life Sciences and the A&M System's vice chancellor for agriculture. Murano, the first female and first Hispanic president in the university's 132-year history, was a celebrated internal choice in January 2008.

For various reasons, however, Murano's tenure as president seemed doomed from the start. Some of the issues were no fault of her own, but she also didn't win friends by dismissing high-level administrators whom Gates had hired. And in the summer of 2008, she forced the resignation of a popular and highly regarded vice president of student affairs.

Additionally, during her tenure, an internal audit on athletics reviewing a span from September 2007 to December 2008 generated more tensions, concluding that the "Texas A&M athletic department lacked control of its finances." Among other things, the twenty-five-page report noted that prior recommendations from facility assessments of Kyle Field performed in 2002 and 2004 had not been substantially implemented. The report represented more negative news for Bill Byrne, who'd also been mentioned in Murano's annual review earlier in 2009, which revealed that during Gates's tenure as president, the University had loaned the athletic department $16 million. That resulted in a stringent repayment plan, and Byrne was forced to eliminate seventeen jobs in the athletic department to cut costs.

While the relationship between the president's office and A&M athletics was strained further under Murano, those tensions could probably be traced back to Dr. Ray Bowen, who served as A&M president from June 1, 1994, to July 31, 2002. Bowen, an A&M graduate from the class of 1958, did an outstanding job running the university in an extremely difficult time following the November 1999 collapse of Bonfire, one of the key Aggie campus traditions, killing twelve Aggie students and injuring twenty-seven more. But Bowen's legacy as president was tied to the launching of the Vision 2020 plan. In 1997, Bowen appointed a task force made up of more than 250 faculty, staff, students, former students, local residents, and various private- and public-sector representatives. This group devoted more than two years to examining all aspects of the University and studying benchmark peer institutions before unveiling its "Vision 2020" challenges and imperatives in 1999. The primary goal of Vision 2020 was to achieve recognition of Texas A&M as a consensus "top ten" public university by the year 2020.

Deservedly, Bowen received plenty of praise for Vision 2020, which played a large role in A&M earning an invitation to join the prestigious Association of American Universities (AAU) in 2001. Founded in 1900, the AAU is an organization of leading research universities in North America devoted to maintaining a strong system of academic research and education. Bowen viewed Vision 2020 strictly as an academic plan, and consequently, the final document listed twelve imperatives that focused on academic issues. During its deliberations, the task force considered many ideas that were ultimately not incorporated into the final twelve imperatives because of the predominant focus on academics. Among the areas that were considered for mention, but not included in any great detail, were athletics. The final Vision 2020 document included only one paragraph regarding athletics under the heading of Imperative Three (Enhance the Undergraduate Academic Experience). That rather vague paragraph stated:

"Intercollegiate athletics is an important part of Texas A&M University's history, and it can and should play an overwhelmingly positive role in the University's future destiny. Intercollegiate athletics has a broad and unique opportunity to add to the diversity of Texas A&M University while increasing unity on campus. Athletics can be a focal point for encouraging former students to be actively involved in the institution. The University can be assisted by athletics in achieving a more positive national prominence. Athletics can play a major role in the spirit of the University while setting enviable standards for educational and character development. A number of our best peer institutions have demonstrated the reality that, properly managed with an appropriate set of core values and beliefs, there is no dichotomy between excellence in academics and athletics. Texas A&M University intends to be in that group of admired and respected institutions, and we advocate being held to those high standards."

That was the entirety of the Vision 2020 document dealing with athletics. I was told that its brevity and the perceived minimizing of the importance of athletics in the plan disappointed many officials and supporters of the athletics program at Texas A&M. Furthermore, according to various donors and sources within the 12th Man Foundation (the fundraising organization for A&M athletics), Bowen was initially opposed to major gift fundraising for athletics facilities, which played a significant role in A&M falling behind some of its key competitors such as Texas and Oklahoma in the overall quality of its athletics structures. Bowen certainly was not opposed to maintaining a quality athletics program at Texas A&M, and he frequently attended A&M athletic events. But in my opinion, he did not appear to be a promoter or defender of athletics while he was president. The early 2000s were difficult times for many of A&M's athletics programs, especially football.

At about the same time that Robert Gates took over in August 2002, Bill Byrne was hired to replace the former athletic director, Wally Groff, who was a great accountant and had run athletics in a fiscally sound way. But many thought he wasn't particularly proactive in terms of marketing, and he was not perceived as a visionary leader. Gates also added a "thirteenth" imperative to the Vision 2020 document that included an increased emphasis on the role of athletics at A&M. But Gates purposely distanced himself far from the day-to-day operations of athletics under its new director, allowing Byrne a great deal of autonomy. Byrne, who'd earned the nickname "Dollar Bill" while he was the director of athletics at Nebraska, was the polar opposite of Groff in many ways, including his budgetary practices. Byrne's free spending at A&M led to the detrimental financial conditions within the athletic department that were subsequently revealed in Murano's internal audit.

Murano resigned as A&M president on June 14, 2009, one day before the A&M System's Board of Regents was scheduled to discuss the University's leadership. Earlier that month, the University System had released a negative performance review of Murano. Texas A&M System Chancellor Mike McKinney had previously told the *Bryan-College Station Eagle* that regents were considering merging the positions of chancellor and president to save money.

Regardless of who was right and who was wrong, it was an extremely difficult time at A&M. In the midst of all this upheaval, I received a phone call at 10:30 on Sunday night, June 14. As a vice president based in Galveston, I had routinely been on the College Station campus as much as twice a week. It wasn't a surprise to any of the vice presidents that instability existed in the president's office. I had been told that Elsa Murano and Mike McKinney were not even talking anymore. McKinney and I talked in early June in Houston, and he informed me that changes could be made soon. So, I was not shocked to hear the news that Murano was stepping down. The phone call from the chancellor's chief of staff, however, was surprising because she requested a copy of my resumé and informed me I was on the short list to fill the role of interim president at Texas A&M.

I seriously doubted I had any chance, and I did not allow myself to ponder the possibilities of the position that night. But at 1:04 p.m. on June 15, my phone buzzed. It was Dr. Rodney P. McClendon, then–vice president for administration at Texas A&M. He had sent me a short text message, stating "you are interim." At that point, I hopped in my car and started driving north. Five minutes later, Mike McKinney called my cell, confirming Rodney's text and providing further details. I was honored, but I also knew I was moving into a turbulent situation. I was busy throughout the summer of 2009, often working sixteen-hour days, trying to settle things down and assure faculty and staff that I would do my best to restore modus operandi to the president's office at Texas A&M.

As I attempted to ease the concerns of faculty and staff and provide some stability and unity in the president's office, I had a couple of other encounters in June 2009 that were strong indicators of things to come. First, I was invited to the 12th Man Foundation's summer meeting of the Council of Athletic Ambassadors in Orlando. I would have loved to attend the meetings, but I simply had too many loose ends to tie up and too many dots to connect. Prior to leaving for Orlando, Miles Marks, the former president and CEO of the 12th Man Foundation, came to my office with Bill Byrne and informed me that the athletics department was in a deficit situation, and that Byrne had asked for $1 million to cover the operational costs for the rest of the fiscal year. Marks said the 12th Man Foundation, a separate 501(c)3 organization that does not fall under the umbrella of the University, would transfer $1 million to athletics. Somewhat hesitantly, I blessed the transfer and moved forward because I had so many other things on my plate. I figured that was the last I would hear of the issue.

After the meeting in Orlando, however, Miles Marks called and asked me, "Why did you guys change your mind?" I was not aware of what he was referring to, but then Miles informed me that in Orlando, Byrne had made an official request for the transfer in front of the Board of Trustees for a larger amount than I had approved. It was suddenly apparent to me why the athletic department had major financial issues. As soon as Byrne returned from Orlando, I scheduled an appointment with him in my office. It was not a pleasant conversation, and I intentionally used some strong language, but I felt that I had to make a point.

Whether I had the word "interim" before my title or not, I was the president. Byrne had run the athletic department during the presidential regimes of Gates and Murano without many checks or balances. He rarely met with them, and I believed it was important that the two of us meet regularly. By the end of the summer of 2009, Byrne said that he had met with me more often in the couple of months of my presidency than he had met with the president during the entirety of the Gates and Murano years.

The other eye-opening event within my first couple of weeks on the job was attending my first Big 12 Conference meeting on June 26, 2009, in Dallas. I had no idea what to expect as I flew up to the Metroplex in the Texas A&M System plane. All the Big 12 presidents attended the meeting except for Texas Tech's Guy Bailey, who sent a substitute. As I later discovered, it was unusual to have so many presidents in attendance. In most of the other Big 12 meetings that I attended later, it was common for many of the presidents to send substitutes.

That particular meeting didn't have much meat to it. The big discussion then and moving forward involved television rights and what might be coming down the pike in terms of different ways to do business. There was a discussion about the possibility of individual conference members owning their own networks, along with conversations regarding the possibility of a Big 12 Network. But the major revelation I made at that first meeting was that not all parties at the table were viewed equally by the others. Nor was there equity in the distribution of funds among members.

University of Texas president Bill Powers served as the chairman of the conference Board of Directors at the time, and it was quite interesting to me to see how the discussion shook out among what I viewed as the haves and have-nots. Nebraska's Harvey Perlman, Oklahoma's David Boren, and Powers seemed to be perceived as leaders of the most successful football schools. As a representative of Texas A&M, I felt as though we were at a "secondary level" that included Missouri, Texas Tech, Colorado, Kansas, and Oklahoma State. Then there was what I saw as the "third tier" represented by Kansas State, Baylor, and Iowa State. Remember this was 2009! On the surface, everyone was civil and accommodating, but there wasn't, from my perspective, a sense of unity in the room. I sensed a degree of tension as the "haves" justified and defended unequal distribution. Perlman even addressed the records of each school, such as listing how many BCS football games each school had made in order to prove that the historic "power" schools deserved more than the others. I was quite uncomfortable during and after the meeting in June 2009, and I grew more so when I began investigating the forced union of the Big 12. Even after just one Big 12 Conference meeting, I began to "feel" that a major storm was brewing on the horizon.

Ironically, time would later reveal that when I left Galveston Island, I ventured right into the eye of another storm that I could have never imagined. As anyone who lives on the Gulf Coast knows, summertime typically produces the most violent storms. The summer of 2009 certainly produced some stormy conditions for me personally, but riding the rough waters in 2009 provided good practice for the monsters that were yet to come in 2010 and 2011.

CHAPTER 4

Don't Worry about It?

I didn't read the article when it was first printed, and even if I had scanned it back then it would not have likely made a lasting impression on me. After all, when the story first appeared in the March 29, 2009, edition of the *New York Times*, I was still the CEO at Texas A&M at Galveston, attempting to restore some sense of normalcy during our first full semester back on the island following the devastation of Hurricane Ike.

At that point in time, I couldn't have told you the difference between Larry Scott the sports administrator, Larry Scott the former bodybuilder, or Larry the Cable Guy. But in my research for this book, I stumbled across an article about the sports administrator Larry Scott on the *New York Times* website. It focused on the spark igniting the realignment firestorm that consumed our thoughts at Texas A&M and reshaped college athletics conferences in the summers of 2010 and 2011. The article detailed a somewhat surprising and nontraditional move made by the Pac-10 Conference, which introduced Scott, the former chief executive and chairman of the Women's Tennis Association (WTA), as the league's new commissioner. In the lead of the story about Scott leaving the WTA, reporter Pete Thamel prophetically wrote that the move "will reverberate in college athletics."

It did, indeed. The innovative and imaginative Scott, a former standout Harvard tennis player who invigorated the WTA with major sponsorship and television deals in his six years with the organization, nearly orchestrated the most significant and momentous conference reorganization in the history of college athletics. Scott's grand vision of a sixteen-team league that would have stretched from the Pacific Northwest to Central Texas would have generated seismic shifts and powerful aftershocks rumbling across the entire country. It would have been a game-changer on many levels.

Proponents of the Pac-16 claimed it would be great for college football, as did media and fans who longed for a more elaborate playoff system. As soon as the news broke regarding Scott's prospective plans for the Pac-16, sports media across the country began speculating about the possibility of four mega-conferences (most likely, the SEC, Big Ten, ACC, and Pac-16) and a sixty-four-team structure that could have generated a natural sixteen- or eight-team playoff format among the NCAA Football Bowl Subdivision (FBS) schools that would be similar to its Football Championship Subdivision (FCS) model. The two divisions would have existed side by side, with the FBS utilizing the bowl game system. Most of those who favored a playoff system, especially those who were confident that their own school would be among the sixty-four programs to be included in the four mega-conferences, seemed to applaud Scott's plan.

On the other hand, Scott's Pac-16 scenario could have spelled imminent doom for the Big 12, which would have been sliced in half by the exodus of six schools. And if the four mega-conferences formed, the other leagues—like the Mountain West, Conference USA, the American Athletic (formerly the Big East), the Mid-American, and the Sun Belt—would have probably been raided. For better or worse, Scott's Pac-16 plan could have revolutionized college athletics, making Scott the most powerful and well-known college sports executive in the country.

Within a year of taking over as Pac-10 commissioner in the spring of 2009, Scott had strategically and secretly—at least for the most part—devised a detailed plan to build the nation's largest collegiate conference and unveil the most lucrative conference-affiliated television network that had ever been constructed. His proposed league included seven states, two divisions (north and south), twenty-seven percent of the nation's television viewers (26.4 million), and twenty-eight percent of the country's population (86.5 million). Before any plans were leaked or discovered, Scott had already calculated annual potential revenue payouts for each of the sixteen schools and had drawn up tentative conference schedules for football, men's and women's basketball, baseball, softball, volleyball, and soccer. From the Emerald City to the South Plains, Scott had all of his ducks in a row. He'd even partnered with what he must have perceived to be the ultimate cash cow (the Texas Longhorns), whose officials later behaved as if they believed that the other invited Big 12 schools would happily follow wherever the

Longhorns led them. In any case, Scott appeared to have athletics administrators and some of the highest-ranking officials at the University of Texas in his corner.

He had outlined three tiers of television distribution strategies for the new league. He had projected rights fees for each of the member institutions for fifteen years into the future, and he eventually had his legal team draft eight-page contracts extending official invitations to six of the members of the Big 12 Conference. To kick-start the most far-reaching domino effect in the history of college athletics, Scott seemed to need only one thing: Texas A&M's signature on the agreement.

With Texas already on board for the Pac-16 formation, Texas A&M would have become the critical cog in the realignment wheel. Our decision would likely have affected everyone and everything else. University of Texas officials later did a splendid job of convincing many media outlets that it was they who chose not to join the Pac-16 and that, by doing so, the Longhorns mercifully saved the Big 12 and pre-vented the have-nots of college football from falling into obscurity. But I can attest that's not the full story.

In fact, Texas was "already gone" and fully prepared to sing their vic-tory song. While UT president Bill Powers and athletic director DeLoss Dodds may not actually have mapped out Scott's Pac-16 flight plan, I came to believe they were its copilots, at the very least. That is the only conclu-sion I can draw from Bill Powers's statement to me on two different occa-sions: "Don't worry. Whatever happens, we will take care of you."

Whether he intended to sound consoling, caring, or considerate, I took his response as condescending. Texas A&M University didn't need UT to take care of us. We were confident in our leadership team's ability to chart our own course. We were determined that Texas A&M University would stand on its own without the University of Texas watching out for us like a protective big brother.

As I quickly discovered, Texas was playing an elaborate, behind-the-scenes chess game, strategically making moves in its own best inter-est and treating virtually all other schools like expendable pieces. We had no interest in playing that game.

When I actually received the phone call from Larry Scott in April 2010, I was not the least bit surprised that he wanted to travel to College

Station to visit with me. The major shakeups were yet to come, but college administrators, athletic department personnel and sports media members had been aware of muffled realignment rumblings for a full year before Scott called me. In the spring of 2009, before his name was tainted by the Jerry Sandusky sexual abuse scandal, Penn State head coach Joe Paterno was banging the expansion drum.

On several occasions, Paterno strongly suggested that the Big Ten should expand from eleven to twelve schools for the purpose of creating a championship game in football. Paterno even pointed out three schools—Syracuse, Rutgers, and Pittsburgh—that he thought the Big Ten should seriously consider. In response to Paterno's comments, Big Ten commissioner Jim Delany initially said that expansion was a "back-burner issue" for the league. But on December 15, 2009—following the conclusion of the regular season—Delany changed his public stance. On that date, the Big Ten Council of Presidents and Chancellors issued a statement, saying the group believed "that the timing is right for the conference to once again conduct a thorough evaluation of its options" regarding expansion. The council also announced that it had given Delany twelve to eighteen months to provide recommendations.

On that same day, Missouri's then–chancellor, Brady Deaton, told the *Kansas City Star* in a prepared statement that Mizzou would entertain an offer if the Big Ten approached the school about becoming an expansion candidate. Three days later, Missouri Gov. Jay Nixon echoed Deaton's comments. In an interview with the *Associated Press*, Nixon said, "If a significant conference with a long history of academic and athletic excellence talks about you joining them, you shouldn't just say, 'We're from the old Big Eight and I remember when . . . ' If they want to talk, we should talk, and we should listen."

While the Big Ten ultimately never invited Missouri to join the league, all the commentary about the potential changes in the Big Ten toward the end of 2009 made it clear that the realignment train would soon be leaving the station, even though the destination at that time was unclear. And the Missouri-focused comments from Brady Deaton and Gov. Nixon clearly displayed how one addition to the Big Ten could directly affect the Big 12 and Texas A&M. Besides, there were some other mumblings toward the end of 2009—none of which were reported by the media—that led me to believe that the University of

Texas was also involved in the behind-the-scenes Big Ten expansion discussions. Again, I wasn't sure of the destination or details, but I had heard from some sources that Texas moving to the Big Ten could be a possibility.

My suspicions were essentially confirmed when Texas A&M vice president for government relations, Michael O'Quinn, and I drove over to Austin for a meeting with Bill Powers and one of his vice presidents in February 2010. Laying groundwork for the 2010 legislative session, the four of us talked about common strategies for the upcoming year, but once the business portion of the meeting was concluded, I asked for a moment of private conversation with Powers. When the other two men left the room, I asked him about the realignment rumors. He told me, "Don't worry; we'll take care of you."

Later that same month, we hosted a meeting at the Clayton W. Williams Alumni Center in College Station between the leadership of Texas A&M's faculty senate and what the University of Texas refers to as its faculty council. The location of the meeting rotated between College Station and Austin every other year, and in 2010, we hosted it at the Clayton W. Williams Alumni Center. Bill Powers and I both spoke, as did the two provosts from each school. After a roundtable discussion, social interaction, and lunch, I asked Powers to accompany me to my office. For the second time he told me that, while he couldn't give me any real information, I shouldn't worry; Texas was going to take care of us.

Like anyone who is told not to worry, I worried. My radar shifted from "curious" to "high alert." In fact, by this time, every major conference in the country was suddenly the subject of some sort of rumor.

On February 8, 2010, when the Big 12 presidents and chancellors were in Dallas for a regularly scheduled meeting, commissioner Dan Beebe had initiated preliminary discussions regarding the potential impact of conference realignment. Beebe acknowledged that the rumors were rampant and that one domino could certainly affect other leagues, including our own.

The very next day, Larry Scott held a press conference in San Francisco, essentially saying that he was more than willing to push the first domino. Officially, the press conference was held to introduce former Big 12 commissioner Kevin Weiberg as the Pac-10's new deputy commissioner and chief operating officer. Weiberg, who would accompany Scott on a visit to my office later that spring, was an extremely interesting choice because he had served as deputy commissioner in the Big Ten from 1989 to 1998, and his biography stated that he "was instrumental in the integration of Penn State into the conference." In other words, he had expansion experience. He also had obvious ties to the Big 12, having served as its commissioner from 1998 to 2007, helping to double the annual revenue distributed among member schools from $54 million in 1998 to $106 million in 2006. Finally, Weiberg had returned to the Big Ten in 2007 to oversee the launch of the Big Ten Network, and TV contracts were at the heart of the realignment rumors.

At Weiberg's introductory press conference, Scott went public on his expansion plans, even drawing a potential timeline. "It is really over the next six to twelve months that we'll start having serious analysis and serious evaluations (about expansion)," Scott said. "If the Pac-10 is going to think about expanding, now is our window. If you're going to consider a reconstruction of the conference, there's a value proposition associated with that. Given that we're about to have negotiations regarding our media rights, it makes sense that if you're going to do it, do it when you can monetize it and get value from it commercially."

It was becoming apparent that there was some truth to the rumors of Texas moving to the Pac-10. One day later, however, the *Lawrence (Kansas) Journal-World* reported that the Big Ten "has had preliminary exchanges" with Texas. While that seemed somewhat confusing, it definitely confirmed that Bill Powers, DeLoss Dodds, and the rest of the University of Texas' leadership team were at the forefront of expansion talks. Perhaps they were hedging their bets by engaging more than one conference, but I was convinced more than ever before that the University of Texas was a prominent player in the realignment discussions.

During the next couple of months, a dizzying array of rumors was reported by media members, innuendos that surfaced through both academic and athletics grapevines, prompting internal university meetings to discuss the speculation, followed by poker-faced posturing and preemptive positioning by practically every party who might be involved in the realignment process. For example, on February 19, 2010, Dan Beebe e-mailed Big 12 CEOs and athletic directors with a talking-points memo that included instructions for how to discuss realignment possibilities with the media and staff. Within the e-mail,

Beebe included what amounted to a Big 12 public relations message, highlighting the league's successes on the fields and courts, and reminding member institutions of how the league had developed and maintained rivalries that made geographic sense. He also reminded us to be kind and show appreciation when discussing the league with reporters. "I request that your public comments express the positives about the Big 12," Beebe wrote in the email. "To the degree you feel you have to placate constituents who would like for you to express interest in another conference, I hope you can indicate that your institution is a proud member of the Big 12, but that you will monitor the environment."

In late February 2010, the *Milwaukee Journal Sentinel* reported that the Big Ten had hired a firm to research potential candidates for expansion and that the initial report included fifteen schools. In early March, a story in the *Chicago Tribune* confirmed that the report, prepared by the Chicago-based investment firm William Blair & Company, analyzed whether five different schools (Missouri, Notre Dame, Pittsburgh, Syracuse, and Rutgers) would add enough revenue to justify expanding the league beyond eleven teams. "We can all get richer if we bring in the right team or teams," an unidentified source told the *Tribune*. Meanwhile, Big Ten commissioner Jim Delany stated that the conference's two priorities for potential additions were to gain a foothold in the South and to expand its growing television network. Closer to home in Big 12 territory, the *Boulder* (Colorado) *Daily Camera* projected in a story running on March 6, 2010, that it would likely cost the University of Colorado $9 million in forfeited revenue distribution if the Buffs left the Big 12 to join the Pac-10.

The documented stories and proposed scenarios were so prevalent that it would have been absolutely foolish not to anticipate shuffling and shakeups on the horizon. Bill Byrne and I continued to meet regularly to discuss financial matters, and our conversations often included the latest realignment news. With everything that was going on privately behind closed doors and all that was being debated publicly in media circles, I was virtually certain that a call would come my way from someone involved in another conference to gauge A&M's interest in leaving the Big 12. When Larry Scott did call, we scheduled a meeting in the conference room of my office at Texas A&M. Larry did not go into great detail on the phone about why he wanted to meet in person, but it stood to reason he was not flying 1,800 miles from the Pac-10 headquarters in Walnut Creek, California, to ask me about computer engineering or artificial intelligence. One day later, Bill Powers called me, confirming my suspicions by informing me that I would hear from Larry Scott soon. I told Bill I had already fielded that call.

Bill Byrne and I were the only two A&M representatives in the meeting.

When he arrived, Scott made quite an impression on me. He was young—in his mid-forties at the time of our meeting—energetic, sharp, ambitious, and focused. He possessed an air of confidence, and he had an impressive track record as a sports executive. After becoming the CEO of the WTA in 2003, Scott had been the driving force behind the WTA's unprecedented six-year, $88 million deal with Sony Ericsson, the largest sponsorship deal in the history of women's sports. He worked to secure equal pay for women and men at Grand Slam events, and he pulled it off.

Although Scott was a surprise choice as Pac-10 commissioner to many media observers and sports fans along the West Coast, his directive from the league's member schools was clear: make the Pac-10 more relevant in the national consciousness. But what impressed me most about him at our initial meeting was his attention to detail. I later learned that the Pac-10 had hired Hollywood-based Creative Artists Agency (CAA) to explore expansion opportunities and to advise the conference on its next media rights deal. One of the reasons the Pac-10 opted for CAA was the agency's numerous entertainment connections in Hollywood, Scott told the *Sports Business Journal*. CAA had also been involved in preparing the presentation that Scott made.

It quickly became clear that Scott was intent on transforming the Pac-10 into the most prominent and powerful conference in America. As Scott explained, the Pac-10 in its current alignment incorporated four states and sixteen percent of TV households in the United States, which barely ranked ahead of the Big 12 at the time (fifteen percent) and behind the SEC (nineteen percent), the ACC (twenty-one percent), and the Big Ten (twenty-three percent). But with the proposed addition of Texas A&M, Texas, Texas Tech, Oklahoma, Oklahoma State, and Colorado, Scott showed that the Pac-16 would both surpass every other conference with twenty-seven percent of TV households in the United States and include seven of the country's top twenty TV markets (Dallas, Houston, Los Angeles, San Francisco, Phoenix, Seattle, and Sacramento). Those numbers would obviously bode well for the proposed Pac-16 Network. And then Scott showed us even more enticing projections.

Remember that the unequal revenue distribution the Big 12 provided to its institutions was a sore point for many of its members. The conference annually dispersed fifty percent of its revenue equally among the conference members, but the other fifty percent was based upon the number of football television appearances for each school. Generally speaking, that method favored the more high-profile schools like Texas, Oklahoma, and Nebraska. In 2007–08, the University of Texas received a league-high distribution of $10.2 million, while Baylor was the lowest at $7.1 million. Texas A&M was No. 4 among the twelve schools in 2007–08 at $9.22 million. One year later, Oklahoma led the league at $12.2 million, followed by Texas at $11.8. Texas A&M was again near the middle of the pack at $10.2 million, while Baylor ($9.1 million), Iowa State ($8.9 million), and Kansas State ($8.4 million) rounded out the bottom of the Big 12.

None of the major programs in the Big 12 were particularly pleased with any of those numbers, especially in light of the published reports on revenue distribution in the Big Ten. The Big Ten Network launched on August 30, 2007, and soon began to have a significant impact on revenue for Big Ten schools, with individual revenues increasing from $14 million for the fiscal year 2006–07 to $22 million for the fiscal year 2007–08. To put that into context, that $8 million one-year increase represented as much as the total Big 12 payout to Colorado ($8.0 million), and it exceeded the payouts to Iowa State ($7.4 million), and Baylor ($7.1 million) for fiscal year 2007–08.

According to Larry Scott's projections, however, a Pac-16 configuration and the resulting conference network would have a similarly positive effect for all sixteen members of the restructured league. Scott and CAA representatives had already been in preliminary discussions with executives at Fox Sports Networks, and Scott presented Bill Byrne and me with Tier 1, 2, and 3 projected rights fees and cash flows showing that each of the sixteen schools would receive roughly $18 million in the first full year of the Pac-16. By year five, the projection was $22 million apiece.

While the financial numbers were impressive, Bill Byrne and I both expressed serious concerns regarding travel costs and demands on our student-athletes. Yet Scott had anticipated those objections in advance and presented us with scheduling plans that had obviously been thoroughly researched and discussed by Pac-10 officials for weeks—maybe months—in advance of our meeting. The key to limiting travel costs and minimizing negative effects on our student-athletes and coaches, Scott said, was the formation of two divisions. The North Division would feature California, Stanford, Oregon, Oregon State, UCLA, USC, Washington, and Washington State, while the South would comprise Arizona, Arizona State, Colorado, Oklahoma, Oklahoma State, Texas, Texas A&M, and Texas Tech. Scott pointed out that the average distance between all existing Pac-10 institutions was 599 miles. But within his proposed new divisions, the average distance between schools in the North would be 497 miles, while the average distance between the South schools would be 547 miles, which seemed reasonable to manage. After all, the average distance between all Big 12 schools was 434 miles, and once a team boards an airplane, 113 miles doesn't make much of a difference. On the other hand, I was a bit concerned about being in a conference spread across three time zones. Returning to College Station from the west after a night game would be challenging for our athletes, coaches, and fans.

For football in particular, Scott and his team had projected Texas A&M's conference schedules for eight years, from 2012 to 2019. Each year, we would play three nonconference games, seven intradivision conference games (full divisional round-robin), and two rotating interconference games. In other words, we would travel to California four times every eight years and to the Pacific Northwest four times every eight years. The 2012 proposed schedule featured five home games against Arizona State, Oklahoma State, Texas Tech, Texas, and Washington, with four road trips to Arizona, Oklahoma, Colorado, and California. In 2013, we'd have five conference road trips to Arizona State, Oklahoma State, Texas Tech, Texas, and Washington State, while the four home games would be against Arizona, Oklahoma, Colorado, and Stanford. At the end of an eight-year span, Texas A&M would have played each school from the North Division twice, once at home and once on the road.

All this seemed quite reasonable, as did the eighteen-game conference basketball schedules for men and women, which featured fourteen games each season against schools from within one's own division and one two-game road swing to either California or the Pacific Northwest each year. For example, the proposed 2012 conference schedule called for Texas A&M to travel to face California and Stanford, while UCLA and USC came to College Station. The following year, the Aggies went to Oregon and Oregon State, and Washington and Washington State came to A&M's Reed Arena.

Other sports involved even less travel. For baseball and volleyball, the league would have been divided into three five-team divisions because Colorado doesn't play baseball and Oklahoma State doesn't play volleyball. In baseball and softball, A&M would never be required to travel to California or the Pacific Northwest for regular-season conference games, while in volleyball and soccer, the Aggies would alternate traveling to California or the Pacific Northwest one time every other year.

Overall, Scott's presentation was notable, as he had anticipated virtually every concern that we might have in advance of the meeting. The *Wall Street Journal* reported in 2013 that Scott was the highest-paid commissioner in college athletics in 2011–12 (in excess of $3 million), thanks primarily to the more than $1.4 million he made in bonuses and additional compensation. That didn't surprise me. I could tell from our first meeting that he was bright, prudent, intuitive, and meticulous. He'd done his homework.

He also mentioned that he had been in planning discussions for some time with officials from the University of Texas. Naturally, I had suspected this from the moment when he first began detailing the annual revenue distribution possibilities. Clearly that is what Bill Powers had meant when he told me—on two different occasions—not to worry about any rumors, because the University of Texas would take care of us.

Larry continually spoke of equality among all sixteen schools in every area, including revenue based on television. But previous Big 12 meetings and conversations with Bill Powers had alerted us that the

University of Texas envisioned creating its own television network. It seemed clear that Texas was really not interested in being a totally equal partner with other schools. The Longhorns believed that their brand was big enough to be a television ratings magnet in all sports, making them feel that they should command a greater share of revenues. My understanding was that Texas wanted its share of guaranteed conference distribution money—revenues from Tier 1 football broadcasts, bowl tie-ins, conference NCAA tournament appearances, and so forth—and then on top of that, wanted to broker the best deal possible for its own television network.

I didn't mention this to Larry Scott at our initial meeting, nor, quite frankly, did he officially extend an invitation to Texas A&M to join the Pac-16 at that time. But two things seemed certain: he had at least an informal agreement in place with the University of Texas and Texas A&M was now at the top of his wish list.

After the meeting with Scott, I informed key members of the Texas A&M University System Board of Regents that there was truth to the rumors we'd been hearing. I told Regent Jim Wilson and Morris E. Foster, the chairman of the Board at that time, about the specifics of the meeting with Scott and about the distinct possibility that Texas A&M would soon be invited to join the Pac-16. Foster's wise words were, "One option is no option." In other words, no matter how good the Pac-16 looked on paper—and it looked enticing on many fronts—it was now our job to explore other possibilities.

The most obvious "other" option was to stay right where we were, in the Big 12. But if Texas was already committed to joining the Pac-16, would Texas Tech, Oklahoma, and Oklahoma State follow along, regardless of what we did at Texas A&M? If that happened, the Big 12 would almost certainly fold and we would have no option at all. Larry Scott hadn't told me whether he'd visited yet with Texas Tech, Oklahoma, Oklahoma State, or even Colorado, which seemed like a natural fit in the expanded Pac-10. Based on our conversation, though, it seemed that Texas A&M had been the first stop he had made on his confidential "information tour." So we needed to act quickly, before we were pressured—or forced—into making a move we didn't fully embrace. To me, this meant that it was time to explore possible membership opportunities in the Southeastern Conference—some twenty years after A&M officials had first looked into that possibility. Understanding our persistent interest in the SEC requires knowing a bit about the conference's history and how it came to be one of the most dominant leagues in collegiate athletics.

In football—the one sport that matters most in terms of finances, power, prestige, and public perception—the Southeastern Conference has become the nation's premier league. It hasn't always been that way, though. From 1985 to 1994, the SEC produced only one team that finished the year among the top three schools in the final Associated Press polls, and that was when Alabama won the 1992 national championship. During that stretch, schools like Miami, Florida State, Nebraska, Notre Dame, Penn State, Oklahoma, and Colorado produced some of the highest winning percentages nationally. But then, a couple of key decisions helped to transform the SEC's image from run-of-the-mill to king of the hill.

First, the league expanded in the early 1990s with the addition of Arkansas and South Carolina. Next, former SEC commissioner Roy Kramer divided the league into two divisions, added an eighth conference game for each school, and organized the first Division I-A conference football championship game. The SEC Championship Game—sarcastically dubbed the "Kramer Bowl" by many skeptics—was initially quite unpopular among the league's coaches. When Alabama head coach Gene Stallings first learned of the extra game, he was adamantly opposed to it and predicted that it would negatively affect the league for generations to come. "The SEC will never win another national championship," Stallings said, as documented in Ray Glier and Phil Savage's book, *How the SEC Became Goliath: The Making of College Football's Most Dominant Conference.*

Stallings himself, however, immediately proved his own prediction wrong. Alabama defeated Florida in the 1992 SEC Championship Game at Legion Field in Birmingham, Alabama, and the Tide went on to whip Miami in the Sugar Bowl, winning the national championship. From then on, the nationally televised "Kramer Bowl" became a showcase for the SEC. "The SEC Championship Game was one last audition for voters before the final polls, and it came when many teams had finished their regular seasons," Glier wrote. "More than that, the SEC Championship Game and the eight-game schedule were booster rockets for the conference schools. . . . Until the Big 12, then the ACC and the Big Ten, and the Pac-12, added their own conference championship games, the SEC was on the national stage by itself with the SEC Championship Game in early December. When the game was moved to the Georgia Dome in 1994, it became a spectacle."

The television deals forged by Kramer and the SEC were equally important. While other conferences partnered with ABC/ESPN, which often typically broadcast different games in different regions of the country, the SEC's deal with CBS called for a national game of the week each Saturday in the fall at 2:30 p.m., central standard time. "The SEC went from a very strong regional brand to a national brand," said Tony Barnhart, SEC columnist and CBS analyst, as reported by Dirk Chatelain of the *Omaha World-Herald* on December 31, 2011.

The SEC's national brand earned the league higher revenues, and SEC schools also benefited from higher season-ticket sales and seat-licensing revenue. The average attendance at SEC games in 2013, for example, was 75,674, the best in the country for the sixteenth straight year. In comparison, the average attendance at Big 12 games in 2013 was 58,899, while the Pac-12 averaged 53,619. SEC schools have used these revenues to hire top coaches. According to *USA Today*, eight of the top twenty highest-paid coaches in college football in 2013 were from the SEC. The Big Ten and Big 12 were next, with five of the top twenty highest-paid coaches.

The SEC schools have also invested in outstanding facilities, which have helped attract some of the nation's best athletes. Additionally, the shifting population demographics in the United States have helped the SEC. According to the *Omaha World-Herald*, in 1980, the nine states that now comprise the Big Ten footprint had a cumulative population of 62.1 million. The SEC's nine states at that time totaled 39.5 million. In the ensuing thirty years, Big Ten states grew by 12 percent, while SEC states grew by 49 percent—even before the addition of Texas A&M and Missouri.

Beginning on January 8, 2007, SEC schools claimed an unprecedented seven consecutive BCS National Championships. This remarkable run began with Florida demolishing Ohio State, 41-14, in the Tostitos Fiesta Bowl. It ended—barely—on January 6, 2014, when

Florida State edged Auburn, 34-31, in Rose Bowl Stadium. The closest any conference has come to this feat since the AP poll began is three consecutive national titles, claimed by the Big Ten in the early 1940s and by the SEC from 1978 to 1980.

All of those factors—and more—have combined to make the SEC the most powerful and prestigious collegiate conference in America.

Bill Byrne's son, Greg, had been named as the new athletic director at the University of Arizona in March and was slated to begin his position in Tucson in early May. Prior to being selected as the Arizona AD, Greg Byrne had served as Mississippi State's director of athletics, in which position he was the youngest athletics administrator in the SEC and the youngest to lead an athletics program at the NCAA Division I-A level. I thought Greg might have some interesting viewpoints on the pros and cons of the SEC versus the Pac-10, and that from his time in the SEC, he could easily put us in touch with Mike Slive, the conference commissioner. Accordingly, Greg gave his dad Slive's mobile number, and Bill gave it to me.

I called Mike. Just as I wasn't surprised when Larry Scott called, Slive had anticipated that he might hear from me. I shared with him my concerns about the future of the Big 12 and also the possibility of joining an expanded Pac-10. "There are some attractive aspects to that," I told him, "but deep down, it doesn't seem like the best place for Texas A&M for several reasons. Is there any chance that we could meet to discuss the possibility of Texas A&M joining the SEC?"

Mike was a practicing lawyer for many years who'd once been the assistant executive of the Pac-10 from 1979 to 1981. He was the director of athletics at Cornell University from 1981 to 1983, and he began serving as the commissioner of the SEC in 2002. He'd also earned the trust of many Texas A&M former students and insiders close to the Aggies' athletic department during the late 1980s. Those were turbulent times for A&M's football program, as the school came under intense scrutiny from the NCAA. Ultimately, the NCAA placed the A&M football program on probation for two years in 1988 for infractions that occurred during the coaching tenure of Jackie Sherrill, who was later forced to resign. Arno W. Krebs, now a retired partner with Fulbright & Jaworski LLP, served as the president of the 12th Man

Foundation in 1988 and has been a strong supporter of A&M athletics since his time as a student in the early and mid-1960s. Krebs, who has been listed in *The Best Lawyers in America* and *Who's Who in American Law*, served as outside counsel to Jimmy B. Bond, the A&M System General Counsel at the time. It was Krebs's recommendation that A&M hire Slive and his partner at that time, Mike Glazier, because of their expertise and experience in representing universities in matters before the NCAA. Bond agreed and hired Slive and Glazier as outside counsel to represent A&M. "They represented us well," recalled Krebs, a personal friend of mine. "Mike Slive was a good guy to work with; very thorough, very bright and committed to honesty and integrity. Having them involved in that case was the beginning of A&M establishing credibility with the NCAA, which [former A&M Director of Compliance] Tedi Ellison took to a whole new level."

From his previous involvement, I knew that Slive understood the culture of A&M and the importance that athletics played in Aggieland. He took my call and said he would like to discuss the benefits of our membership in the SEC, but he would rather not meet on our campus or at the SEC offices in Birmingham, Alabama. He quickly arranged a meeting at D. W. Hooks Memorial Airport near Tomball, Texas, a suburb of Houston. I drove down to the public-use airport with Scott A. Kelly, the Texas A&M University System's deputy general counsel. We were joined at the airport by Houston resident Andrew Strong, then the general counsel of the Texas A&M System.

Slive flew into town with Greg Sankey, the SEC's executive associate commissioner and chief operating officer, and associate commissioner Charlie Hussey. Scott's presentation had impressed me, but the professionalism of Slive and his staff was mesmerizing, especially since they were responding barely a week after I had placed my initial call to Slive. The three SEC executives showed up with an extraordinary presentation, presenting me with a brand new iPad that was loaded with an array of charts, graphs, and statistical information that confirmed my inclination that Texas A&M might find an ideal home in the SEC.

Understated and reserved, Slive was extremely careful and calculated with his choice of words. Like Larry Scott, Mike Slive did not at this time invite Texas A&M to seek membership in his conference. But it was clear that Slive—like Scott—was intrigued by what Texas A&M

could bring to his conference. And unlike the Pac-16, the SEC was unconditionally interested in Texas A&M . . . and not just as a package deal with someone else.

As we drove back to College Station later that evening, my mind was racing. Our next move was not absolutely certain, nor could we know how this would all play out. But at the very least, we could report back to Board Chair Morris Foster that Texas A&M now indeed had multiple options, including one that seemed to be a natural fit . . . maybe even a perfect fit.

CHAPTER 5

Some Historical Context

"Aggie jokes," which were once so prevalent when I was growing up in a small town just southeast of College Station in the 1950s and 1960s, have all but disappeared. The typically crass tales usually contained punch lines in which the connotation was that Aggie students or former students were inferior on an intellectual level to students at other universities.

Did you hear about the Aggie who won an Olympic gold medal? Punch line: *He was so proud he had it bronzed.*

All of us "old Ags" heard our share of similar jokes during that time frame. Not anymore. Texas A&M is now viewed as one of the premier public universities in the country, ranking third nationally in enrollment in 2013 with more than 58,000 students, including 12,000 graduate students on the main campus. It is one of sixty-two members in the prestigious Association of American Universities, and in 2012, *U.S. News & World Report* ranked A&M second in the nation among public universities in the "great schools, great prices" category. *Washington Monthly* ranked A&M second nationally among public and private universities based on research, service, social mobility, and contributions to society. And Texas A&M ranked first in Texas among the state's public colleges in *Kiplinger's* 2013 "best values." The Aggie jokes now go something like this:

What do you call an Aggie ten years after graduation? Punch line: *Boss.*

Nevertheless, even during my time as president at Texas A&M, I continued to sense that many administrators and graduates of UT-Austin often viewed Texas A&M as the Longhorns' "little brother." It wasn't necessarily a superiority complex, as most Texas exes and administrators I encountered possessed an authentic respect for how Texas A&M had evolved from an all-male, military college into a diverse, world-class university. Texas officials also recognized A&M as a partner in the state-run, multibillion dollar mineral rights endowment for both universities called the Permanent University Fund (PUF). Yet, I often noticed that, even in the midst of recognizing A&M's growth and advancement, many people affiliated with UT did not—or at least would not—fully regard Texas A&M as its equal.

Perhaps that has everything to do with history that dates back more than a century.

Pulitzer Prize–winning author Pearl S. Buck once noted, "If you want to understand today, you have to search yesterday." Similarly, American novelist and essayist James A. Baldwin wrote, "People are trapped in history, and history is trapped in them." Those two philosophical quotes seem quite applicable in trying to explain why some UT-Austin officials and alumni viewed Texas A&M's interest in possibly joining the SEC in 2010—and again in 2011—as yet another "Aggie joke." Some of those representatives and graduates could simply not believe that Texas A&M was seriously considering going out on its own in its search for a conference home without being accompanied by Texas or without even seeking Texas' approval. To them, Texas A&M was still the tag-along little brother, a tolerated annoyance with a shared PUF inheritance.

I'm convinced that those individuals were trapped in history, because the two schools were not originally intended to be equals. The Morrill Land-Grant Act, passed by the United States Congress and signed into law by President Abraham Lincoln in 1862, provided for the establishment of a land-grant college that became the Agricultural and Mechanical College of Texas, which formally opened as the state's first public institution of higher education on October 4, 1876. According to the Texas State Historical Association, in the same year as A&M's official opening, the Constitution of 1876 specifically provided that a "university of the first class" be established at a site selected by a vote of the people and that it be called "The University of Texas."

Even though the Agricultural and Mechanical College of Texas opened its doors seven years before Texas did on September 15, 1883, state lawmakers clearly implied that A&M was a second-class institution in comparison to the one being planned in Austin. The Texas legislature also wrote into the constitution, which was never amended, that A&M was "to serve as an annex or a branch of the main university in Austin."

All along, lawmakers planned for the university in Austin to feature a diverse and broad-based academic curriculum, while A&M would be limited to agricultural and mechanical studies and military training: the elite of Austin versus the working class of College Station. The entrepreneurs and business leaders would attend Texas; the farmers and foot soldiers could train near the railroad stop that became College Station. That's how things were designed by the state of Texas; it was all part of the master plan.

But things have changed dramatically since the Constitution of 1876 was adopted. Texas A&M evolved from its original second-class designation and became a world-class institution. Gen. James Earl Rudder, chairman of the Board of Regents Sterling Evans, and other leaders transformed the University's future by opening the doors to female students and making membership in the Corps of Cadets non-compulsory; the Aggie jokes slowly began fading away as enrollment grew dramatically in the 1970s, 1980s, and 1990s; College Station evolved as a community; and Texas A&M's reputation prospered nationally and flourished internationally.

Yet, some perceptions among many University of Texas administrators, students, and graduates did not advance at the same rate as A&M's reputation. Many of the administrators associated with UT-Austin figured that Texas A&M would always be at least somewhat dependent on the Longhorns, especially in its athletics relationships. Those of the burnt orange persuasion often poked fun at Aggies, pointing out that A&M was so obsessed with beating Texas on athletics fields and courts that the second verse of the Aggie War Hymn—originally written in 1918—opens with the words, "Goodbye to Texas University."

Perhaps because of the formative history of the two universities, many fans, alums, and administrators affiliated with UT-Austin could simply not fathom a day when Texas A&M would ever have the courage to say those words—"Goodbye to Texas University"—and really mean it. Maybe they really thought the Aggies were kidding by inquiring about membership in the SEC.

But times and universities change. And little brothers grow up enough to pack their own powerful punch instead of merely being the brunt of punch lines.

CHAPTER 6

Forming the Tentative Ten

On the morning of June 3, 2010, the sports world empathized— collectively, regretfully, and genuinely—with Detroit Tigers pitcher Armando Galarraga. The Venezuelan-born starter had been on the cusp of becoming the twenty-first pitcher in major league baseball history to throw a perfect game the previous night, retiring the first twenty-six batters he faced. All that stood between Galarraga and the first perfect game in Tigers' history was Cleveland's Jason Donald.

Donald grounded a ball toward the hole between first and second. First baseman Miguel Cabrera ranged far to his right, as Galarraga raced over to cover the bag and took the throw from Cabrera. Replays clearly showed Cabrera's throw to Galarraga beat Donald to the bag by at least a half step. Detroit teammates began rushing toward the infield to celebrate with Galarraga, but first base umpire Jim Joyce then emphatically and erroneously ruled Donald to be safe.

The following morning, sports media were still buzzing about the blown call. White House Press Secretary Robert Gibbs even opened his morning press briefing on June 3 by saying, "I hope that baseball awards a perfect game to that pitcher." It was one of those stories that transcended the sports world, at least in part because the timing of the call was so utterly distressing for the pitcher. If the umpire's mistake had been in the early innings, it still would have been a major news story, but the timing of the call seemed particularly gut-wrenching for Galarraga.

Little did I know, on the morning of June 3, that later that day I would essentially have a ringside seat for another one of those "can-you-believe-the-bad-timing?" moments that would rock the sports world. It certainly didn't make the nation empathize with then–Big 12 commissioner Dan Beebe in the same manner the country wanted to console Galarraga. But as I sat next to my new friend, Baylor University president Ken Starr (he'd just taken over as president two days earlier), at Kansas City's Intercontinental Hotel, I couldn't help but feel some sense of compassion for Beebe, who seemed to be attempting to draw a tenuous line in the sand just as cataclysmic events slammed against the boundaries of the Big 12, shaking the league to its core.

Typically, the Big 12 Conference's spring meetings had been mundane, uneventful gatherings where "big agenda" items involved discussions regarding the locations of future championship competitions. But the anticipation for the 2010 meetings, scheduled for June 1–4, had built to a crescendo of media speculation as reporters from across the country pondered the potential fallout if a few of the rumored window-shoppers within the league (most notably Nebraska, Missouri, Colorado, and Texas) chose to relocate to a new and more lucrative conference neighborhood. Rumors regarding those schools had been rampant entering the Big 12 spring meetings, and Beebe had addressed the issue in late May. "The importance of these meetings can't be overstated," Beebe told the *Kansas City Star*. "This is a critical point in the time of the Big 12, and there needs to be some honest discussion about what must happen to solidify the members' standing in the conference." His comments to the *Dallas Morning News* entering the meetings were similar: "I'm going to put to our membership that they quit deciding how to react and just go forward. We're going forward, this plane is going to take off, and we're going to see who's onboard."

Media members flocked to the Intercontinental Hotel in hopes of seeing a showdown at the KC Corral. Could Beebe, against the longest of odds, somehow persuade the band of Big 12 brothers to stay together? Would Beebe give Nebraska, Missouri, and Colorado an "in-or-out" ultimatum? Would Nebraska and Missouri profess their allegiance to the Big Ten? Would Colorado bolt for the Pac-10? And what about Texas? The Longhorns appeared to have plenty of options, but was staying in the Big 12 still a viable one for UT-Austin?

To the disappointment of the camera-toting media assembled in the hotel's hallways and lobbies, the meetings opened harmoniously. Athletic directors and league officials met on June 1 and 2 with nothing particularly newsworthy to report. Nebraska athletic director Tom Osborne and Missouri's Mike Alden both told the media that the initial meetings went well. Beebe reiterated his belief that the Big 12 was a strong league that made geographical sense and pointed out that the current, twelve-school configuration would likely command a significant increase in revenues when he opened negotiations the following April on a new television agreement with Fox, as he hoped to do. The closest thing to a controversial statement came from Texas AD DeLoss Dodds, who told the media on June 1: "You've known me for very long; I am not hanging back. I'm not waiting to see what other people are going to do. I'm going to know what our options are, so that's not going to change. My hope is that the Big 12 survives, and you and I retire knowing it's a great conference. It's been very viable, and if it stays in place, it will continue to be very viable."

Dodds then noted that the University of Texas had not been responsible for starting the nationwide realignment talks. "If we need to finish it, we'll finish it," Dodds said. "We're going to be a player in whatever happens."

Personally, I found it interesting at the time that Dodds made no mention of the Pac-10. From my meeting more than a month earlier with Larry Scott in College Station, I was fully aware of the University of Texas' involvement in plans to create a Pac-16 super conference. I also presumed that the other presidents and athletic directors whose schools would be directly affected by that potential move—Guy Bailey and Gerald Myers of Texas Tech, David Boren and Joe Castiglione of Oklahoma, Burns Hargis and Mike Holder of Oklahoma State, and Bruce Benson and Mike Bohn of Colorado—had met with Scott and were also aware of the proposed westward expansion.

Since my meeting with Scott, I had not seen anything leaked to the media about the comprehensive proposal of the Pac-16, but that all changed on June 3 when the Big 12 athletic directors and school presidents were scheduled to hold joint meetings in Kansas City. That afternoon, a website that I had not heard of previously—but one I would come to know quite well in the next couple of weeks—released news that sent shock waves across the country and rocked Beebe's world. According to a story by Chip Brown, an Austin-based columnist for Orangebloods.com, the Pac-10 was "prepared to make a bold move and invite Texas, Texas A&M, Texas Tech, Oklahoma, Oklahoma State, and Colorado to join its league, according to multiple sources close to the situation. Left out would be Iowa State, Baylor, Kansas, Kansas State, Nebraska, and Missouri." That article by Brown, a former reporter for the *Associated Press* and *Dallas Morning News*, also noted that Texas A&M might have other options. "According to a source close to the situation," Brown wrote, "A&M officials have had serious conversations with the Southeastern Conference about the Aggies joining that league."

When that news broke, that day's meeting essentially ended. It wasn't just an elephant in the room; it was the entire zoo. Beebe had been scheduled to hold a press conference later that afternoon with Texas' Bill Powers, then the chair of the Big 12 presidents/chancellors. But in the aftermath of the Orangebloods.com revelation, Beebe, suddenly looking as panicked by the ambush as Custer at the Battle of Little Bighorn, cancelled the press conference. Meanwhile, news traveled instantaneously across the country. Colorado AD Mike Bohn told the *Boulder Daily Camera* later Thursday afternoon that he believed the Pac-10 might extend invitations to the six Big 12 schools as soon as the weekend, pointing out that the Pac-10 meetings started Friday, the same day the Big 12 meetings in Kansas City concluded. Meanwhile, on the West Coast, Larry Scott responded to the breaking news of the day by issuing the following prepared statement:

"We are aware of a story filed today by an Orangebloods.com columnist, speculating about possible expansion plans for the Pac-10 Conference. While many interesting scenarios have been suggested in numerous news reports around the country, we remain focused on a thorough evaluation process that examines all of the options for increasing the value of the conference for our member institutions, our student-athletes, and our fans. We have not developed any definitive plans. We have not extended any invitations for expansion, and we do not anticipate any such decisions in the near term."

Perhaps because I had been sitting earlier in the day next to Ken Starr, the namesake for the "Starr Report," the purposeful vagueness of Scott's remarks reminded me of President Bill Clinton's infamous quote, "It depends upon what the meaning of the word 'is' is." Scott's plans seemed rather "definitive" to me when he presented them in my office, but I suppose that since no contracts had been signed, nothing regarding the proposal was set in concrete. It was certainly true that Scott had not yet extended Texas A&M an invitation, but I was definitely perplexed by what "near term" might have meant. Regardless, I understood that Scott was being vague so that he would not be dishonest. I also realized I would need to choose my words extremely carefully the following day, as I anticipated that Beebe would draw that line in the sand, asking the presidents and chancellors to commit to the future of the Big 12.

Realignment news pushed Armando Galarraga off the front pages of many sports sections across the country on the morning of June 4, and it wasn't all focused on the Pac-16 proposal. The *Columbus* (Ohio) *Dispatch* released a story that morning, showing that at least one prominent member institution of the Big Ten had been in direct contact with the University of Texas. Through a public records request, the newspaper confirmed that Ohio State University president Gordon Gee had sent a cryptic email to Big Ten Commissioner Jim Delany on April 20. "I did speak with Bill Powers at Texas, who would welcome a call to say they have a 'Tech' problem," Gee wrote in an email obtained by *The Dispatch*. I suspected right away what that likely meant.

It appeared to me that Powers had been exploring a move to the Big Ten, and he'd already anticipated political pressure from within the Lone Star State to include at least A&M and Texas Tech in any realignment plans. But the Big Ten had made it clear months earlier, when the conference announced it would consider expansion, that it was seeking schools that were members of the Association of American Universities, the prestigious alliance of research-minded universities. While A&M and Texas were members of the AAU, Texas Tech was not. Perhaps the "Tech" problem in the Big Ten is what caused Powers to turn his full attention to the Pac-10. Perhaps he hoped that the West Coast–based conference did not have an issue with the possibility of adding three non-AAU institutions (Oklahoma, Oklahoma State, and Texas Tech).

The big realignment news of June 4, however, involved speculation regarding the final day of the Big 12 spring meetings. As all the presidents, chancellors and key conference administrators gathered inside one of the meeting rooms at the Intercontinental Hotel, Dan Beebe looked as if he were sweating bullets. The Big 12 appeared to be on the brink of a collapse, and the handwriting could be on Beebe's wall. As calmly as he could, Beebe asked each of the presidents for a commitment to stay in the Big 12. When it was my turn to speak, I said that Texas A&M was committed to the Big 12 "as it is today." I was quite deliberate in stating that we were committed to staying in a twelve-school alliance, but I was not willing to pledge allegiance to a league that might only be held together with duct tape and baling wire. Missouri and Nebraska refrained from making any commitment. Nebraska's statement, by the way, was delivered not by Chancellor Harvey Perlman, but rather by AD Tom Osborne. Meanwhile, the comments from Colorado's Bruce Benson made it clear to me that the Pac-10 was the future home where the Buffaloes would roam. University of Oklahoma president David Boren was absent from the meeting, having sent his chief of staff. Before the meeting concluded, Beebe did his best to at least place the twelve-member conference on life support, extending an "unequivocal, unconditional" deadline of Friday, June 11 to commit to the Big 12.

I left those meetings with the feeling that it was only a matter of time before the Big 12 was done . . . and the doomsday clock had officially begun its countdown with the report from Orangebloods.com. From my perspective, losing Colorado certainly wasn't a death knell for the conference. The Buffs could be replaced with another school that might make even better geographical and financial sense. But the possibility of losing Nebraska and Missouri to the Big Ten would significantly weaken the league. In a story that later appeared in the *Omaha World-Herald*, Nebraska president Harvey Perlman acknowledged that he left those spring meetings in Kansas City and placed a call to Delany as he was driving back to Lincoln, telling the Big Ten commissioner, "This is not an ultimatum to you, but . . . if I don't have something definitive from the Big Ten, I'll have to commit to the Big 12."

As I returned to College Station, my mind was racing, and I knew it was time to make some decisions on A&M's behalf. We had put together an informal realignment discussion group within the Board of Regents, consisting of Jim Wilson, Morris Foster, and Gene Stallings, the former head football coach at both Texas A&M and Alabama. All of us believed that if the Big 12 did collapse, our best option would be to go to the SEC. But I would soon discover that our former students, as well as fans, faculty, staff, current students, and even some members of our Board of Regents, were not united on which conference direction would be best for Texas A&M's long-term future.

The days immediately following the conclusion of the Big 12 spring meetings were chaotic and sometimes confusing. On a personal and professional level, I was extremely disappointed with the vast majority of sports media during the summers of 2010 and 2011, because so many reporters seemed more focused on tweeting rumors than actually reporting sourced and correct news. Perhaps it's a sign of the times, but immediacy in the media often seems more important than accuracy, and I was—and still am—particularly disturbed by how many reporters were comfortable citing "unidentified" sources who were allegedly "close to the situation." Especially in the Twitter world, even some "old-school" journalists didn't mind reaching to report the rumored news. With conflicting information being reported hourly, it was often difficult to decipher fact from fiction.

We were not making our decisions at Texas A&M based on media reports, but some of those reports definitely influenced the time frame of when decisions needed to be made. It had crossed my mind in the days after the Big 12 spring meetings that perhaps the University of Texas was expediting the decision-making process by providing details of the Pac-16 plan to a Rivals.com-affiliated website tailored to Texas fans. And maybe the timing of that breaking news release during the final days of the Big 12 meetings was not coincidental, either. If UT officials wanted to accelerate the super conference formation—as I suspected they did—the Orangebloods.com article had certainly set some wheels in motion, as Beebe's deadline had suddenly placed every Big 12 member on the clock. I didn't initially spend much time pondering whether Texas officials were purposely leaking information to specific media outlets, but it did cross my mind as I traveled back from the Big 12 meetings. It also disturbed me that Chip Brown was reporting that Texas A&M was already in serious discussions with the SEC, according to "a source close to the situation." Who was that source? It wasn't me or Mike Slive, and I felt certain it wasn't any of our Regents. But I wondered if someone within our inner circle was talking.

My "conspiracy theory" thoughts would essentially be confirmed the following week (June 7–11). That eventful week began with the news that the Pac-10 presidents and chancellors had given Larry Scott authority to advance the process of possible expansion. Speaking to reporters after the close of the Pac-10 meetings in San Francisco, Scott said: "I don't have any grand proclamations or announcements to make here. I have the authority to take (expansion) in different directions, depending on various scenarios. We absolutely could move more quickly if we needed to, but we're under no pressure to decide anything before the end of this year."

Scott didn't wait until the end of the year . . . or even the end of the week. On Wednesday, June 9, the Pac-10 made its first and safest move, extending an invitation to the University of Colorado. Quite frankly, the Buffs had been more flirtatious with the Pac-10 than a group of high school girls seeking prom dates, and practically everyone knew that CU would accept the conference's invitation when Scott offered. The Colorado invitation temporarily silenced many Baylor fans and officials who had argued and pleaded publicly after the Orangebloods.com article that the Bears would be a more valuable addition to the Pac-10 than the Buffs.

At Texas A&M, we had a conference call on June 9 that included Regents Morris Foster, Jim Wilson, and Bill Jones, along with General Counsel Andrew Strong, Bill Byrne, and me. We discussed Colorado's certain departure, the likelihood that Nebraska would join the Big Ten by the end of the week, and our strategy moving forward, including the meeting we had scheduled for the next week in Austin with a contingent of UT administrators and Board of Regents members. In the aftermath of the June 3 Orangebloods.com story, I had received hundreds upon hundreds of emails, texts, and phone calls from Texas A&M former students and fans, who expressed varying opinions on what conference would be the best fit for Texas A&M. At that point, there was certainly no strong consensus among the A&M family, as our constituents appeared fairly equally divided about their preferences. During our teleconference, we discussed possible scenarios and determined that our best strategy might be to simply see how things unfolded instead of making any declaration or any long-term decisions. In this high-stakes poker game, we didn't feel pressured by any declarations, calls, or perceived bluffs. If the Big 12 fell apart, we believed we could play our ace in the hole by making one phone call to the SEC.

The *New York Times* also released a story on June 9, indicating that the Big Ten was taking a proactive approach to expansion. "Everyone is picking up the pace," Ohio State president Gordon Gee said. "We can't sit there in uncertainty." That same evening, Donnie Duncan, a former Big 12 associate commissioner and one of Beebe's advisors, received a call from the distraught commissioner. "(Beebe) was very emotional," Duncan told Wendell Barnhouse of Big12Sports.com. "He felt he had let the (conference office) staff down."

As expected, Colorado accepted the Pac-10 invitation on June 10, the same day our team of A&M representatives traveled to Ashbel Smith Hall in Austin. Our intent in meeting with the Texas contingent (Board of Regents chairman Colleen McHugh, Regent James Huffines, Vice Chancellor and General Counsel Barry Burgdorf, General Counsel to the Board of Regents Francie Frederick, Powers, Dodds, and Regent Steve Hicks, who participated via conference call) was to inform them that we were considering multiple options. But upon our arrival, Wilson, Jones, Strong, Byrne, and I (Foster also participated over the phone), quickly discovered that UT officials expected our rubber-stamp approval of the Pac-16 plans. The tone of the meeting was initially tense, as I detected a sense of urgency among the Texas representatives to move forward with the westward expansion plans. They informed us that they had already scheduled a special meeting of the UT System Board of Regents for 11:00 a.m. the following Tuesday (June 15), clearly implying that they planned to approve the move to the Pac-10 on that date. We were also told that regents at Texas Tech had scheduled a meeting on the afternoon of June 15.

We pointed out that we couldn't possibly schedule a meeting so quickly, even if we were in agreement that moving to the Pac-16 was Texas A&M's best course of action. By Texas state law, after all, regents meetings are required to be posted seventy-two hours in advance of the actual meeting. We said we needed more time, more discussions, more evaluations, and more process before drawing any conclusions. At that point, the tone of the meeting became increasingly strained. My sense was that Texas wanted to move quickly to avoid the type of political hurdles that had derailed the Longhorns' realignment plans back when the Big 12 was formed in the mid-1990s. Especially after the Pac-10 made its invitation to Colorado, Baylor representatives dropped their public pleas and once again began rallying support from elected public officials in an attempt to either keep the Big 12 together or to be included—somehow, some way—in any expansion plans.

One of Baylor's regents had called Jim Wilson, telling him that "A&M and Texas leaving would be a rifle shot to the head for Baylor athletics." Two Baylor-affiliated men even showed up in Austin on June 10, demanding that they be able to speak during our meeting. University of Texas officials denied their demands, but the Baylor "spokesmen" did stick around until the meeting adjourned. Wilson spoke to them after the meeting, but he soon grew tired of their lawsuit threats and venomous tone. Wilson attempted to explain to them that Texas A&M was not driving any Pac-10 expansion plans, but he finally had to end the discussion abruptly.

By that time, we'd been exposed to enough verbal threats for one day. The Texas representatives simply couldn't understand why we would possibly consider joining the SEC instead of joining them in the Pac-16. Again and again, they explained that other schools were already onboard with their proposal and that everything was already prepared. They seemed stunned and dismayed by our desire to consider other options. During one break in the two-hour meeting, Wilson observed DeLoss Dodds shaking a finger toward Bill Byrne, cursing at him and threatening to never play the Aggies again if we dared to go against the grain. Wilson noted that Byrne didn't say much to defend himself. That certainly wasn't because he was intimidated by Dodds. Byrne wasn't the type of person who backed down from confrontation, and he was often adamant and up-front regarding his disdain for UT-Austin, which dated back to his years as the director of athletics of Nebraska (1992–2003). But my opinion was that Byrne did not view the SEC as a positive option for A&M. Although he never said it to me directly, I believe the Pac-16 had a strong appeal to him. Not only had he been a successful athletic director in the Pac-10, serving in that position from 1984 to 1992 at Oregon, but I also sensed that Byrne liked the idea of being in the same conference as his son, Greg, who had taken over as director of athletics at Arizona on May 3, 2010.

Ultimately, the contentious meeting in Austin probably did more harm than good, especially when it was over. Before we even made it all the way back to College Station, Chip Brown had posted a new story on Orangebloods.com filled with information about the meeting we'd just left. There was some misinformation in the report, but according to Brown's story, Texas, Texas Tech, Oklahoma State, and Oklahoma were merely waiting for a formal announcement by Nebraska about joining the Big Ten before announcing that they were leaving the Big 12 for the Pac-16. At the latest, Brown projected that those four schools would wait until after the weekend to make the official announcement "to allow some time to pass following Nebraska's anticipated Friday announcement."

From our standpoint, the most maddening and frustrating part of Brown's report was the following three sentences: "But sources say Texas A&M is still seriously exploring joining the Southeastern Conference. That charge is being led by A&M Regent Gene Stallings, who, of course, won a national title in 1992 at Alabama as head coach. But if Texas A&M waits too long to commit to the Pac-10, the Aggies could be put on the clock, possibly opening up their invitation to another school, sources close to the Big 12/Pac-10 merger said."

Although I couldn't actually prove it, I was thoroughly convinced that information was intentionally being leaked to pressure us into joining the Pac-16. But that's not all that bothered me about the article. Brown reported that Powers and Dodds had met with UT coaches on Wednesday and told them they had "done everything they could to save the Big 12 but were unsuccessful."

From my viewpoint, that was so misleading that it was laughable. So was the contention that Mike Slive was "pulling out every enticement he can to lure Texas and Texas A&M to the SEC, including possibly moving two teams from the SEC West to the SEC East to allow Texas and Texas A&M in the SEC West, one source with knowledge of the SEC said. But Texas does not appear interested in the SEC, no matter what." That was not even laughable because it was so inaccurate. I never asked Slive about his interest in UT-Austin, but he certainly wasn't concocting numerous incentives to lure A&M to the SEC. He merely answered my call and developed a proposal at our request that would include the addition of Texas A&M as the thirteenth member of the SEC.

Nevertheless, the Orangebloods.com information was cited by more traditional news agencies across the country, as the story went viral in a matter of minutes. While I felt betrayed by the leaks coming out of our meeting in Austin, I did not feel pressured into doing anything that was not in Texas A&M's best interests. Nothing had changed.

We were staying the course, holding our cards as close to our vest as possible, and if Texas truly wanted to break up the Big 12 and leave schools like Baylor, Kansas, Kansas State, Iowa State, and Missouri scrambling to find other options, it would be the Longhorns making that call. Besides, we had scheduled meetings over the weekend with both Larry Scott and Mike Slive, and we were in no rush to make a decision.

Before those meetings ever occurred, Friday, June 11 delivered some definitive realignment news, as opposed to mere speculation. In a somewhat unforeseen move, Boise State announced it would leave the Western Athletic Conference and join the Mountain West in 2011. And to the surprise of no one, Nebraska's Board of Regents voted on June 11 to join the Big Ten Conference in 2011, giving that league twelve members. At the press conference announcing Nebraska's move, then–Huskers athletic director Tom Osborne insinuated that the Huskers felt forced to find another solution because of the Pac-16 plans. "One school leaving does not break up a conference," Osborne said at the press conference. "Two schools does not. Six schools leaving breaks up a conference."

I spent much of the day on June 11 analyzing whether Texas A&M should be one of the schools leaving the Big 12. I compiled a document in which I listed various criteria that we should consider before choosing Texas A&M's future conference destination.

For example, I considered factors such as conference structure, travel, national exposure, cultural similarities, and so forth, to determine whether it would be best for A&M to stay in the Big 12 with ten schools, move to the Pac-10 with sixteen schools, or pursue membership in the SEC with thirteen or fourteen schools. Weighing the pros and cons of each conference, I then made a decision as to which conference option was most advantageous to Texas A&M. Putting everything on paper made it clear to me that, if the Big 12 fell apart, the SEC was undoubtedly a better option for A&M than the Pac-10, even if it meant severing ties with Texas and other traditional rivals. On the other hand, I knew that politicians in the Lone Star State were working feverishly to keep the Big 12 together, and I continued to believe that would be a viable option for Texas A&M.

Criterion	Big 12 Remainder (10 teams)	PAC-10 (16 Teams)	SEC (13 or 14 Teams)	Advantage
Conference Structure	Single Division; No Championship Playoff (<12 members); Automatic BCS Invitation; 8 Bowl Invitations (likely decrease); Nine-Game Conference Schedule	Two Divisions; Championship Playoff Game (?); Automatic BCS Invitation; 6 Bowl Invitations (likely increase); Nine-Game Conference Schedule	Two Divisions; Championship Playoff Game; Automatic BCS Invitation; 9 Bowl Invitations; Eight-Game Conference Schedule	SEC
Welfare of Student-Athlete: Travel Impact	Increased Travel in Single Division Conference	1 West Coast Football Game/Regular Season; Time Zone Disadvantage	1 East Coast Football Game/Regular Season Time Zone Advantage	SEC
Conference Member Revenue	Probable Decrease Over Future Contract Value*	Substantial Increase (Risk regarding success of PAC-10 Network)	Substantial Increase (Guaranteed)	SEC
National Exposure	Some Diminution Likely	Some Increase Possible	Increase Certain	SEC
Merchandise Licensing	No Appreciable Change	No Appreciable Change	Increase Likely	SEC
Ability to Compete in Football	No Appreciable Change	No Appreciable Change	Decrease Likely (initially)	Big 12/PAC-10
Ability to Compete in Men's BB	No Appreciable Change	Decrease Likely	Increase Likely	SEC
Recruiting Capability	No Appreciable Change	Retain 3 of 4 Texas Schools for Conference Play; Opens Texas to AZ and CA Recruiting (and vice versa)	No Texas Schools for Conference Play; Opens Texas to SEC Schools for Recruiting (and vice versa)	Big 12
Academic Prestige	No Appreciable Change	Substantial Increase	Substantial Decrease	PAC-10
Reputation (Recruiting, Compliance, etc.)	No Appreciable Change	No Appreciable Change (although recent USC sanctions by NCAA are substantial); 2 NCAA investigations underway	Perceived Decrease (academic program quality; non-compliance)	Big 12/PAC-10
Texas A&M Independence & Leadership	No Appreciable Change	No Appreciable Change (except dilution due to size of conference)	Greatly Enhanced	SEC
Game Attendance	No Appreciable Change	Few West Coast Opponent Fans at Home Game (may also apply to AZ schools); Small Decrease Possible	Likelihood of all Conference Home Games Selling Out (possible exception with East Coast team)	SEC
Traditional Rivalries	Can Be Retained; Retaining Arkansas Game Leaves 2 Non-Conference Games Open	Can Be Retained; Retaining Arkansas Game Leaves 2 Non-Conference Games Open	Potential Loss of Annual Texas Game; Restoration of Historic LSU Rivalry; Arkansas Becomes Conference Game	Big 12/PAC-10
Land-Grant Mission	5 (of 10)	7 (of 16)	9 (of 13)	SEC
Culture of Conference Members	No Appreciable Change	Likely Culture "Clash" with Some West Coast Schools	Similar Cultures; Some Common Economic Factors (e.g., oil and gas industry; agriculture)	SEC

Facility Comparison	No Appreciable Change	Favorable	Unfavorable	PADC-10
Current Student Opinion	Favorable	Unfavorable	Very Favorable	SEC
Former Student Opinion	Favorable	Mixed (leaning against)	Mixed (leaning for)	SEC
Faculty Opinion	Favorable	Very Favorable	Unfavorable	PAC-10
External Academic Opinion	No Appreciable Change	Favorable	Unfavorable	PAC-10

*New information will be provided based on conversations with the Big 12 Commissioner.

Morris Foster had informed me that key members of the Texas legislature were flexing their muscles to keep the Big 12 and the traditional rivalries intact. I later learned that State Rep. Dan Branch, R-Dallas, chair of the House Committee on Higher Education, called a meeting for Wednesday, June 16 "to discuss matters pertaining to higher education, including collegiate athletics. Invited testimony only." Officials from Texas A&M, Texas, and Texas Tech, as well as collegiate conference officials, were scheduled to give testimony. I was also notified that Lieutenant Governor David Dewhurst, House Speaker Joe Strauss, and others, including Steve Ogden, then chair of the Senate Finance Committee, were rallying support to keep the Big 12 together.

Meanwhile, Big 12 commissioner Dan Beebe was preparing for what was probably the biggest and most exhaustive weekend of juggling and negotiating of his professional life. "I have perseverance and a pretty positive outlook," Beebe told the Associated Press after all the dust had settled in July 2010. "I can be down 21–0 with four minutes left and I'm going to play until the final whistle. I was in that mode (heading into the weekend of June 12–13)."

On Saturday, June 12, in Kansas City, administrators from Baylor, Missouri, Kansas, Kansas State, and Iowa State agreed to forfeit their shares of the exit penalty fees that were being levied against Colorado and Nebraska by the Big 12 for leaving the conference. Those administrators, in a last-ditch attempt to save the conference, gave Beebe permission to use that money to entice Texas A&M, Texas, and Oklahoma—the three marquee schools left—to remain in the Big 12. That was Beebe's first victory of the day. The second was even more significant.

The Big 12 had a $480 million deal with ABC-ESPN that ran through 2015–16, and a $78 million contract with Fox Sports Net through 2011–12. Beebe entered the weekend hoping both networks would agree to continue honoring the numbers in those contracts, guaranteeing the remaining ten schools in the conference would receive larger cuts. It would require a big concession, especially by ABC, because with ten schools, the Big 12 could no longer hold a conference football championship game (twelve schools is the minimum for a league to hold a title game). According to Joel Lulla, the Big 12's television strategist, on Saturday Beebe received confirmation that ESPN would not reduce its payout to the Big 12. "When we got ESPN to agree to not cut our right fees—they probably could have reduced our deal by $75 million to $100 million over the final six years—that put us in a better position, because we were getting the same money and having to distribute it to two fewer schools," Lulla told Wendell Barnhouse of Big12Sports.com. According to various reports, Beebe continued to work the phone lines throughout the day Saturday and into the wee hours of Sunday, gathering information and assurances from the Big 12's remaining television partners. Apparently, he was also providing updates to Big 12 schools "that had multiple options," but I was not in regular contact with him, which was a source of considerable frustration for me. I tried reaching Beebe several times on Saturday and Sunday, but it wasn't until Monday that I actually spoke to him.

I was frustrated that Beebe had not returned my calls during the weekend, and I was also angry with Byrne because, in what amounted to one of the most critical weekends in Texas A&M's history as a member of an athletic conference, he was in Idaho. He'd left the Lone Star State for Idaho shortly after the Thursday meeting in Austin, even though he knew Mike Slive was coming to College Station on Saturday and Larry Scott was arriving on Sunday. I expected him to cancel or postpone his family trip to Idaho to be a part of these historic meetings and decisions, but that was not the case.

Slive and other SEC officials flew into Easterwood Airport on Saturday. Jim Wilson, General Counsel Andrew Strong, Deputy General Counsel Scott Kelly, and I met with the SEC representatives at Easterwood Airport, and we reaffirmed Texas A&M's interest in seeking membership in the SEC if the Big 12 was no longer an option. Slive, understanding the uncertainty of the times and the delicacy of the situation, essentially assured us that the SEC would act accordingly if we officially requested to join the conference. We were not yet at that stage, but I felt comfortable with Slive, and I was absolutely confident that A&M would be a great fit in the SEC. It was never our intention to play any kind of a role in the breakup of the Big 12, and we were intent on honoring our existing relationship with the conference and its remaining members. If the Big 12 was no longer a viable option, however, the SEC was Texas A&M's best fit. The majority of our Regents agreed with that assessment, and I was confident that they would have voted accordingly if it had come to that.

One day after Slive and the SEC officials visited College Station, the Pac-10's Scott and deputy commissioner Kevin Weiberg met with Wilson, Strong, Kelly, and me in the same location where we'd met with SEC representatives the previous day. Scott had spent Saturday on the other side of the Red River, meeting with officials from Oklahoma and Oklahoma State. He presented us with an eight-page contract that officially invited Texas A&M to become a member of the Pac-10, effective July 1, 2012. The contract stated that if Texas A&M wished to accept the invitation, I needed to respond by sending the signed contract to Scott via facsimile by noon central time on June 17. We had a good visit, and I told Scott that we were considering all of our options, including the Pac-16. He wasn't surprised by our thoroughness and informed us that he was also considering various scenarios. He also mentioned that his itinerary for the rest of the day included stops in Lubbock and Austin.

At that point, Jim Wilson asked Scott point-blank what he planned to do with the Longhorns' proposed television network. Scott looked dumbfounded. He then said, "There will not be a Texas network. We've already discussed that with the (administrators at Texas)."

I then reemphasized my concern about UT-Austin's intentions. From everything I could gather, I believed that the Longhorns planned on delivering the three Texas schools and two Oklahoma schools to the Pac-10, and then indeed planned on pursuing their own TV network. On two occasions, Scott had explicitly described to me his intent to start a Pac-16 network and to distribute revenues equally among all the member institutions. But I cautioned him to make certain that he and the UT-Austin officials were absolutely, positively on the same page, sharing the same vision. I made it as clear as possible that I did not think Bill Powers and Texas planned to merely share television revenues equally among fellow members of the Pac-16. I believed that Texas wanted to be part of the Pac-16, but that the Longhorns also wanted to start their own network, profiting from their own tier-three broadcasts (explained more fully in chapter 8). Scott thanked me for my concern, asked us to seriously consider the invitation he had presented to us, and went on to Lubbock.

Back in Dallas, Beebe was making more progress with the Big 12 television partners. By the end of the day he said he was confident that, based on his discussions with ABC, ESPN, and Fox, the Big 12's distributions to each of the existing ten member institutions would jump from between $7 million and $10 million annually (as was the case with the twelve-school Big 12 in 2009) to roughly $17 million in 2012, when the league's new TV contract would be in place. Furthermore, because of the assurances he'd already received from Baylor, Kansas, Kansas State, Iowa State, and Missouri, he was willing to guarantee that linchpins Texas A&M, Texas, and Oklahoma would receive a minimum of $20 million annually, regardless of how many times the schools appeared on television. That was certainly comparable to the numbers Scott was projecting for Pac-16 payouts. Beebe's plan also stipulated that individual institutions would be allowed to pursue their own networks, which was obviously aimed directly at UT-Austin's interests. I was privately concerned that this policy would continue and even aggravate the problem of uneven distribution of conference revenues. However, it was important to the Board members with whom I spoke.

The media was buzzing with reports on Sunday, and former Baylor Regent Drayton McLane held a teleconference with various reporters that evening, reminding them how important the Big 12 was to the Texas economy. The Twitter world was also wild with rumors, including one that claimed Texas A&M had rejected the Pac-10 invitation. Upon hearing that rumor, Jason Cook comprised an official statement that I approved Sunday evening: "As (athletic director) Bill Byrne and I have said on several occasions, our desire was for the Big 12 Conference to continue. With the departure of two universities from the conference last week, the Big 12 is certainly not what it was. We are aggressively exploring our options, one of which is for the Big 12 to continue in some form. We also have had extensive discussions with other conferences over the past two days. We continue to evaluate our options in a deliberate manner, as we work toward a decision that is in the best long-term interests of Texas A&M."

I cannot say with certainty exactly what happened behind closed doors in Austin on Monday, June 14. But by 4:00 p.m. that day, Texas had abandoned months of planning, positioning, and posturing to stay right where it had been since 1996. Bill Powers called Dan Beebe in the commissioner's "war room" in Irving, Texas, with the announcement that the Longhorns had turned down the Pac-10 invitation and were staying in the Big 12. My suspicion—purely my own opinion that I cannot prove—was that Scott specifically addressed the Longhorns' network visions during the meeting on Sunday in Austin, making it clear that Texas would be required to turn over their media rights to the Pac-16, just like every other school in the conference. My guess was that the two sides could not come together over that issue, which was the major sticking point.

At the end of July 2010, Scott addressed what he believed ultimately doomed his Pac-16 scenario at the Pac-10 media days in Pasadena, California. Speaking to a group of reporters on the floor of the Rose Bowl, Scott downplayed the proposed network's role in the unraveling of the Pac-16. "(Inviting Texas) wouldn't have gotten that far if it was about a few dollars here or there or a TV right here or there," Scott said. "There were bigger issues." In Scott's opinion, the bigger issues involved Lone Star State politics. "Texas and Texas A&M separating with Baylor created a tsunami effect," he said, as reported by Dennis Dodds of CBSSports.com. "It got way too hot for the politicians. We wanted to get Colorado first. We knew there were some political efforts in the state of Texas that might derail it. Time was of the essence. In twenty-four hours (from Sunday to Monday), it went from happening to not happening. In hindsight with a few months to reflect, fundamentally it was Texas political issues that derailed it."

Scott did take that opportunity to confirm another one of my suspicions during that chaotic two-week time frame that began with the start of the Big 12 meetings on June 1 in Kansas City. Scott believed—like many of us at Texas A&M—that UT-Austin officials were leaking information to Chip Brown at Orangebloods.com. "We weren't trying to publicize what we were doing," Scott said at the 2010 Pac-10 media days. "We were going about it for four months quietly behind the scenes. It's really Texas (that) leaked the plan as they were going into those Big 12 meetings in Kansas City, I think, hoping to keep Nebraska, hoping to keep the Big 12 together. I don't know . . . It could only be a small (amount of people) who knew what was going on."

I tend to disagree with Scott's assessment of why UT-Austin officials leaked the information. I believe they were first trying to expedite the Pac-16 process and that they were later trying to pressure us at Texas A&M into making a move.

Regardless, Chip Brown vehemently denied Scott's accusation and our assumptions. "Larry Scott is living in a fantasy world if he thinks DeLoss Dodds or Mack Brown leaked information to me," Brown said in response to Scott's press conference. One year later (in June 2011), Brown offered his perspective on those two weeks and how he became, according to Sports Illustrated.com, the leading source on the realignment news of June 2010: "People have asked me repeatedly how Orangebloods.com was able to stay ahead of the Big 12 Missile Crisis, seemingly from start to finish," Brown wrote on June 3, 2011. "And I've said the same thing over and over again. We had valuable information not many people had. Others involved in the story with information began calling me. And we began to trade information. I probably started the story with three great sources and finished with about a dozen. The bottom line is I've never been a part of a faster-moving, more complex story with so many ramifications than that one."

Whatever the case, we at Texas A&M learned some valuable lessons from how everything unfolded in June 2010 and how UT-Austin officials managed to shape and define the entire story in the media, all the way to the end on June 14. By announcing that afternoon that Texas was rejecting the Pac-10 invitation, Powers, Dodds, and the rest of the Longhorns were lauded publicly for saving the Big 12. That irked me and practically everyone else associated with Texas A&M University. UT-Austin officials did make the announcement first on June 14 that the Longhorns were staying in the Big 12. But in reality, it was also Texas who first threatened to break up the Big 12, and it was Texas A&M who slowed the westward expansion plans down long enough to allow Beebe to develop alternative plans, as well as permitting the process to play out. The politicians whom Scott said were, in his opinion, the biggest factor in the undoing of the Pac-16 plan would have never likely had the time to unify and mount an offensive if we at Texas A&M had not purposely dragged our feet.

At the end of the day on June 14, we believed we had acted conscientiously and dutifully in representing the best interests of the Aggie family throughout the realignment process. Beebe's financial plan made sense to us, offering as much in guaranteed revenues as Scott's theoretical projections. By staying in the Big 12 as opposed to joining the Pac-16 or seeking membership in the SEC, we would also maintain our long-standing traditional rivalries with Texas, Texas Tech, and Baylor. And perhaps most important, we were best representing the desires of our constituents by staying in the Big 12. From the thousands of texts, emails, or phone calls my office had received since the Orangebloods.com story broke on June 3, it was obvious to me that there was no consensus among the Aggie family. People were torn on what we should do. As such, we believed it was best to stay where we were—in the Big 12.

Shortly after Powers's phone call to Beebe at 4:00 p.m. and the ensuing media frenzy regarding the news from Austin, we at Texas A&M then followed up by posting this letter from me on the Texas A&M University website:

June 14, 2010
To the Aggie Family:

The past two weeks have been a whirlwind of speculation as Texas A&M University and several other institutions in the Big 12 Conference evaluated our athletic affiliations. At the end of the day, ten of the twelve schools in the Big 12, including Texas A&M, have determined that the conference was definitely worth saving due to our collective strengths in academics, national competitiveness, geographic fit, and overall financial value.

Throughout the conference evaluation process, I was encouraged by something that I already knew: Texas A&M is incredibly strong and the passion of our current and former students, as well as our faculty and staff, is unmatched anywhere. As evidence, I have been overwhelmed by thousands of emails, phone calls, and Facebook posts from Aggies in support of any of the three options we were considering: remaining in the Big 12, or joining the Southeastern Conference or Pac-10 Conference.

Let me be clear: This decision was made in the best interests of Texas A&M and was not made in haste. As I mentioned to the Faculty Senate Monday afternoon, our top consideration was the demands placed on our student-athletes, in terms of academics, time away from the classroom, and the overall level of competition. There were also many other factors considered, including maintaining Texas A&M's strong foothold in the State of Texas and preserving our natural athletic rivalries, many of which date back more than one hundred years. And, ultimately, by remaining a member of the Big 12, we were able to more than double our financial return to the levels being offered by other conferences.

I understand that some Aggies are disappointed, but I am confident this decision will serve Texas A&M well in the years to come. As Athletic Director Bill Byrne and I stated numerous times throughout this process, our hope and desire was for the Big 12 to continue. And we both agree that this is an exciting, new day for our league.

I appreciate all of your feedback and thoughts on this important issue. As Aggies, I know that you will rally around our Texas A&M student-athletes as they train over the summer and begin Big 12 competition this fall.

Thanks again, and Gig 'Em!

Dr. R. Bowen Loftin '71

Immediately after we made the decision to stay in the Big 12, I went to a quiet corner of the Board of Regents' meeting room and placed a call to SEC commissioner Mike Slive, thanking him for his sincere interest in Texas A&M and letting him know that, in my opinion, the timing was just not right for the Aggies to move to the SEC. Deep down, I knew A&M would be a great cultural fit in the SEC. And, quite frankly, I believed the Big 12 was still on life support, especially since there was now such clear separation between the "haves" and "have-nots" in the conference. So much had happened in a couple of weeks, exposing the fragility of the conference. I believed that Beebe's plan offered only a temporary fix, and I asked Slive if he would be receptive to hearing from me again in the future if it turned out that the Big 12 no longer seemed like a viable option to Texas A&M. He assured me that the SEC would welcome a call from Texas A&M if that were ever the case.

Two days after we posted the letter to the Aggie family, Larry Scott exercised his Plan B option, as Utah accepted an invitation to join the Pac-12. Meanwhile, flowers were delivered to my office in College Station from Baylor President Ken Starr, who obviously recognized that we at Texas A&M had been critical in keeping the Big 12 alive and keeping Baylor, as well as several other schools, in a power conference.

As I traveled across the state representing Texas A&M throughout the rest of the summer of 2010, Aggies had a number of opinions that they shared with me about the realignment chaos. While some were happy that we stayed in the Big 12 and others were disappointed that we had not chosen to go to the SEC or the Pac-16, the one consistent sentiment I heard from Aggies was that they were disappointed by how Texas had shaped the court of public opinion by its use of the media. I agreed with that sentiment, and I assured the Aggie family that we had learned much in the entire process. Unfortunately, in the summer of 2010, we'd been thrust into a reactive mode instead of being proactive, as we tried—much like Detroit Tigers pitcher Armando Galarraga had done at the start of June 2010—to make the best of an imperfect situation.

If anything happened in the future like what had transpired in early June 2010, I assured all those with whom I spoke that we would be proactive in promoting Texas A&M and managing the message in the media. Little did we know then how quickly we would be able to apply the lessons we learned in 2010. We had weathered some tenuous times, but more major storms were on the horizon.

September 26, 2011 was one of the more memorable days of my life as the SEC celebration was held at The Zone at Kyle Field. From left, Regent Jim Wilson, SEC Commissioner Mike Slive, University of Florida President Bernie Machen, and Regent Richard Box enjoy the moment with me. (Photo courtesy of Glen Johnson/Texas A&M Media Relations).

Mike Sherman was a great recruiter and role model, but his teams had a difficult time finishing games. The 2011 Aggies blew double-digit leads in five of six losses. (Photo courtesy of Glen Johnson/Texas A&M Media Relations).

Bill Byrne (shown here with his wife Marilyn) was the Director of Athletics at Texas A&M from January 2003 until May 2012. (Rusty Burson photo)

Mike Slive (center) joins Director of Athletics Eric Hyman and me on the field prior to the first-ever SEC game at Kyle Field on September 8, 2012. Slive made sure our home SEC opener was a marquee matchup, as Florida visited Aggieland. (Photo courtesy of Glen Johnson/Texas A&M Media Relations).

It didn't take long to realize that Kevin Sumlin was the right man at the right time for Texas A&M. (Photo courtesy of Glen Johnson/Texas A&M Media Relations).

Kevin Sumlin and strength and conditioning coach Larry Jackson lead the '12 Aggies through the tunnel walk prior to a home game. The coaches brought a new attitude to Aggieland when they arrived prior to the 2012 season, and the team reflected their toughness. (Rusty Burson photo).

Kevin Sumlin, shown here being interviewed by ESPN's Samantha Steele at the 2012 Home Depot College Football Awards Show, made Texas A&M "cool" to recruits across the state and the region. (Rusty Burson photo).

Johnny Manziel became the first freshman ever to win the Heisman Trophy and gave a memorable acceptance speech that garnered rave reviews. (Rusty Burson photo).

Immediately after he won the Heisman Trophy on December 8, 2012, Manziel's likeness appeared on a massive electronic billboard in the heart of Times Square in New York City. (Rusty Burson photo).

Manziel and the 2012 Aggies capped the season in impressive fashion, stunning Oklahoma, 41-13, on January 4, 2013 in the Cotton Bowl. (Photo courtesy of Glen Johnson/Texas A&M Media Relations).

Kevin Sumlin is joined by Tommy Bain (left) and Mike Baggett (right), who are both former Texas A&M students and members of the Cotton Bowl Board of Directors, following the blowout win over OU. (Photo courtesy of Glen Johnson/Texas A&M Media Relations).

Jason Cook was instrumental in our marketing, branding and public relations efforts as we moved from the Big 12 and entered the SEC. (Personal photo).

CHAPTER 7

New Year's Salutations

As 83,453 fans shuffled quietly out of Kyle Field on the afternoon of October 16, 2010, Texas A&M's football season appeared to be collapsing. The Aggies had slipped to 3-3 with their third consecutive defeat, and this most recent setback—a 30-9 whipping at the hands of Missouri—was particularly disheartening and demoralizing. In the aftermath of that humiliating home loss, however, head coach Mike Sherman made a few moves that changed the complexion of the season.

On the Tuesday following the loss to the Tigers, Sherman tossed the Missouri game plan and video into a trash can and set it all on fire. His message then was that no one—not even the coaches—had done an adequate job in preparing for that contest. Forget it and move forward.

That was not all that Sherman did to light a fire under the team. He also decided to allow backup quarterback Ryan Tannehill to split time with starter Jerrod Johnson in the next game against Kansas, and he started reserve tailback Cyrus Gray in front of Christine Michael. Together, Tannehill and Gray transformed a struggling offense into one of the more prolific units in school history.

Beginning with a road victory at Kansas on October 23, 2010, the Aggies finished the regular season with six consecutive victories to grab a share of the Big 12 South Division championship. In the process of going 9-3 during the regular season, A&M beat Texas Tech, Baylor, and Texas in the same season for the first time since the formation of the Big 12.

Perhaps the signature victory of the season came on November 20, 2010, when Gray ran for a career high-tying 137 yards (his fifth straight 100-yard performance) before a Kyle Field record-setting crowd of 90,079, as the Aggies beat Nebraska 9-6 in the final regularly scheduled Big 12 game between the two schools for the foreseeable future. This was the most thrilling game I had witnessed since we beat Texas on Thanksgiving Day in 1967. I was on the sidelines for the last five minutes of the game, and the noise level was incredible. Seeing the white towels float down from the east side was a sight I'll never forget. It was a feel-good win in so many ways, and our team followed up that victory with yet another memorable moment.

On Thanksgiving Night in Austin, I was euphoric watching Gray rushing for 223 yards and making two long touchdowns, helping Number 17 Texas A&M beat Texas 24-17, sending the Longhorns to their first losing season since 1997. Gray had touchdown runs of 84 yards in the second quarter and 48 yards in the third. Von Miller intercepted a tipped pass at the A&M 11 yard line with 2:37 left, killing what could have been a game-tying TD drive for Texas. It was A&M's sixth win in a row, giving the Aggies a share of the final Big 12 South title. It was also Texas' fifth home loss of the season. The setback kept the Longhorns (5-7, 2-6) from becoming bowl eligible, just one season after playing for the national championship.

After all that had transpired during the summer of 2010—especially in our face-to-face dealings with officials at UT-Austin—I must admit that the stretch run of the 2010 football season was particularly rewarding. Winning six games in a row to end the season also earned the Aggies their first January bowl bid since the 1999 Sugar Bowl. Texas A&M accepted an invitation to play LSU on January 7, 2011, at what was then known as Cowboys Stadium in Arlington, Texas.

During the course of football games, I don't actually watch much of the game. I've learned that it is best to wait for the DVD on Monday and watch it later, because my role during most games is to visit with our former students, current students, fans, and key representatives from the school we are playing. Among other things, I typically make my rounds through the suites, greeting as many people as possible. As fate would have it, my journey on the night of January 7, 2011, took me into a suite where I found SEC commissioner Mike Slive. I had run into Mike on the field prior to the game, and I told him I thought we should talk. He gave me the location of his suite, and as I entered, he greeted me warmly. Mike and I had developed a friendship during the spring and summer of 2010, and I thoroughly respected him personally and professionally. Before I left the suite to continue meeting and greeting others during the game, I asked Slive to step into the corner—away from everyone else who was watching the game—for a moment of privacy. He obliged.

"Mike, I know I asked you this back in June, but I wanted face-to-face confirmation here," I said to him. "If there ever comes a point in time when it is obvious that Texas A&M's best interest is to pursue membership in the SEC, is that door still open?"

Mike smiled, shook my hand and reaffirmed that the SEC would welcome a call from Texas A&M if the timing was right. We shook hands and parted ways.

Texas A&M lost the game that night to LSU, 41-24. But as I looked back on the previous seven months—from early June 2010 to early January 2011—I believed we had been the big winners. Texas A&M had stood its ground and now was proactively prepared to shape its own future. Undoubtedly, 2010 had been a year to remember. And 2011 would be one we'd never forget.

CHAPTER 8

The Devil Wears Burnt Orange

Hollywood has long recognized that nothing unifies an audience quite as quickly and as fervently as a diabolically despicable villain. Think about it. Did moviegoers in 1977 really love and immediately connect with Luke Skywalker, Han Solo, and Princess Leia, or were they more united by their absolute disdain of the dark, merciless, helmet-and-cloak-clad Darth Vader, whose menacing, mechanical breath served as a second-by-second reminder of his sinister and wicked plans for the entire galaxy?

Likewise, what made *Dallas* such a popular television series during that same time frame, and again nearly thirty-five years after its original debut in 1978? It certainly wasn't the likeability factor of Bobby, Jock, Pamela, or Sue Ellen Ewing. Instead, viewers were emphatic in their hatred of J. R. Ewing, the conniving, backstabbing eldest among the Ewing siblings. Throughout the summer of 1980, the most prevalent question on the minds of many Americans—perhaps even more than the upcoming presidential race between Jimmy Carter and Ronald Reagan—was, "Who shot J. R.?"

Even in real life, villains tend to unify the country unlike practically anything else. In the sports world, Nancy Kerrigan might well have attracted only minimal attention outside the figure skating community during the 1994 Winter Olympics in Lillehammer if not for the villainous schemes of Tonya Harding and her ex-husband Jeff Gillooly. And unless they were wearing the uniform of your favorite team, who didn't enjoy rooting against notorious professional sports figures like Latrell Sprewell, Dennis Rodman, John Rocker, Terrell Owens, and Ndamukong Suh? Rooting against Rodman could actually unite Lakers and Celtics fans, just as booing Suh could bring even Packers and Bears fans together. And who hasn't witnessed the way that one of the "bad boys" of professional wrestling can electrify an entire coliseum, as every single spectator shouts "Boo!" at the top of his or her voice?

Similarly, one thing truly brought Texas A&M's former students, current students, fans, faculty, and staff together in the summer of 2011, uniting practically all Aggies in their pursuit and support of a move to the Southeastern Conference: the Longhorn Network (LHN). To the fans of the maroon and white, LHN was a villainous lightning rod, the equivalent of the light saber–wielding Darth Vader, the flesh-eating Hannibal Lecter and the ruby slipper–coveting Wicked Witch of the West all rolled up into one rules-bending antagonist. We needed a dragon to slay, and LHN became our fire-breathing, claw-baring, wing-flapping serpent in burnt orange.

To be honest, the network was not really the final straw for Texas A&M, at least from an administrative standpoint. Honestly, each of us had probably thought about a network of our own to show a nonconference game—according to the original understanding in the conference—and to air nonrevenue sports and other events. But UT-Austin began to stretch its intentions for the LHN far beyond the parameters any of the rest of us thought we had agreed to. Thus, many other factors, such as the lack of leadership in the Big 12 Conference and the preferential treatment the league seemed to brazenly extend toward UT-Austin, led many Texas A&M administrators and Board of Regents members to conclude that staying in the league was simply not in the Aggies' best interests. And, for a lot of us, it appeared that many of those infuriating decisions and manipulative tactics occurred in closed-door meetings among conference administrators or via memos sent from the league's offices in Irving, Texas.

The Longhorn Network, on the other hand, was certainly a high-profile, well-publicized reminder to Aggies that the University of Texas, with the financial backing and clout of ESPN, planned to test and stretch the boundaries of the NCAA's authority. And more than once it seemed that Dan Beebe was perfectly willing to provide rubber-stamp approval for virtually anything that Texas proposed, regardless of whether it was favorable to the rest of the league or only UT-Austin.

The network itself was not actually the issue. After the events of June 2010, practically everyone who followed college athletics expected that UT-Austin would launch its own network. Thus, no one was surprised on January 19, 2011, when school officials, ESPN, and the Longhorns' multimedia rights partner, International Management

Group (IMG) College, announced a twenty-year contract agreement to create the nation's largest twenty-four-hour television network dedicated to a single university's intercollegiate athletics programs. The contractual figures were impressive, as Texas stood to receive $300 million over the life of the contract. From a presidential perspective in an age of higher education cutbacks, I also found it interesting that UT athletics would contribute $5 million per year to academics in the first five years of the deal with ESPN.

While the financial numbers were most certainly appealing from an outsider's perspective, we at Texas A&M wondered if UT-Austin's network, with all of its anticipated time demands and logistical challenges, might become as much of a burden to the Texas coaches and student-athletes as it was a financial benefit. In other words, we anticipated that Texas would truly earn its income from LHN, and we were not opposed to UT-Austin operating its network and benefiting from it financially.

What ultimately bothered us—as well as many other universities in the revised Big 12—was how Texas and ESPN seemed to be conspiring to use the network. Even before LHN had ever broadcast a single minute of air time, several issues were brought to light that gave us considerable concern. In May 2011, the *Austin American-Statesman* reported that the Longhorn Network contract stated that it would replace any on-air talent that UT-Austin determined "[did] not reflect the quality and reputation desired by UT for the network based on inappropriate statements made or actions taken." In other words, ESPN, arguably the biggest name in all of sports broadcasting, would hire the talent for LHN, but UT-Austin would have the power to do the firing. At Texas A&M, we perceived immediate conflict of interest concerns. It was one thing that LHN and ESPN were now inseparable, but it was another that LHN had leverage over ESPN talent. Would Texas' commanding influence eventually extend beyond the Longhorn Network and into other areas of the ESPN family?

We believed it was a fair question, and we were not alone. "No matter how ESPN spins it, the Longhorn Network is a PR arm of Texas," wrote Richard Deitsch, a media columnist for SI.com.

Another ESPN-related issue brought us even more concern. Dave Brown, the Longhorn Network's vice president for programming and acquisitions, announced in a June 2011 interview on ESPN Austin affiliate KZNX 104.9 FM that the Longhorn Network planned to air as many as eighteen high school football games.

"We're going to follow the great [high school] players in the state," Brown said in the interview. "Obviously a kid like [then unsigned UT-Austin verbal commit and Aledo High School senior-to-be] *Johnathan Gray*—I know people are going to want to see [him]. . . . So we're going to do our best to accommodate them [on LHN] and follow the kids who are being recruited by a lot of the Division I schools, certainly some of the kids Texas has recruited . . . and everyone else the Big 12 is recruiting. . . . I know there's a kid [unsigned Texas verbal commit] *Connor Brewer* from Chaparral High School in [Scottsdale] Arizona. We may try to get on one or two of their games as well so [LHN viewers] can see an incoming quarterback that'll be part of the scene in Austin."

Such comments raised a major red flag. We believed that airing high school games featuring players in whom UT-Austin had recruitment interest would give Texas a significant and unfair recruiting advantage over every school in the Big 12 and throughout the region. Upon further inspection, we also believed that such coverage could potentially violate three elements of Title 13, Section 10 of the NCAA rulebook. Among other things, that section prohibits colleges from arranging radio or TV appearances for prospective student-athletes and prohibits schools from allowing prospects on shows conducted by coaches, or shows in which coaches are participating. We at Texas A&M, along with other universities in the Big 12, pointed that out. Texas A&M also contacted the NCAA for an interpretation.

In response, UT-Austin athletic director DeLoss Dodds said the Texas athletic department would not be involved with selecting high school games on LHN. "ESPN will select the games based on what they feel is best," Dodds said, as reported in the *Houston Chronicle*. "We understand that this is a new world and that we're leading the way in an area that is new to us and new to the NCAA and new to ESPN. Like everything else, we will do it in a first-class way, in the light of day, and we will do it the right way." Apparently, Dodds thought that would make everyone at Texas A&M, Texas Tech, Oklahoma, and elsewhere feel better, but it did not.

Following conference calls with Big 12 athletic directors and university presidents, Beebe, on July 20, 2011, announced that telecasts of high school football games on LHN were at least temporarily placed on hold, pending decisions by the NCAA and the Big 12 about how to handle school and conference networks. "It's not going to happen until and unless the conference can make it happen with benefit to all and detriment to none," Beebe said. Then in early August, the Big 12's athletic directors agreed at a meeting in Dallas to a moratorium on high school content delivered on institutional or conference media platforms for a minimum of one year. Later in August, the NCAA banned school-affiliated networks from showing high school games and highlights, determining it would be an unfair recruiting advantage—just as we at Texas A&M had stated immediately after the interview on the Austin radio station.

That solved one issue, but there were others that concerned us even more. In April 2011, the Big 12 Conference and Fox Sports Media Group had officially reached a thirteen-year agreement for exclusive cable rights to forty football games per season (twice as many as the previous contract allowed), as well as to a variety of Olympic sports events and conference championships. The deal, which was scheduled to start during the 2012 football season, would pay the conference roughly $90 million a year. Along with the Big 12's deal with ABC/ESPN, the Fox arrangement delivered enough new revenue streams that the "conference would be able to provide an annual average per institution television revenue at the highest levels in college athletics," stated the official conference press release that was distributed to media and posted on the Big 12 website. That release also contained the following specific nuggets of information regarding programming under the new contract:

- No warehousing of rights (networks signing for rights to conference events, but only televising a small number and "warehousing" the rest).
- No exclusive windows except for football telecasts.
- Institutions have the option to retain rights to *one* home football game per season [my emphasis] for distribution via institutional distribution platforms [the Longhorn Network, for example].

Finally, the press release contained some creatively crafted general questions and answers for media and fans, such as:

How does this impact the future of the Conference?

"This landmark agreement positions the conference with the best television arrangement in collegiate sports, taking into account revenue, exposure, and preservation of institutional rights. It achieves these benchmarks while solidifying the long-term commitment of the member institutions to one another. Add to this that we will be back in the marketplace in four years with our Tier I football and men's basketball rights, and you can see why we believe that the best days of the Big 12 Conference are yet to come."

In theory, the deal looked extremely promising, and Beebe was praised prominently in the media for keeping the league together in the summer of 2010 and making good on his promises to deliver much bigger revenues in the near future. The April 2011 deal with Fox seemed to assure that every school in the conference would receive at least $20 million, which had been promised in June 2010 to only Texas A&M, Texas, and Oklahoma, regardless of how many times those schools appeared on Tier I telecasts. At the end of July 2010, though, according to Brent Zwerneman of the *San Antonio Express-News*, Beebe told a handful of reporters at the Big 12 football media days that "UT and OU had declined an offer from five of the league's schools—the desperate ones who were going to be left behind had the league dissolved—for their share of the exit fees of Nebraska and Colorado."

From Texas A&M's viewpoint, that gesture from Texas and Oklahoma was certainly not as magnanimous as the general public may have construed it. The Longhorns and Sooners were practically assured of appearing on the Big 12's Tier I telecasts often enough to earn the $20 million because they were playing so well on the field. Texas A&M, at that time, did not have the same assurances, because the Aggies had struggled on the field in recent years. Entering the 2011 football season, A&M's combined overall record during the past eight seasons (2003–10) under Dennis Franchione and Mike Sherman was just 51-48. During the same time frame, Texas went 84-19, and Oklahoma was 86-22. Obviously, the Longhorns and Sooners were appearing more often on major networks and in marquee time slots than the Aggies because of their successes on the field. I had pointed out in July 2010 that a key part of A&M's decision to remain in the Big 12 was the commissioner's commitment that A&M would receive a minimum of $20 million annually in future conference distributions. We were prepared to do whatever was required to ensure that payment.

In the aftermath of the Fox deal, however, Beebe said that the Big 12 now had "one of the best television arrangements in college sports." Furthermore, he told Jimmy Burch of the *Fort Worth Star-Telegram* that the new deal would make the pledge to A&M, UT, and OU "moot in 2012 and beyond. We're counting on that [minimum] going forward."

Again, everything initially looked good on paper, and we all seemed like one big happy Big 12 family at the 2011 spring meetings in Kansas City in early June—exactly one year from when all hell broke loose on the realignment front in 2010. Unlike 2010, only a handful of media members even bothered to cover the 2011 league meetings. "We couldn't get through that hallway out there last year," Oklahoma athletic director Joe Castiglione said jokingly in reference to the difference a year had made, as reported by the *St. Louis Post-Dispatch*.

The big news that was actually reported by the media was that our ten-school conference had decided to keep the same name and logo that we had been sporting since 1996. "We decided it is best that we don't try to update our logo at this time," Beebe said to the media. "There were time concerns about instituting a new logo at the ten member schools. Placing a new logo on fields, courts, scoreboards, uniforms, venues, printed, and video materials can be a time-consuming process."

In other words, there wasn't any dirt to report, because the meetings generally hummed along with a harmonious tone. But that doesn't mean we didn't address some important issues. First, the chancellors, presidents, and athletic directors discussed the need to rework and reword the language of the Big 12 bylaws as we went from twelve to ten schools. Some of the bylaws were confusing, no matter how many schools were in the league. A committee led by Baylor president (and former lawyer) Ken Starr was formed to address and clarify the legality of the wording in the bylaws and to recommend necessary changes. I also served on this committee.

For example, membership was based on a five-year term, so every five years the conference essentially had to renew itself. That renewal process had never happened in a formal way. Under the bylaws, though, each member institution had to opt in again every five years. If a school chose to withdraw from the conference within that five-year period, the amount of the exit penalties would differ, depending on how many years had passed since the last five-year agreement. In theory, penalties were assessed to schools on a sliding scale based on how many years had passed since the last five-year contract. But as we found out in the mediation with Nebraska and Colorado, the wording of the bylaws was vague and confusing. So, the bylaws committee was also tasked with addressing and clarifying the withdrawal procedures, but we deferred doing anything about this matter until we had made the first cleanup pass in the bylaws.

My major contribution to those 2011 Big 12 spring meetings was to raise the issue of establishing—once and for all—complete equality in revenue distribution. If the conference was ever going to gain any true, long-term stability, I believed equality was essential, especially in the Tier I and Tier II television revenue distribution. We eventually agreed to do so for the new Fox deal, and I hoped we could eventually do it for the Tier I deal as well. While UT-Austin or any other school was free to cut the best deal possible for Tier III rights, I made the point that the near-implosion of the conference a year earlier clearly showed that revenue inequality would be a source of unrest forevermore unless we addressed it as quickly as possible. The new Fox deal gave us some financial flexibility to really tackle the issue, and the initial feedback I received at the meetings was positive. I didn't leave the meetings singing "Kumbaya," but I was encouraged.

I was falsely encouraged, as I soon discovered. Texas had already scheduled its home game against Rice on September 3, 2011, to be the first-ever football game on LHN, which was officially set to start broadcasting on August 26. Later in June, though, it was reported that ESPN had been in talks with Fox Sports Net about picking up at least one more UT football game—preferably a conference game—for the LHN. And it was soon reported by Kirk Bohls of the *Austin American-Statesman*, and confirmed by Redraidersports.com, that Texas Tech had been approached by ESPN to place its game against Texas on November 5 on the LHN . . . and that Beebe had essentially blessed such a deal. Ultimately the board gave Beebe the power to make this decision. I was the lone dissenter.

Obviously, that was not what we had all signed off on back in March and not what the Big 12 official release had stated after the Fox contract news in April. Remember this point in the league's official release: "Institutions have the option to retain rights to one home football game per season for distribution via institutional distribution platforms." What part of "one" was so difficult to understand? At Texas A&M, we initially planned to use pay-per-view for our single nonconference home game. University of Oklahoma senior associate athletic director Kenny Mossman confirmed in January 2011 that OU was planning to have its own TV channel up and operating at some point during 2011. And every other school was looking into its own options and possibilities. I even engaged a consultant to look into partnering with another university in a network that would spotlight Texas A&M. We talked about going beyond athletics, with the proposed network's coverage to include academic content and much more. I had also contacted the Texas A&M AgriLife Extension Service to gauge its interest in being a part of the network.

The bottom line was that I was never worried about Texas having one nonconference game to sell, because every other school in the Big 12 also had the same thing. We each had an equal opportunity to air one nonconference game in the way we deemed to be the most beneficial to our respective universities. But then UT-Austin began pushing the envelope of the agreement and appeared to be manipulating Beebe however they wanted. Not only were the Longhorns now seeking more than one game, they were also venturing into the conference slate.

Much of the media couldn't understand why the second game on the LHN bothered us so much. But it is important to understand how the television rights work in practically every major conference. Tier I and Tier II rights are generally controlled by the conferences, which sell them—either separately or combined—to national networks like ABC/ESPN, CBS, and Fox. The Tier I rights holder, which was ABC in the Big 12, receives first pick of the conference's weekly football games for over-the-air broadcasts. The unselected games then pass to the Tier II rights holder (Fox, in this case), and games chosen at that level are generally aired on cable networks.

The definition of "Tier III" varies from conference to conference, but it mostly consists of what remains after the first two tier selections have been made. For most conferences, Tier III rights belong to the conference members, who are free to monetize them as they see fit. In Texas' case, it was with the Longhorn Network. Again, we at Texas A&M didn't have a problem with the LHN in principle, but we had a big issue with how LHN, in combination with ESPN, was pursuing games beyond the limits of the conference agreement. And it wasn't just us. As Jon Mark Beilue wrote in his lead paragraph for a story in the *Amarillo News*, "The Longhorn Network . . . is about as popular to the rest of the Big 12 as a rat floating in a punch bowl."

Beilue's story—along with many others on the same topic—confirmed another worry we had about Beebe, ESPN, and the LHN. Right from the start, we were concerned about the possibility of collusion that would intentionally allow LHN to broadcast games that should have been on Tier I or Tier II networks. If that happened, the LHN would have some fabulous games to broadcast, while the rest of the league's schools would eventually suffer from lost revenue when the Tier I contracts were renegotiated. According to numerous media reports, that was already happening before the LHN ever went on the air. Texas Tech officials were reportedly told in the summer of 2011 that the Red Raiders' November 5, 2011, game in Austin would not likely be carried by ESPN or its partner, ABC. That seemed odd, to say the least, as the Texas Tech–Texas series had been one of the more entertaining rivalries in recent years. When that news broke, it appeared clear to many of us that the LHN/ESPN/Big 12 triumvirate was already manipulating a system that had only been put in place with the Fox deal in April.

Tech chancellor Kent Hance immediately rejected that possibility, reportedly saying, "I don't want a Tech fan to have to give one dime to the Longhorn Network." President Guy Bailey and athletic director Kirby Hocutt also publicly backed Hance's statement. While Tech stood strong, Beilue pointed out that other schools might have a more difficult time taking such a stance, as LHN now gave UT-Austin unprecedented leverage. "While ESPN tried to make it attractive for Tech to play on the Longhorns' personal network, what's to keep ESPN from playing hard ball with, say, Missouri or Baylor?" Beilue wrote. "'You don't play on the LHN? Fine, then we (ESPN) won't be televising certain games you wanted down the road.' This Longhorn Network is going to get very messy down the line, so much so that it wouldn't surprise me if Texas A&M and Oklahoma, if they can't start something like that themselves, eventually bolt to the SEC."

By the time that story was written in early August 2011, we at Texas A&M were already completely convinced that a move to the SEC was in the Aggies' best interest, and we were in detailed discussions with conference officials. Dating back to the summer of 2010, every discussion I had with Jason Cook, Jim Wilson, and others close to the situation had focused on three issues regarding realignment as it pertained to Texas A&M:

- The institution's brand exposure/awareness;
- The stability of the conference;
- Enhanced financial opportunities.

In all three of those areas, we were sold on the SEC being the best fit for Texas A&M. As such, we intermittently continued our discussions with key members of the Board of Regents throughout the fall of 2010 and into the winter and spring of 2011 regarding the shifting landscape of college athletics, the health of the ten-school Big 12, the Longhorn Network, and the best options for Texas A&M. We were not yet, by any means, determined to leave the Big 12. After the summer of 2010, though, we were adamant about being proactive in our approach to conference realignment. We would not be forced into a reactionary mode by other universities or events. Nor would we be caught off guard by anything that might happen to further undermine the strength of the Big 12.

This approach required us to make some tough decisions and to take what some might regard as radical steps. First, we made a conscious decision to keep the inner circle of decision makers and informed administrators extremely tight. We did not want any of our plans or internal discussions to immediately become media tweets and sound bites. Initially, the circle was more of a triangle that included Cook, Wilson, and me. When we included other key Regents, such as Richard Box, Jim Schwertner, and Cliff Thomas, we were extremely guarded about those with whom we shared information. Because conference alignment decisions were the responsibility of the president and the Board of Regents and would ultimately be made solely by them, we did not include any Texas A&M athletic department personnel in our highly restricted contingent of informed decision makers. While this would prove upsetting to some top administrators within the athletic department, we believed it was necessary to prevent any information leaks.

We also continued to maintain contact with high-ranking officials at the SEC, including Commissioner Slive and the SEC's television consultant. We discussed conference television issues from a national perspective, the newly proposed Fox deal in the Big 12, and an array of possibilities in the future. We did not lay any groundwork for Texas A&M's move to the SEC at that time, nor did Slive mention any plans to expand his league. This was purely an informational, stay-connected effort.

Meanwhile, Cook continued his stellar work with the media, using his strong connections to shape the message that we wanted to deliver at the right time. While we had been open to the possibility of Texas A&M continuing its membership in the Big 12 after the conference's 2011 spring meetings concluded in Kansas City in early June, one news item after another regarding the LHN, ESPN, and related matters forced us to change our plans and objectives. We could no longer trust UT-Austin, Dan Beebe, or the Big 12's long-term viability as one of the power conferences in the nation. Also, the Longhorn Network had now united Texas A&M fans, former students, and current students in a manner that we could not have predicted back in the summer of 2010. It was apparent by mid-July 2011 that the Aggie family would not only support a move to the SEC, but would positively welcome it.

We had a regularly scheduled Board of Regents meeting set for Thursday and Friday, July 21 and 22. The Board then publicly called and posted a special executive session to discuss conference realignment, the Big 12, and the Longhorn Network. That closed-door session would be held at the Board Annex at the west end of the Memorial Student Center (MSC), and it was during that meeting that I made the case to the executive committee of the Board of Regents that the time was right for Texas A&M to seek membership in the SEC. The committee essentially blessed my recommendation to move forward. When the closed-door meeting ended, we all left the annex to go across the street for the regularly scheduled Board of Regents meeting inside the Zone Club on the third floor of the north end zone at Kyle Field. Before leaving the MSC, however, I had a short interview with three reporters: Brent Zwerneman, the Texas A&M athletics beat writer for the *Houston Chronicle* and the *San Antonio Express-News,* Vimal Patel, the higher education reporter for the *Bryan-College Station Eagle,* and Steve Fullhart, a reporter and anchor for KBTX-TV, the local CBS affiliate.

Zwerneman had been identified by Cook as one of the key media members who was objective and would not be swayed by the court of public opinion. UT-Austin had controlled the media message in 2010—often through the reporting of Chip Brown at Orange-bloods.com—and we were determined not to allow that to happen in 2011. We were not trying to manipulate the media—no one can control today's media—but we were intent on making sure that stories were reported objectively, without a burnt-orange slant. Jason Cook was the perfect person to handle the job.

His background, which included media relations at Mississippi State and at a *Fortune* 500 sports medicine company—and that of his wife, an Aggie who had worked for the SEC for nine years—could not have been any more suited for what we were preparing to do. Cook understood the sports media and their needs as well as anyone; he was intimately acquainted with the SEC; he had reliable contacts through-out the SEC footprint; he was experienced in public relations at both the university and system level; and he had a firm handle on the culture of Texas A&M, the politics of Texas, and the precarious condition of the Big 12. More than all of that, though, Cook was a masterful marketing and media relations professional who was fully prepared for this moment in time.

At the beginning of the summer of 2011, Cook had worked with Steve Moore to hire a television consultant on our behalf and had con-ducted a media analysis. He concluded early that Texas A&M was unlikely to receive favorable media coverage in Austin, Lubbock, or Waco, and that Dallas was somewhat questionable. Within Texas, Zwerneman was a key media contact for many reasons, including the fact that his stories were printed in both Houston and San Antonio.

Cook also had a good relationship with Zwerneman and believed he could be counted on to report the information provided to him in an accurate and unbiased manner. Cook also identified some other key media members in the state such as Chuck Carlton of the *Dallas Morning News* and Billy Liucci of TexAgs.com. Liucci, a 1998 Texas A&M graduate and part owner of TexAgs, also became an extremely valuable distributor of information when we were targeting messages specifically to the Texas A&M family. Brandon Jones, TexAgs.com president and CEO, reported that the website was flooded with millions of page views each day as the story of the move to the SEC evolved. "During the SEC stuff for two months in 2011, we were averaging a thirty-day snapshot of fourteen to fifteen million page views on our mobile product," Jones said. "When you add the main site with that, it was about sixty million page views for thirty days. It was an enormous amount of traffic."

Liucci reached that audience each day with his Aggie-nuanced content, and we trusted absolutely that he had Texas A&M's best interests in mind. Whenever Liucci contacted him, Cook provided him with great insight. Liucci was so accurate and reliable in his reports that he eventually began appearing on ESPN and on radio stations across the country. We knew, of course, that Liucci would be perceived as wearing maroon-colored glasses, which is why Zwerneman's reputation as an unbiased professional was so valuable.

Cook also identified key media he knew personally from SEC strongholds, such as CBS Sports' Tony Barnhart, a longtime reporter with the *Atlanta Journal-Constitution*, Jon Solomon of the *Birmingham News*, and Ron Higgins of the *Memphis Commercial Appeal*, who had been covering the SEC for more than thirty years. Cook also cultivated certain national media figures such as Andy Staples, a college football reporter for *Sports Illustrated*. We did not ignore all other media members, by any means, but we focused our efforts on keeping a handful of reporters informed with accurate and timely information that would combat the unsubstantiated claims, rumors, and innuendos that had run rampant in 2010. Cook would call or text his key media members regularly, providing a context for what was happening.

Most of these reporters had contacts within the A&M athletic department and throughout the Big 12 and SEC member institutions. But conference realignment was happening at a presidential level, and the sports media often didn't have many of those contacts. Cook was able to fill them in on both perspectives, and he knew all the reporters. He was also able to police the Twitter world, and he wasn't afraid to call a reporter—or the news agency for which the reporter worked—when the information being tweeted was inaccurate or downright venomous in nature.

Unfortunately, our fears of slanted media coverage would eventually be justified. But we were prepared and able to continue providing accurate information to the more reliable and trusted sources, starting with the July 21–22 Board of Regents meetings in College Station. In advance of those meetings, Cook had been in touch—off the record—with Zwerneman, who reported on July 19 that "a Texas A&M insider" said that Longhorn Network would be discussed during the closed-door executive session, and that the official agenda item had been titled "Big 12 Conference."

Two days later, Zwerneman, Patel, and Fullhart were waiting for me as I exited the closed-door session. I spoke to the three reporters briefly before taking a golf cart ride with Cook from the MSC to the Zone Club on campus. As Zwerneman noticed and later reported, I used one word over and over again regarding the Big 12: uncertainty. The reporters also asked me if I had been in contact recently with the SEC. I told them only that I had not been in touch with the SEC in the last several months.

I then hopped on the golf cart for a short drive across the street to the official Board of Regents meetings. Zwerneman, who was relatively new to the Twitter world at that point, pulled out his laptop and tweeted what I had said about the existing "uncertainty" in the Big 12. He later said that within an hour, he had picked up thousands of followers as the information was retweeted and favorited. That's what really started the ball rolling from a public perception standpoint, and that's how our "unofficial" media campaign began. Zwerneman eventually won a national journalism award for his reporting on that day and beyond in his coverage of Texas A&M's move to the SEC.

As Zwerneman's tweet took on a life of its own, I stepped off the elevator in the Zone Club, pulled out my cell phone, and walked onto the smoker's patio overlooking the Zone Plaza and the MSC. It was time to give Mike Slive another call. Slive answered and informed me that he was sitting on his back porch in Birmingham, smoking a cigar with Chuck Gerber, the SEC's media consultant and the former ESPN vice president of college sports programming. I chuckled as I pictured that scene and then told the commissioner the reason for my call.

"Mike, let's start talking again," I said.

He knew exactly what I meant and welcomed the news. I had called him the previous spring (2010), looking for another conference option, but this time was different. Now we were looking for a permanent new home for Texas A&M. We had a vision and a plan. A familiar (to Texas Aggies, at least) villain had emerged that had united our fan base. And we had just officially set the wheels in motion.

CHAPTER 9

A Tortuous (but Not Tortious) Path

At 4 o'clock in the morning on May 29, 1953, Edmund Hillary and Tenzing Norgay awoke in camp and prepared themselves for what they intended would be the final leg of their historic climb to the summit of Mount Everest. Before the climb could even begin that morning, however, Hillary, a New Zealand beekeeper, discovered that his boots had frozen overnight. It was yet another unexpected obstacle that delayed him from reaching his dream destination, and he spent the next two hours defrosting his boots. Undaunted, the two men finally left camp at 6:30 a.m., knowing that eight previous British expeditions had failed to reach the top of the 29,035-foot mountain, and a number of expedition members who had preceded them in the attempt had died in the process. The final stages of the climb were especially dangerous, as the air grew thinner and the snow and ice thickened near the top.

Hillary and Norgay, the mountain guide, had begun their climb up the world's tallest mountain a full seven weeks earlier, and Hillary had spent much of his life dreaming of completing this climb. At 11:30 a.m., Hillary and Norgay ultimately reached the summit of Mount Everest, becoming the first men to ever successfully reach the top. Hillary reached out to shake Tenzing's hand, but Tenzing embraced him. After risking their lives on a daily basis for nearly two full months, the two men spent only fifteen minutes at the top of the world, because the scanty air supply made it difficult to breathe. After taking photos and enjoying the amazing view, the two men began their descent. According to numerous reports, Hillary, who died in 2008, offered a rather irreverent perspective of his accomplishment when he returned to the base camp after the ascent and saw his friend and fellow New Zealand climber George Lowe, who was also part of the expedition. "We knocked the bastard off," Hillary told his friend in a proud and satisfactory tone.

I could have easily uttered those exact same words after I finally received the phone call on September 25, 2011, from Commissioner

Mike Slive, informing me that all legal hurdles had been cleared and that Texas A&M's request to join the SEC was now finally and unconditionally accepted. To be completely accurate, though, I would have needed to change the direct object of Hillary's quote to plural, not singular. In my mind, there were at least a couple of people who could have fit that irreverent description at the time.

Nevertheless, I really was overcome by the combination of complete euphoria and total exhaustion that I have read about climbers experiencing once they reach the summit of any challenging peak. The journey to the top is a supreme mental, physical, and emotional test, a financially costly endeavor, and a risky expedition that most climbers would never want to repeat. But once atop the summit, climbers often pause momentarily and realize that the arduous trek was worth every laborious step.

Such was the case for Texas A&M's two-month journey in 2011 that officially started with my phone call to Slive from the smoking patio of the Zone Club in late July and culminated with a celebration for the ages in the Zone Club in late September. A public celebration and press conference welcoming Texas A&M as the thirteenth member of the SEC was held in the Zone Club on September 26, 2011. It included Slive, University of Florida president and SEC chairman of the presidents and chancellors Bernie Machen, A&M System Board of Regents members, university officials, yell leaders, the Aggie Band, A&M's collie mascot Reveille, and hundreds upon hundreds of fans. This sensational, gratifying event was long overdue. But the moment I will truly never forget was receiving the phone call from Slive the previous day.

"It's done," Slive said. "Texas A&M is in. Unconditionally."

I was by myself when I received that call, and my mind started racing as I allowed those words to soak in and contemplated the historical significance of the phone call. After hanging up with Slive, it seemed that I should mark the moment by doing something. I briefly considered leaping into the air, shouting out triumphantly, pouring myself a drink, or at least pumping my fist victoriously, something that would serve as a distinctive memory that I could look back on for many years. Instead, I simply called Jim Wilson, who had also invested so much time and effort in the process.

If this was my Edmund Hillary moment—my fifteen minutes at the top of Mount Everest—then Wilson was my Tenzing Norgay, as we had been brothers in arms throughout 2010 and 2011. Wilson often talked me down off the ledge and vice versa. We'd been through so much together, and I thought it was appropriate for him to be the first person I called with the news. I believe his initial one-word response was, "Hallelujah!"

During the two months leading up to that phone call, Wilson and I—along with Jason Cook and a few key members of the Board of Regents—believed that the SEC would eventually welcome Texas A&M to its ranks. But there had been many trials that tested our resolve, and unexpected obstacles were continually tossed in our pathway. When Slive finally called on that particular Sunday in late September, it truly felt as if a burden had been lifted off my shoulders and Texas A&M could at long last celebrate the SEC scenery from atop the mountain.

Following my phone call to Mike Slive a few weeks earlier on July 21, I began speaking to him on an almost daily basis, usually around 7:15 a.m., before either of us had left for the office. Although we had first started talking the previous summer, the actual process of adding a new member to the league was new territory for Slive and practically everyone who was then working in the SEC offices in Birmingham. Since its formation in 1933, the SEC had only twice expanded to add institutions outside of its original charter members. Both of those additions came in 1991, when South Carolina and Arkansas joined the conference. At that time, Roy Kramer was the commissioner of the SEC, and Mike Slive was just embarking on a new career as commissioner of the Great Midwest Conference, which subsequently dissolved in 1995.

Clearly, a methodical process needed to be accomplished before the SEC could formally welcome Texas A&M, upon our request, as a member of the league. Likewise, there was also a process—a rather convoluted and confusing one, as we had all seen in the summer of 2010—needed for our withdrawal from the Big 12.

When Colorado had announced it was leaving the Big 12 in 2010, that institution's chancellor, Phil DiStefano, had assessed the Big 12 bylaws and asked for a two-year withdrawal period. One day later

Nebraska withdrew, and its chancellor, Harvey Perlman, requested a one-year withdrawal period. Both chancellors had examined the bylaws and had drawn different conclusions regarding the necessary course of action. Ultimately, the remaining Big 12 presidents and chancellors determined that, in order to avoid scheduling difficulties, it would be much easier to go from twelve schools to ten in one year instead of going from twelve to eleven one year, and then from eleven to ten the next year.

Nevertheless, the Big 12 board of directors treated the two schools differently in assessing withdrawal penalties. The Big 12 board treated Colorado as if it was withdrawing over a two-year time frame and assessed the Buffs a lighter penalty, withholding $6.863 million from Colorado for the 2010 calendar year. Meanwhile, the Big 12 board viewed Nebraska's departure as a one-year procedure and levied a stiffer penalty, withholding $9.255 million from revenues otherwise distributable to the Cornhuskers in 2010. In the grand scheme of things, however, neither school was assessed particularly onerous exit fees because—as best as I could tell from the confusing bylaws and where each school stood in its five-year membership window in the league—Nebraska and Colorado had both provided notice they were leaving prior to July 1, 2011, when a new five-year window opened.

So, frankly, I was initially unsure of how Texas A&M's exit would be perceived and administered, especially from the standpoint of exit fees. In August and September of 2011, some of the media's financial speculations on exit penalties were daunting, to say the least. One interpretation of the Big 12's bylaws suggested that Texas A&M would forfeit ninety percent of conference revenue for 2010–11 and 2011–12, an amount that could have totaled in excess of $35 million. When all the realignment and negotiating was said and done, Texas A&M and Missouri each were assessed $12.41 million in exit fees. However, the net penalty was less for us, since I argued successfully that A&M was entitled to its share of the Fox sign-on bonus. Although the mediation was held for both schools at the same time in Kansas City, our cases were handled separately, and I was not privy to the discussion between the Big 12 representatives and Missouri.

Long before any of the detailed exit negotiations began, Beebe volunteered some interesting pronouncements in a highly public setting at the 2011 annual Big 12 football media days in Dallas. Typically, those two made-for-media days don't generate much major news, as coaches and players from each member institution fly into town to answer reporters' questions about the upcoming season, the depth chart, off-season developments, preseason rankings, coaching changes within the league, and so forth. For the most part, this event provides an opportunity for reporters to socialize and for the conference to toot its own horn in what amounts to an official kickoff for the upcoming season.

But when Beebe stepped in front of the media on July 26, 2011, he presumed to speak on behalf of the Texas A&M community as if he had some great insight into the entire Aggie family. On the previous day, ESPN.com's Big 12 reporter David Ubben wrote in his blog that he had spoken to various A&M officials (he did not speak directly to me) regarding what percentage of the Aggies' fan base would support a move to the SEC. Ubben wrote, "My estimation was 60 percent, based on interactions, emails, and comments I've heard from Aggies fans. [A&M officials] agreed that the number was somewhere in the 60 percent ballpark, adding that it was up to that number from probably 30 to 40 percent last summer, when a move to the SEC was a possibility."

Whoever the A&M "officials" were who spoke to Ubben, they were in my view grossly underestimating the unity of the Aggie family, for the Longhorn Network had brought A&M fans to near unanimity in favor of a move to the SEC. In my estimation, the Aggie family was at least 85 percent—if not more—in favor of leaving the Big 12 for the SEC by the end of July 2011.

But when Ubben asked Beebe about his 60 percent number at the Big 12 media days, the commissioner retorted, "I don't know where [A&M officials are] getting that from; that's not the sense that I have from those folks," Beebe said to Ubben and other reporters. "That issue [the SEC] has been around that institution for a long time, but thankfully most of the coaches and administrators and others are adamant about wanting to be in the Big 12."

As if that were not enough, Beebe elaborated. "I was trouncing around this neck of the woods back in my [NCAA] enforcement days," Beebe continued, as reported by Brent Zwerneman. "There is a contingent at Texas A&M of thoughtful people, I'm sure, who for twenty or more years have wanted to go to the . . . somewhere else. Whenever something happens, that group is going to come out and say 'this is our chance, let's go.' I remember back when I was an [NCAA] investigator coming through here, I'd hear that in the early 1980s, before the Big 12 was even a concept. That's understandable. I'm thankful, I'm grateful that the majority of A&M graduates and fans do not feel that way. I'm strongly of the belief their coaches don't feel that way, and their administration and the professionals who work there don't feel that way."

Zwerneman pressed the issue further, however. In a follow-up question directed to Beebe, Zwerneman said that he had been told that there was plenty of "uncertainty" at Texas A&M regarding the Big 12's future. Beebe attempted to dismiss the assertion, saying he didn't know why Zwerneman or anyone else would make that conclusion. But Zwerneman told the commissioner it was because he had been present when I first used the word "uncertainty."

Nevertheless, Beebe's comments at the Big 12 media days were beyond befuddling or patronizing. For him to state publicly that he had special insight into the pulse and overall sentiment of the A&M community seemed to me to be a headfirst dive off the deep end of reality. And when Ubben pressed him a bit more, asking him what A&M fans would be thinking ten years later if the Aggies left for the SEC, Beebe went even further out on his limb: "Then they would be saying 80 percent of our people [wanted] to stay in the Big 12," Beebe said with a smile, "and thought that we made a bad decision."

Even as Beebe misspoke for the maroon masses, I was continuing my regular discussions with Slive. In early August, we arranged for a meeting of SEC and Texas A&M officials at an airport in New Orleans. The A&M contingent included Regents Jim Wilson, Richard Box, Jim Schwertner, and Cliff Thomas, along with deputy general counsel Scott Kelly, and me. Slive was accompanied by Chuck Gerber, the SEC's media consultant, along with Robert Fuller, an attorney with Robinson, Bradshaw, & Hinson, PA, a corporate and commercial law firm based in Charlotte, North Carolina. Fuller had previously represented the SEC in 2008 when it entered into a fifteen-year broadcast agreement with CBS and ESPN. He also represented the NCAA in 2010 when it entered into its fourteen-year agreement with CBS and Turner Broadcasting for the rights to the NCAA men's basketball tournament. We soon discovered that Fuller was extremely conservative in his approach to such agreements.

It was apparent right from the start that the SEC wanted to avoid litigation, and to that end, we made it abundantly clear that we approached the SEC, not vice versa. But Fuller was concerned about the murkiness of the Big 12 bylaws and the possibility of exorbitant exit fees. We had an extended conversation about specific details regarding the process of withdrawing from the Big 12 and seeking membership in the SEC, and we all shook hands and parted ways with the understanding that Texas A&M would continue moving forward in a systematic and guarded method, based on the advice and directives of Scott Kelly, Fuller, and the rest of the respective legal teams. Slive and I continued to talk regularly in the ensuing days. Meanwhile, at Texas A&M, our internal discussions focused on outlining a step-by-step time line for withdrawal from the Big 12.

That schedule was expedited by a couple of events that transpired shortly after our nationally ninth-ranked football team reported for the beginning of fall camp on Monday, August 8, 2011. First, Texas governor Rick Perry, perhaps the most famous former yell leader in A&M history, was asked by *Dallas Morning News* statehouse reporters on August 10 about speculation regarding A&M's possible desire to leave the Big 12 for the SEC. Perry kicked the media ant bed with this response: "I'll be real honest with you," Perry said, as reported by the *Morning News*. "I just read about it the same time as y'all did. As far as I know, conversations are being had. That's frankly all I know. I just refer you to the University and the decision makers over there."

The media wasted no time in seeking quotes both from me and from Board of Regents members. I did not want to comment, because I did not want to be misleading. Jason Cook released the following, intentionally vague statement: "President Loftin is committed to doing what is best for Texas A&M not only now, but also into the future. We continue to have wide-ranging conversations regarding all aspects of the University, including both academics and athletics."

While the statement didn't really convey much, the Board of Regents' action on Friday, August 12, spoke loud and clear to anyone who was paying attention. Their meeting was originally scheduled for August 22, but on August 12, it was posted—as required legally—that the meeting would be held on Monday, August 15 at 3:00 p.m., and item 15 on the Regents' public agenda stated: "Authorization for the President to take all actions relating to Texas A&M University's athletic conference alignment." This was a clear signal that Texas A&M was now shifting into a higher gear in its realignment efforts. And one of the boldest moves was made by A&M System Board of Regents Chairman Richard Box.

I was on stage at Reed Arena with Jason Cook—in full graduation regalia—during the morning commencement ceremonies on Friday, August 12, 2011, when Box first learned that the Texas House of Representatives had called a hearing for the following Tuesday, August 16, and that legislator Dan Branch had requested his presence. State law requires a house committee or subcommittee holding a public hearing during a legislative session to post notice of the hearing at least five calendar days before the hearing. But Box, wishing to avoid having Texas A&M's decision constrained by anything that might occur at the Branch hearing, contacted Board of Regents executive director Vickie Spillers to determine the earliest date possible for a telephonic meeting of the Board of Regents. She responded that if the call was posted with the office of the Texas secretary of state by 6:00 p.m., the meeting could take place on the following Monday. Box instructed Spillers to post the call, and the Regents meeting was scheduled for Monday, August 15, to precede the House of Representatives hearing. I didn't find out about all the strategic posturing until I stepped off the commencement stage to go to lunch, but I was thoroughly impressed by Chairman Box's courageous decision to make sure that Texas A&M would be permitted to make decisions regarding the future without further political pressuring.

This was also the week when much of the media's coverage of A&M, both regional and national, turned from informational to downright condescending, hostile, and even venomous.

- Jerome Solomon of the *Houston Chronicle* tweeted on August 10: "I have no doubt that A&M fans are talking about going to the SEC. Get back to me when the SEC is talking to A&M about coming there."

- Stewart Mandel of *Sports Illustrated* wrote on August 12: "It hardly seems worth diluting the best on-field product in college football today for a few extra millions, which is exactly what the SEC would be doing in welcoming A&M, a program that last won a national title in 1939 (five different SEC schools have won one just in the BCS era) and has rarely even contended for a Big 12 title (winning its sole crown thirteen years ago). Since the Big 12 began in 1996, the Aggies have won 106 games, which would tie them for seventh-best in the SEC over the same time period. Would the SEC reconfigure for a seventh-place team?"
- Pete Thamel of the *New York Times* wrote on August 13: "The same forces that drove expansion in 2010—ego and money—have reemerged this summer. Only in this era of college sports could a university like Texas A&M prompt potential seismic changes in the landscape. Consider that the Aggies' last Big 12 title in football was in 1998 and their lone bowl victory since 1995 came in the Galleryfurniture.com Bowl. But as they walk the plank to be devoured in the SEC—hello, Louisiana State, Alabama, and Auburn—at least Texas A&M's leaders can revel in having the college sports world breathlessly follow them for a few days in August."
- Tim MacMahon of ESPNDallas.com tweeted on August 13: "Got no dog in the fight, but I really hope the SECede movement blows up in A&M's face. [Two] good reasons: 1) I like watching Big 12 football, especially the South rivalries; 2) Humiliated Aggies are hilarious."

In all sincerity, I was most taken aback, not by the hostility of the media, but rather by the short-sighted nature of such reports (and there were many others that were similarly spiteful). It's rather common for Texas A&M, often regarded as one of the most conservative universities in the country, to receive unbalanced coverage from the national press. But this was sports, not politics. The move to the SEC was a 100-year decision for Texas A&M based on brand exposure and awareness, financial opportunities, and the stability of the conference over the next century—not the next season.

For the SEC, moreover, Texas A&M's addition would represent a major expansion of the conference's brand, footprint, and financial strength. Admittedly, Texas A&M's football program had struggled at times in the post–R. C. Slocum era, but this move was not about a ten-year snapshot. It was about the full, panoramic, big picture. I found it difficult to believe that so many respected media representatives couldn't understand all the reasons why the SEC would be interested in Texas A&M.

In my view, there are at least twenty-six million good reasons (the estimated population of Texas) why the SEC would want to expand into the Lone Star State. Texas A&M, with an enrollment in excess of 50,000 students, would also instantly become one of the largest universities in the SEC and one of its leaders in academic standing (joining only Florida and Vanderbilt as members of the prestigious AAU). And the cultural fit was very appropriate. Jason Cook was later quoted by the Associated Press: "I always tell people that Texas A&M has always been an SEC school in terms of our traditions, our spirit, and our passion. We've just been positioned in the wrong conference."

We now had the perfect opportunity to reposition favorably. And though it was frustrating at times that so much of the media did not understand—or at least did not want to acknowledge—the mutual interest between A&M and the SEC, we were undaunted.

Nevertheless, it was not the least bit surprising to me that the media was overwhelmingly negative on Sunday, August 14. That was the day that we had first hoped to receive an invitation from the SEC chancellors and presidents. In fact, Jason Cook says that one of his funniest memories is of the Twitter pictures of me at my church on that Sunday morning, checking my phone for updates. As I pointed out to Jason, however, those of my fellow parishioners who tweeted those images were also using their phones for something other than biblical research.

But that was not to be the day that Texas A&M received its invitation. Instead, Bernie Machen, president of the University of Florida and chair of the SEC leadership board, issued this statement following the August 14 meeting: "The SEC presidents and chancellors met today and reaffirmed our satisfaction with the present twelve institutional alignment. We recognize, however, that future conditions may make it advantageous to expand the number of institutions in the league. We discussed criteria and processes associated with expansion. No action was taken with respect to any institution, including Texas A&M."

Within minutes, Stewart Mandel of *Sports Illustrated* tweeted that the SEC had "Passed" on Texas A&M. Yael T. Abouhalkah of the *Kansas City Star* wrote: "Sports fans saw a weird story unfold this past week, when Texas A&M tried as hard as it could to leave the Big 12 and join the Southeastern Conference. Fortunately, the SEC on Sunday rejected that request, for now, which should leave Texas A&M feeling mighty embarrassed." Wes O'Donnell of BleacherReport.com wrote: "Nowhere in that [SEC] equation does Texas A&M fit in. For a lot of reasons, the potential expansion would be good, but for now, the conference has wisely decided to table the move for Texas A&M. . . . Texas A&M may stand to gain more money by joining the SEC, but these two sides don't stand to gain much from joining forces right now." And in an especially scathing commentary, Jean-Jacques Taylor of ESPNDallas.com wrote: "We can say a lot of things about the Aggies, but questioning their passion and devotion to anything maroon and white isn't one of them. Their brotherhood is admirable; their incessant whining is not. It will be surpassed only by their embarrassment if the SEC decides they're not worth the trouble or potential litigation. On Sunday, the SEC released a statement that said it's happy with (twelve) teams for now. That would qualify as yet another body blow to A&M's massive ego if it weren't able to join the SEC. . . ."

Fortunately, Jason Cook's carefully cultivated relationships with others in the media proved helpful in combating the negativity of these stories. More accurate reports were published by Billy Liucci of Tex-Ags.com, Brent Zwerneman of the *San Antonio Express-News* and *Houston Chronicle*, and Andy Staples of *Sports Illustrated*. Although we knew that Machen's statement was merely legal posturing, we realized that Texas A&M needed to take even more proactive steps in the process.

Liucci alleviated the fears within the Aggie family when he wrote, "What the league didn't do was reject Texas A&M's interest in joining the conference. The league did, however, tap the brakes and slow down the process . . . because the real sticking point surrounds the SEC's desire to avoid the threat of extended litigation at all costs. Whether it's a Baylor Bear/Texas Longhorn-led legal 'dream team' or the Big 12 itself, someone created just enough uncertainty to give the SEC reason for pause."

Zwerneman spelled out the situation for readers across Texas: "My understanding is this is simply part of the (convoluted) legal process of A&M bolting the Big 12 for the SEC—that it must be documented that A&M courted the SEC, not vice versa, to avoid potential lawsuits. The A&M Regents are still expected to hold a teleconference on Monday to discuss 'conference alignment.'"

And Staples wrote an outstanding article in *Sports Illustrated* on August 14 in which he actually called out his colleague, Mandel, for being inaccurate in his assessment. Staples wrote: "The language [of Machen's statement] was pure legalese meant to slow a boulder rolling downhill. Here's a more accurate translation: *'If we can make more money from our TV contracts, we're probably going to expand. But no one has applied for membership yet. So we didn't vote today. If we had voted to extend an offer to a school that hadn't applied for membership, we might have left ourselves exposed to a big, fat lawsuit. So don't sue us, Big 12. If someone—perhaps a land-grant institution based in College Station, Texas—happens to authorize its president to seek new conference membership—maybe at a special Board of Regents meeting Monday afternoon—and that president happens to ask us to consider his school for membership, then we might strongly consider that school.'"*

With his "more accurate translation," Staples nailed the remaining steps in that process. Just as he predicted, at its meeting on August 15, the A&M System Board of Regents unanimously authorized me to act on conference realignment, after which I met with a vast array of media members and fielded a number of questions in a lengthy interview session. This is where I first characterized the move to the SEC by A&M as a "100-year decision." Because there were still other procedural steps to accomplish, I was purposely vague in answering direct questions about joining the SEC and leaving the Big 12. I asked for patience among the A&M family and explained that any move to another league would be a "lengthy" endeavor. Upon direct questioning, I also added that the Big 12 was a strong conference and would be a viable league even if Texas A&M was no longer in it. I also said that if A&M chose to leave for another league, we would still welcome the opportunity to play UT-Austin in an annual nonconference game, preferably around Thanksgiving.

From that point forward, our legal team intensified its study of the Big 12 bylaws and began formulating a plan to issue an official written notification to the conference that Texas A&M was exploring other conference affiliations, similar to the course of action that Nebraska took in 2010.

One of the key members of the legal team was Mike Baggett, a former Texas A&M yell leader. Baggett was chairman and CEO of Winstead PC, a large and respected law firm, from 1992–2006, and has also served as the director of the State Bar of Texas. Actively involved with the 12th Man Foundation for many years, Mike's long tenure as a member of the board of directors for the Cotton Bowl also uniquely positioned him to interpret the Big 12 bylaws and to represent Texas A&M's interests.

Mike and his team were instrumental in helping prepare a letter from me to Dan Beebe that was dated August 25, 2011. It explained that if Texas A&M withdrew from the conference, we would do so in a way that complied with the Big 12's bylaws. Additionally, we noted that Texas A&M would be supportive of the Big 12's efforts to seek a new member of the conference.

Our hope was that the Big 12's board of directors would meet, as scheduled, on August 27 and perhaps release Texas A&M from the Big 12 on that day. While that didn't happen exactly as planned, Texas A&M did receive a written response from Dan Beebe on Monday, August 29, that outlined the conference's position on withdrawal procedures, financial provisions of the Big 12 bylaws, and mutual waivers of legal claims. Naturally, we assumed that Beebe was speaking for the entire conference, including our two closest neighbors, Texas and Baylor.

In my view, the key words in Beebe's letter were "waivers of legal claims." Although negotiations regarding financial exit fees would still continue for some time, we accordingly believed the legal shackles had essentially been removed, and that we were now free to begin leaving the Big 12 and seek membership in the SEC. I wrote the following letter to Beebe on August 31, 2011:

"After much thought and consideration, and pursuant to the action of the Texas A&M University System Board of Regents authorizing me to take action related to Texas A&M University's athletic conference alignment, I have determined it is in the best interest of Texas A&M to make application to join another athletic conference.

We appreciate the Big 12's willingness to engage in a dialogue to end our relationship through a mutually agreeable settlement. We, too, desire that this process be as amicable and prompt as possible and result in a resolution of all outstanding issues, including mutual waivers by Texas A&M and the conference on behalf of all the remaining members."

Back in July, when I first called Mike Slive from the smoking patio at the Zone Club, I had initially hoped—obviously far too optimistically—that all the legal maneuvering involved in changing conferences could be completed before the start of the 2011 football season, which kicked off for Texas A&M on Sunday night, September 4, against SMU. While we didn't hit that target date, I was still convinced, as the calendar flipped from August to September, that it was only a matter of days before we could celebrate Texas A&M's move to the SEC. The SEC board of presidents and chancellors was scheduled to meet Tuesday evening, September 6, and Mike Slive had told me he was confident that Texas A&M would be unanimously voted into the SEC. We were so optimistic about that vote that we had reserved the Zone Club for Wednesday, September 7, and Thursday, September 8, for our SEC announcement and celebration.

Indeed, even after I sent the letter to Beebe announcing our intention to explore another affiliation, I was still a member of the Big 12 board of presidents and chancellors and attended meetings by telephone, though I was not active in any discussions of the league's future or of our withdrawal. In the first meeting following my letter, I appreciated hearing Bill Powers tell the group that A&M's withdrawal should not only be allowed but should be done as quickly and easily as possible. So, my hope that matters would proceed in this way was not entirely unfounded or naïve.

Unbeknownst to me at the time, however, Ken Starr—Baylor's recently appointed president and the man I had sat next to and answered questions from at the Big 12 spring meetings in 2010—was having a change of heart from the way he had voted at the Big 12 board of directors meeting. Part of the reason for that, I now realize, may have been that in just a short amount of time realignment rumors and reports had multiplied, magnified, and expanded to include far more possibilities than merely A&M-to-SEC speculation.

On Saturday, September 3, *The Daily Oklahoman* reported that OU president David Boren had stated that the Sooners would not be a "wallflower" in matters of conference realignment and were being proactive in deciding their conference future. Boren said OU had received interest from multiple conferences. The story also noted that Texas, Texas Tech, and Oklahoma State could also be part of the move to the Pac-12 with Oklahoma. Oklahoma State president Burns Hargis issued a statement on the same day that implied the Cowboys would follow the Sooners' lead. "We are in close communications with our colleagues at the University of Oklahoma and expect a decision soon that will be in the best interest of our institutions and the state of Oklahoma," Hargis said.

Later on Saturday, Pac-12 commissioner Larry Scott, who was in Arlington, Texas, on September 3 for the LSU-Oregon season opener at Cowboy Stadium, acknowledged for the first time in 2011 that his league had, indeed, been contacted by prospective members. "I will say schools have reached out to us," Scott told reporters covering the game. "We are not doing anything proactively. But schools have called us. We certainly are going to listen." According to CBSSports.com, Oklahoma State billionaire benefactor T. Boone Pickens also told an Oklahoma City reporter on September 3, "If you can't fix the Big 12, you might as well go West." But my personal favorite quote from Pickens that day was this gem: "[Dodds] is a friend of mine, but DeLoss had too many cards and he played every damn one of them. I think that's too bad. You get tired of saying 'aaah' while you get something shoved down your throat. The network could have been the straw that broke the camel's back."

Clearly, at least to me, the Big 12 was again in grave danger, which is obviously why Starr changed his opinion from one day to the next. On Sunday, September 4, Starr sent me an email titled, "Your Vital Role," which was later obtained and reproduced by the *Dallas Morning News* through an open records request:

"Bowen:

As you have seen, the Big 12 is now in mortal danger. This can be stopped. If Texas A&M will remain, we can save the conference. I hope and trust that you will consider this admittedly bold step. But the consequences now flowing were, I have no doubt, entirely unanticipated by your Board—and certainly by you personally. As you stated to me early on, the Big 12 could (it was thought) readily recruit another member, namely the University of Houston. That sensible solution proved problematic for reasons that were, in no small part, driven by issues relating to the size and scope of our billion-dollar-plus TV contract. An expansion committee thoroughly discussed this set of issues for some days. The Big 12 Conference board then agreed upon a course of action with respect to replacing Texas A&M, were the SEC move indeed to eventuate, and then to expand conference membership to our original size of (twelve). At every step, that effort has proven to be a profound challenge. In the meantime, other conferences have become restive. The entire national landscape is being reshaped.

I respectfully request the opportunity to discuss this profoundly disturbing set of events with you. The situation is really quite grave for the future of a heartland conference. I believe it can be saved.

Gratefully,

Ken"

I didn't see the email when Starr sent it, as Sunday was the opening game day for one of the most anticipated seasons in recent memory for the Aggie football team. Following the Aggies' 46–14 victory over SMU on September 4, I did send this reply (also printed by the *Dallas Morning News*) on Monday at 6:19 p.m.:

"Ken:

Forgive me for the delay in responding to your email. Yesterday was a game day, and I was totally consumed until midnight. Labor Day is not a holiday for Texas A&M, and I had a full slate of meetings today (that just got done).

As I have often stated, Texas A&M certainly wants the Big 12 to continue to flourish. At the same time, we seek greater institutional visibility and have investigated alternative conference affiliation in order to achieve that goal.

I am certainly willing to talk to you tomorrow if you have time. We have a Board of Regents meeting in the morning that will consider naming John Sharp as our new System chancellor. Hopefully, that will be done by 10 a.m. or so, and I can be available by telephone up until 11:45 a.m., when I have a luncheon appointment. If that time period is unsatisfactory, please let me know when you might be available.

Bowen"

Apparently, my response was not particularly comforting to Starr. He and his Baylor associates went to work on many fronts the next day, September 6. First, on its university-affiliated website, Baylor launched its "Don't Mess with Texas Football" campaign, which featured a green and gold shield logo and this message:

"Nothing is more beloved in Texas than Texas football. Entire towns travel to neighboring communities on Friday nights as rivals meet under the Friday night lights; Saturday mornings find families rushing out to pee wee football games and spending their afternoons with friends tailgating or watching some of the most historic and storied football rivalries in the nation; Sunday afternoons see families gathered in living rooms across the state to cheer on the Cowboys or the Texans.

Football in Texas is more than a passing interest; it is a part of the fabric of this great state.

- Will Texans stand by and watch hundred-year-old rivalries be cast aside as the state's largest universities align themselves with other states across the country?
- Will Texans sit and watch as Texas' flagship universities pledge their loyalties to other states?
- Will Texans stand by as our most promising student-athletes are lured out of Texas by new rivals?
- Will Texans watch as our most precious resources—the great minds of the next generation—are exported to new conference institutions?

Texans must stand up and call the leadership of the University of Texas, Texas A&M, and Texas Tech to clearheaded thinking about the state's future. Texas' flagship institutions of higher learning are the guardians of the state's future—their loyalties must first be to Texas and to her citizens. Ask these leaders to take a stand for Texas and to stop this madness that will lead to the dissolution of the Big 12 and the end of an era for Texas."

After that message, a link was provided so that "concerned Texans" (apparently code for "Baylor fans") could contact members of the Board of Regents and presidents/chancellors of Texas A&M, Texas, and Texas Tech. But in the end, the campaign was more amusing than maddening. Contact from Baylor fans was not going to cause me to reverse course or any of our Regents to change their minds. And my sense was that this time around even the state politicians were staying out of it. In mid-August, for example, I had agreed to meet with Chairman Dan Branch at a Texas House Committee on Higher Education hearing in Austin addressing A&M's potential move, but the meeting was postponed indefinitely. I sensed that the political card that had been played often in previous realignment discussions was no longer in the deck.

Perhaps Starr sensed that as well, making him feel that he had to take so many matters into his own hands. Although the "Don't Mess with Texas Football" campaign was not particularly exasperating to me, Starr's other move on September 6 was infuriating. At some point in the day—before the SEC board of directors' meeting that evening—Starr had placed a call to an SEC official. Starr left two voicemails, threatening a lawsuit against the SEC for "tortious interference." In the most simplistic terms, tortious interference occurs when a third party interferes with an existing contract between two other parties. In other words, if A is in an existing contract with B, then C is not permitted to induce A to break its contract with B. Applying that to Texas A&M and the SEC, Texas A&M was in a contractual relationship with the Big 12. So the SEC couldn't then induce Texas A&M to break that contract.

Obviously, such a suit had no merit whatsoever. First and foremost, Texas A&M approached the SEC, not vice versa. But Starr's voicemails were played for all the SEC chancellors and presidents, causing enough concern on their part to vote Texas A&M into the SEC "conditionally." It was this that caused Machen to issue the following statement on behalf of the SEC chancellors and presidents on Wednesday morning, September

7: "After receiving unanimous written assurance from the Big 12 on September 2 that the Southeastern Conference was free to accept Texas A&M to join as a new member, the presidents and chancellors of the SEC met last night with the intention of accepting the application of Texas A&M to be the newest member of the SEC. We were notified yesterday afternoon that at least one Big 12 institution had withdrawn its previous consent and was considering legal action. The SEC has stated that to consider an institution for membership, there must be no contractual hindrances to its departure. The SEC voted unanimously to accept Texas A&M University as a member upon receiving acceptable reconfirmation that the Big 12 and its members have reaffirmed the letter dated September 2, 2011."

I was livid. On the one hand, I did empathize with Starr's apparent perception that his school was in a desperate position. He was trying to do something—anything possible—to keep Baylor in one of the power conferences. But to pick on Texas A&M's move to the SEC, as opposed to the potential move of Oklahoma, Oklahoma State, Texas Tech, and Texas to the Pac-16, was beyond infuriating to me. As Clay Travis of Fox Sports' OutkickTheCoverage.com so eloquently stated, "Texas A&M's departure for the SEC isn't killing the Big 12. Subsequent departures from the Big 12 could kill the Big 12. So if Baylor wants to sue a conference for ending the Big 12, it should sue Larry Scott and the Pac-12. It's altogether possible that the threat of suing the SEC and Mike Slive is intended as a threat to the Pac-12. Or it could be that Baylor is going to sue everyone. Hell, why not? Remember, just because a suit has no merit doesn't mean it can't be filed. (Especially when you're talking about Baylor president Ken Starr, the king of throw-things-at-the-wall-and-see-what-sticks litigation strategy. This is the same guy who started an investigation into Bill Clinton's real estate dealings, found nothing, and ended up poring through the explicit details of Bill Clinton's sex life)."

I also remembered well that if not for Texas A&M, Baylor might have been begging for membership in the WAC or Conference USA in the summer of 2010, when UT-Austin had, as far as I could see, worked very hard with the Pac-10 for Texas A&M, Texas Tech, Oklahoma, Oklahoma State, and Colorado to join the Longhorns in the Pac-16. On that occasion, UT-Austin had, in my opinion, no consideration of

Baylor's welfare—none. Only by Texas A&M slowing down the process was Baylor kept in the Big 12.

Ken Starr had sent me flowers in 2010. Now, he was devising a bogus lawsuit against the SEC to throw a monkey wrench in Texas A&M's plans. From my viewpoint, calling the SEC and leaving threatening voicemails was the equivalent of hitting below the belt. I had turned sixty-two years old in June 2011. As I have aged, I have usually done a good job of keeping my composure. But when I finally had the opportunity to speak to Starr and Beebe during a three-way conference phone call, though I don't recall using any foul language, I did say numerous things that I later regretted. To put it bluntly, I lost my cool. The audacity of Starr—perhaps in cahoots with Beebe to save the Big 12, Beebe's job, and Starr's reputation—was more than I could take.

The next two weeks were some of the most frustrating days of my professional life. I was furious at Starr for the misguided threat of a meritless lawsuit; I was angered at Beebe for his complete lack of leadership as the Big 12 spent these days on life support; and I was disappointed that the SEC, realizing that Baylor's lawsuit threat was bogus, did not change its stance and extend an unconditional offer to Texas A&M. Meanwhile, the speculation of what might eventually happen in the realm of conference realignment took on a life of its own. Would Oklahoma and Oklahoma State go to the Pac-12, regardless of what Texas decided? Could Oklahoma part ways from OSU to become the fourteenth member of the SEC? If Texas chose to become an independent, what would be Texas Tech's options? If Texas and Oklahoma stayed in the Big 12, could the conference lure Notre Dame into the fold? What schools were the best alternative targets for the Big 12: TCU, BYU, or West Virginia? How about inviting Arkansas to reunite with Texas?

Some of the ensuing speculation was nothing short of ludicrous. Nothing much really happened on the public front for roughly two weeks following Starr's lawsuit threats, but there were some amusing developments that brought a smile to my face in the midst of a frustrating impasse. First, Jason Cook contacted Jay Kimbrough, Gov. Rick Perry's former chief of staff and then a high-ranking official with the Texas Department of Transportation (TxDot), regarding what was an obvious trademark infringement by Baylor's campaign slogan, which leaned heavily on TxDot's longstanding anti-littering campaign, "Don't Mess with Texas." Kimbrough was initially unaware of the Baylor campaign, but after learning about it, TxDot ordered Baylor officials to cease and desist using the slogan. Within thirty minutes after being contacted, BU officials complied and had it removed from the website.

Another smile came courtesy of TexAgs.com and former A&M student Luke Jalbert. From his home in Amarillo, Jalbert rallied some fellow Aggies fans on the website to contribute $100 apiece to purchase ad space on a billboard in Waco near Baylor's Floyd Casey Stadium. The maroon billboard featured these words in white lettering: "Thou shalt not covet thy neighbor's conference deal." Texas A&M University had nothing to do with the billboard, but it did produce a much-needed laugh when I first learned of it.

I continued to talk regularly with both Mike Slive and Bernie Machen throughout mid-September, and Machen assured me that he was working on Texas A&M's behalf to squelch the litigation concerns of the other SEC presidents and chancellors and of its lawyer Robert Fuller, who continued to maintain a cautious outlook. Behind the scenes and at Regent Jim Schwertner's suggestion, Neal Adams, Rick Rickman and Scott Taylor—all lawyers and members at the time of the Board of Trustees of the 12th Man Foundation, the nonprofit fundraising organization of A&M athletics—had prepared documents that guaranteed coverage of up to $3 million of legal costs for the SEC if Baylor did, indeed, file the lawsuit. As time progressed, Fuller began to acknowledge that the tortious interference accusation had no real merit. Machen also continued to make progress with the rest of the SEC leadership.

In the meantime, at the suggestion of Board of Regents chairman Richard Box, Jim Wilson and I contacted leaders in Texas A&M's Association of Former Students and the 12th Man Foundation, as well as Billy Liucci at TexAgs.com, asking each of them to do what they could to mobilize their constituencies to lobby legislators for relief from the political pressure being brought to bear on Texas A&M with regard to the conference decision. At this critical moment, the "Aggie Network" once again proved its value as a powerful force for the good of the university.

I am convinced that even if the Big 12 had dissolved by the end of September and Starr had filed his lawsuit, the SEC would have still unconditionally welcomed A&M at some point in October. Fortunately for all parties, we didn't have to wait that long. Oklahoma president David Boren seemed to have also reached his personal wit's end with UT-Austin and Dan Beebe. Throughout much of September 2011, Boren was involved in a high-stakes game that would ultimately determine Oklahoma's conference affiliation future and whether the Big 12 would survive or not. Kansas governor Sam Brownback later revealed to Berry Tramel of *The Oklahoman* that Boren was playing his cards in hopes of gaining some concessions from UT-Austin regarding the LHN and demanding Beebe's replacement. "Boren finally called [me] back," Brownback told *The Oklahoman*, "and said, 'Look, I couldn't call you back. I was playing poker.' Because he didn't have a deal, as we saw later. He was trying to get them [Texas] to commit, get them to stay. It was a bluff. Boren told me it was. He said, 'I couldn't call and tell you . . . I had to get it tied down or it wouldn't work.'"

But ultimately, it did work as Boren had hoped. On September 20, an unidentified, high-ranking source at the University of Oklahoma told the state's two largest newspapers that OU was considering remaining in the Big 12, but only in a reformed version of the conference that included restrictions on the Longhorn Network and the removal of commissioner Dan Beebe. Two days later—September 22— Beebe was dumped by the Big 12, and the conference announced a plan to bind the nine remaining member schools together. Speaking to the media on a conference call, Boren said all nine remaining schools had agreed to give a six-year grant of their first- and second-tier television rights to the Big 12. Regarding Beebe, Boren said, "I have no negative personal feelings toward our previous commissioner, but I'm alarmed by the fact that in fifteen months we lost three teams, and I'm aware in detail of how some of those situations played out. I don't feel it was inevitable that we lost those three teams." In response, Beebe later told ESPN.com: "I feel like the conference was driving over a cliff, and they turned the bus around and ran me over."

Feelings were obviously hurt, but I definitely agreed with Boren's opinion regarding the need for Beebe to be dismissed. In fact, because I was still a member of the Big 12 Board of Directors at that time, I voted in favor of his dismissal. He was replaced on an interim basis by former Big Eight commissioner Chuck Neinas, and the Big 12 Conference was unofficially taken off life support and declared healthy enough to continue as a league. Personally, I was happy for many of my longtime friends and associates who may have been left scrambling if the Big 12 had died. Professionally and as an Aggie, I was absolutely ecstatic. Keeping the Big 12 together meant Baylor would have a conference home and the SEC would most definitely welcome Texas A&M as its thirteenth member. Technically, Baylor never officially dropped its lawsuit threat, but the SEC no longer cared if Baylor sued or not. As Slive later stated, "To make a long story short, when Oklahoma decided that the Big 12 was where it wanted to be, we felt that the spirit of the letter that we got on September 2 was fulfilled and we were prepared to move ahead." In other words, once OU decided to stay in the Big 12, the SEC was ready to fully embrace Texas A&M.

That historic, emotional, and much-anticipated call came from Mike Slive to me on Sunday, September 25. Later that day, we announced that Texas A&M had been cleared to play in the SEC beginning in the 2012–13 school year. "Texas A&M is a nationally prominent institution on and off the field and a great fit for the SEC tradition of excellence—athletically, academically, and culturally," Slive said in the statement that was carried by media outlets across the country.

Two days later, inside the Zone Club, Slive, Machen, and other SEC staffers joined us on a stage decorated with maroon and white balloons and adorned with A&M's national championship trophies from various sports, as well as the new SEC logo incorporated into Texas A&M's flag. It was a great moment, and it is an event I will never forget. "Good things come to those who wait," I told the audience at the press conference. "We did not anticipate some of the issues that arose that were externally driven. We worked through those and were patient about it, although Aggies are seldom patient about some things. We were certainly patient about this, and I appreciate the perseverance of Commissioner Slive and the presidents and chancellors of the SEC— and my Board, as well—as we worked through issues."

I breathed a sigh of relief. We were at the summit, and the most arduous part of the journey was done.

CHAPTER 10

The Wrong Way, but the Right Move

Following his death in 2012, Art Modell was commended for many things, including negotiating the NFL's first national television contract in 1962, serving as one of former NFL Commissioner Pete Rozelle's most trusted advisers as the league rose to prominence in the 1960s and 1970s, and displaying the marketing savvy that helped him earn a fortune on Madison Avenue. On the other hand, Modell's legacy as an NFL owner was forever tainted among his own team's fans—even before he moved the Browns from Cleveland to Baltimore—by his decision in the early 1960s to fire iconic coach Paul Brown, the namesake of the team. Later, in 1995, long before he came to be recognized as one of the greatest coaches in the history of the NFL with the New England Patriots, Bill Belichick too was fired as the head coach of the Browns . . . by Art Modell.

Likewise, many Dallas Cowboys fans have never forgiven Jerry Jones for firing Jimmy Johnson, who had rebuilt the team and led the Cowboys to consecutive Super Bowl titles at the conclusion of the 1992 and 1993 seasons. For that matter, many Cowboys fans are still livid at Jones for the way he handled the firing of the legendary Tom Landry in February 1989, replacing him with Johnson.

In the college ranks, Tennessee coach Phil Fulmer, who led the Volunteers to the 1998 national title, was fired by his athletic director, Mike Hamilton, in 2008. Hamilton then made two disastrous decisions: first, to replace Fulmer with Lane Kiffin, and next, when Kiffin soon jumped ship, to replace him with Derek Dooley. That duo combined to lead Tennessee to a record of 22-27 from 2009 to 2012. Vols fans fumed, and Hamilton eventually fell on the sword, resigning as AD in 2011. In a similar vein, in 2004 at Notre Dame, school president Rev. John I. Jenkins and the school's board of trustees completely ignored the objections of their athletic director Kevin White, firing football coach Tyrone Willingham after just three seasons (and just two years removed from a 10-3 debut year). Notre Dame then signed Charlie Weis to a six-year, $12 million contract. After the Irish lost to USC, 34-31 in Weis' sixth game as head coach, school officials extended his contract for ten years and between $30 to $40 million. Yes, Notre Dame *lost* a game *and extended* Weis for a decade. In his first two seasons—essentially with Willingham's players—Weis went 19-6. In his final three seasons, primarily with his own recruits, Notre Dame went 16-21. That contract extension was so outrageously damaging that in 2012, when Weis was "guiding" Kansas to a 1-11 overall record (0-9 in the Big 12), Notre Dame was paying more of his salary than the University of Kansas.

In the high-stakes, big-money, intensely scrutinized world of professional and college football, fans and media rarely forget the erroneous firings and misguided hires for which administrators are often remembered, long after they are gone from their positions—and even from this life! Undoubtedly, my wife, Karin, would have reminded me of this fact when, after consultation with others, I ultimately reached the conclusion at the end of the 2011 football season that Mike Sherman needed to be fired as the head coach of Texas A&M. Karin was so upset at me for reaching that conclusion and essentially forcing then–athletic director Bill Byrne to fire Sherman, a man whom my wife had grown to admire immensely, that she would not talk to me for a time. And the despicable manner in which Sherman regrettably learned about his release—via a phone call while pulling into the driveway of a recruit's home after the news had already been tweeted by an Austin sportswriter—only added to my wife's anger. She was certainly not alone in that sentiment.

Although it was definitely not a part of our plan, Sherman's dismissal from Texas A&M was a public relations disaster that still causes me to shake my head in disgust. There's no doubt in my mind that firing Sherman was the right thing to do, but it happened the wrong way on so many levels. The day after the news was leaked and then tweeted, Texas A&M University permitted Sherman to hold an exit press conference. It was an awkward event, to say the least. Most schools wouldn't dream of allowing a fired coach to stand on a university platform in front of sports-beat writers and national reporters to explain, among other things, how badly the termination had been handled. But

Sherman said he needed the press conference for closure, we obliged, and he handled it professionally. When asked about how he found out about his firing, Sherman told the media, "It was disappointing to a degree because my family had the opportunity to find out before I did, because it was released a little sooner than I was told, and that's disappointing. I think we're better than that."

I definitely agreed with Sherman on that point. Internally, we'd made a plan to sit down with Sherman on Friday, December 2, 2011, to inform him, after he had been notified by Bill Byrne, that the decision had been made to let him go. Our plan was to send out a press release, complete with statements from Sherman, to the media; then, a couple of days after the release, to allow Coach Sherman to hold a press conference on his terms. It wasn't going to be a pleasant experience for Sherman, but at least it was going to be handled professionally.

Unfortunately, we never had an opportunity to execute that plan. Information regarding our plan was leaked—probably intentionally, by someone unhappy with the decision to fire Sherman—to a member of the media. I have no proof of who actually leaked that information, but I will say that there were plenty of candidates within the athletic department at that time who had shown they were unhappy with me. Just a few days earlier, on November 29, a high-ranking member of the athletic department had acknowledged publicly that he had written some rather derogatory things about me in the summer of 2011 in a forum on TexAgs.com. I am fairly certain that many in the athletic department held me in low esteem because of the decision I had made to keep Bill Byrne out of the information loop.

For a number of reasons, Byrne was extremely popular among some of the athletic department staff. First and foremost, his track record of hiring outstanding coaches was impressive, beginning with his first hire, women's basketball coach Gary Blair in 2003. Blair completely overhauled what had been an embarrassingly bad program and led the Aggies to the 2011 national championship. Byrne also hired A&M track and field coach Pat Henry, who in 2014 led A&M to its eighth outdoor team national title in either men's or women's track and field.

In fact, Byrne's arrival at A&M from Nebraska in December 2002 initiated ten years of unprecedented Aggie athletic success. Texas A&M had won fourteen Big 12 Conference titles in the first six years of the league's existence, but after Byrne's arrival in Aggieland, Texas A&M won an additional forty-five Big 12 championships and seventeen national titles in track and field, women's basketball, men's golf, and women's equestrian. Byrne took a great deal of pride in his ability to hire coaches, he typically paid them well, and he was genuinely liked and admired by many of the men and women who worked for him.

My relationship with Byrne, however, had become strained, as detailed in previous chapters of this book. Because I sensed that Byrne had grown especially angry toward me throughout the summer of 2011 and into the fall, and in an attempt to keep any sensitive information from being leaked to the media, I didn't include him or anyone else within the athletic department in the information loop when we decided it was time for Texas A&M to seek membership in the Southeastern Conference. As it turned out, that decision was aided by some fortuitous timing, because Byrne had been out-of-pocket when the 2011 push toward the SEC began in full force, accompanying new coach Billy Kennedy and the men's basketball team on a ten-day, four-game tour of Switzerland and France from August 8 to 17.

Nevertheless, I do understand why Byrne wanted to be part of the tight-knit decision-making team and why he asked me about being excluded. We were, after all, making decisions about Texas A&M's athletic future, and Byrne was the top administrator of A&M's athletic department. But we were focusing on Texas A&M's best long-term interests, attempting to look as far as one hundred years into the future. As athletic director, most of Byrne's attention was appropriately fixed on the next season or two, and perhaps especially on how the Aggies would finish in the Learfield Sports Directors' Cup, an annual competition that ranks all college athletic programs based on their performances in all sports.

Byrne was also sensitive to the feelings of his current coaches and whether they believed they could compete right away in the SEC or not. I did talk with many of the A&M coaches in 2010 and 2011, seeking their preferences on conference realignment. For better or worse, though, I did not allow their comments, especially those pertaining to the immediate competitiveness of their teams, to weigh too heavily in my decisions. Likewise, I did not give much credence to Byrne's reservations about leaving the Big 12 for the SEC. Again, I was looking at the big picture, not the upcoming season.

My stance on those issues may have further angered Byrne and ignited an ancestral temper that he himself often referenced. Byrne told Kate Hairopoulos of the *Dallas Morning News* how one of his forebears, Billy Byrne, an Irish revolutionary during the late 1700s, had been hanged by the British because of his temper. Byrne joked frequently about inheriting that temper. It was obvious that he was a passionate leader, which is probably part of the reason he was so admired by the coaches he brought on board. He never fired a single coach at A&M that he himself had hired. (The Dennis Franchione hiring was already in the works when Byrne arrived from Nebraska.) He was obstinately opposed to firing Mike Sherman, and he strenuously voiced his displeasure to me when I called him shortly after the final game of the 2011 regular season and said that I had made the decision that it was time to let Sherman go.

Honestly, that was one of the more difficult calls I've ever made. I would have absolutely loved it if Mike Sherman would have continued to build on the success he had at the end of the 2010 regular season, when the Aggies won six straight games to earn a bid in the Cotton Bowl. Sherman's first two seasons at A&M resulted in records of 4-8 and 6-7 and included a number of rather humiliating losses. But he was recruiting well and he made some outstanding staff changes prior to the 2010 season, bringing in defensive assistants Tim DeRuyter, Dat Nguyen, Terrell Williams, and Nick Toth to rejuvenate a defense that had often been woeful under the direction of the former coordinator.

Following the strong finish to the 2010 season, the Aggies entered the 2011 season ranked eighth nationally. I truly believed—along with many other people who were far more knowledgeable than I about college football—that Sherman had turned the corner and was well on his way to returning A&M to a prominent position among the nation's premier football programs. Although the Aggies lost first-round draft pick Von Miller when he decided to turn pro following the 2010 season, the team returned many key players in 2011, including future NFL players such as quarterback Ryan Tannehill, running backs Cyrus Gray and Christine Michael, offensive linemen Luke Joeckel and Jake Matthews, wide receiver Jeff Fuller, and linebackers Sean Porter and Jonathan Stewart. Like many other A&M fans, I had extremely high hopes entering the season. I even had visions of our fans chanting, "SEC, SEC,

SEC" in the closing minutes of games each week as we rolled toward our final Big 12 title.

Those magnificent visions, however, began to fade from my mind on September 24, 2011, when the Aggies blew a 20-3 halftime lead against seventh-ranked Oklahoma State in the first top-ten matchup at Kyle Field since 1975. OSU took advantage of three A&M turnovers and numerous penalties to score twenty-seven straight points en route to a 30-29 win for the Cowboys. In the closing seconds of that game, the Oklahoma State fans in attendance at Kyle Field began chanting, "Big 12, Big 12, Big 12."

We didn't have to listen to those chants the following week, as the Aggies played SEC member Arkansas at what was then known as Cowboys Stadium in Arlington. Before the game, University of Arkansas chancellor David Gearhart presented me with a commemorative football that celebrated Texas A&M's entrance into the SEC family. After the game, though, I felt like we had instead entered the Twilight Zone. It was a different week, a different opponent, and a different stadium, but our loss to Arkansas was practically a repeat of the Oklahoma State game. The Aggies took an eighteen-point lead to the locker room at halftime, but the Razorbacks dominated the second half and rallied for a 42-38 victory. Texas A&M simply could not stop Arkansas in the second half, and it was apparent to practically everyone in the stadium that the Aggies needed to keep scoring in order to beat the Razorbacks. This A&M team could not afford to play it safe and rely on its defense to hold the lead.

On two instances in the fourth quarter, however, Sherman chose to punt instead of going for first downs on a fourth-and-one and then a fourth-and-two. Sherman said afterward that he didn't want to risk giving his struggling defense a short field if the offense didn't convert. But it just didn't make sense to me that A&M could produce 628 yards of total offense and manage only a field goal in the second half. For most of the game, Arkansas had seemed incapable of stopping Christine Michael, who rushed for 230 yards on thirty-two carries, and although I don't pretend to be a football coach, I would have bet that Michael was quite capable of gaining a first down on fourth-and-short.

The loss to the Razorbacks was A&M's seventh straight setback in games against SEC opponents, dating back to 2000. It was particularly alarming that Sherman was 0-5 against the SEC following the 2011 loss to the Razorbacks. Unfortunately, the blown leads and losses in consecutive weeks to Oklahoma State and Arkansas were not isolated incidents during the 2011 season, but rather signs of things to come. The Aggies would go on to lose three more games in which they held double-digit leads, including one of the most anticipated games in the history of Kyle Field.

Back in 2010, when Texas A&M explored the possibility of moving to the SEC instead of staying with UT-Austin in the Big 12 or joining the Longhorns in the Pac-16, Texas athletic director DeLoss Dodds repeatedly threatened that the Horns would never play the Aggies again if A&M went to the SEC. I thought that was an exceedingly childish, shortsighted statement on Dodds's part, and I continually stated—whenever possible—that it was Texas A&M's desire to continue the rivalry in all sports, "anytime, anywhere."

In collegiate football, many other instate rivalry games involve schools from different conferences, such as Florida-Florida State, Georgia-Georgia Tech, Colorado-Colorado State, Clemson-South Carolina, and Iowa-Iowa State. I didn't see any reason why we shouldn't continue with the storied Thanksgiving tradition of Texas A&M–Texas, even though Dodds was adamantly opposed to it. When we joined the SEC in 2011, Commissioner Mike Slive even assured me that he would be willing to work with A&M from a scheduling standpoint to make certain that the A&M-Texas rivalry continued. But Dodds would not even consider it . . . at least until 2018, long after he planned to retire. (His official retirement announcement was made on October 1, 2013.)

"In my email to Bill Byrne, I wrote that we were not in a position now to look at future football scheduling," Dodds said, as reported by ESPN.com in mid-October 2011. "We're scheduled out with nonconference games through 2018 and our Big 12 schedule is not yet settled. What we have right now is a full schedule, but if any future options are available, the decision will not be made by just one person." By March 2013, however, Dodds had changed his tune somewhat: "We [UT-Austin] get to decide when we play [Texas A&M] again. I think that's fair. If you did a survey of our fans about playing A&M, they don't want to. It's overwhelming. I know. I hear it. Our fans are important to us. I think there's got to be a period where things get different. I think there's too many hard feelings." Yet a year later, in March 2014, new UT-Austin head football coach Charlie Strong said he was ready to play the Aggies. "It's all about the two ADs getting together and getting that figured out," Strong said. "When you look at it, it's been such a huge rivalry game. . . . I think at some point it will get worked out. When there's been so much tradition there, you'd like to see it continue on. That's my feeling on it. I'd love to play it."

Undoubtedly, it will be played again, at least as much on A&M's terms as on UT's. But because Dodds initially declared it would not happen, the A&M-Texas game on November 24, 2011, was thought by many to be the last for some time to come, making it particularly historic and important to both fan bases. Bragging rights would last for years, maybe even a decade or more.

When game time came on Thanksgiving night before an absolutely electric crowd of 88,645 fans inside Kyle Field, we felt there was no way that Texas should have even been in the ballgame. Mack Brown had coached some great teams during his tenure with the Longhorns, but his 2011 squad was not one of them. Talent-wise, A&M was superior to Texas in virtually every aspect of the game, and the Aggies displayed their supremacy by building a 13-0 lead in the second quarter. A&M dominated the first half statistically and led 16-7 at the intermission. Yet just as they had blown big leads in losses against Oklahoma State, Arkansas, Missouri, and Kansas State, the Aggies exhibited no killer instinct in the clutch. They couldn't execute down the stretch and couldn't finish victorious.

A&M allowed an 81-yard punt return in the third quarter and tossed three interceptions, including one that was returned for a TD. In spite of all that, the Aggies still rallied to take the lead at 25-24 late in the fourth quarter. But Texas' Justin Tucker kicked a 40-yard field goal as time expired to give the Longhorns a 27-25 victory that sucked the air out of Kyle Field and ended—at least temporarily—the 118-year rivalry. Texas' final drive was aided by a drastically ill-timed, fifteen-yard personal foul penalty against an A&M defensive back. "They played their hearts out tonight," kicking specialist Tucker said about the Aggies after hitting the game-winning field goal. "But sending them off to the SEC with a sour taste in their mouth feels pretty good."

Blowing another double-digit lead by turning the ball over four times and making just enough blunders to allow a mediocre Texas team to win on the final play of the game was probably a fitting finish to an infuriating, frustrating season for the Aggies. Contrary to what many fans and media have suggested, though, losing that one game was not the only reason that Mike Sherman was fired.

The loss to Texas brought Sherman's overall record in four seasons as a head coach at Texas A&M to just 25-25. Following the 2010 season—Sherman's lone winning season during four years—I was hopeful that Mike had truly adjusted from being a professional coach to being a college coach. Prior to taking over as the A&M head coach in 2008, Sherman had spent the previous eleven years as either an assistant or head coach in the NFL, and there are major differences between the two levels. According to ProFootballReference.com, NFL teams averaged twenty-three points or more per game only three times from 1946 to 2013. In other words, the pro game—at least from a scoring standpoint—has essentially remained the same from decade to decade, ever since the conclusion of World War II. In 1970, for example, twenty-six NFL teams combined to average 19.1 points per game. Twenty years later in 1990, the twenty-eight teams averaged 20.0 points per game; in 2000, thirty-one teams scored 20.6 points per contest; and in 2010, thirty-two NFL teams scored 22.0 points per game.

The college game, however, has undergone massive changes during the same time span. In 1980, Baylor won the Southwest Conference title by averaging 26.4 points per game, while SMU led the league in scoring at 27.0 per contest. TCU's Steve Stamp led the league in passing that year, throwing for 1,830 total yards and fourteen TDs. Ten years later, Houston led the SWC in scoring at 46.5 points per game and UH quarterback David Klingler passed for 5,140 yards and fifty-four TDs—forty more touchdowns than Stamp produced a decade earlier. And in 2011, Big 12 champion Oklahoma State scored 48.7 points per game, and four of the ten quarterbacks in the league (OSU's Brandon Weeden, Baylor's Robert Griffin, Oklahoma's Landry Jones, and Texas Tech's Seth Doege) surpassed 4,000 passing yards for the season.

Despite all the obvious signs that the college game had become a far more high-scoring, roll-the-dice, keep-the-pedal-to-the-metal style, Mike Sherman maintained a conservative, professional football approach: protecting leads, minimizing risks, and playing it safe by kicking field goals or punting. It wasn't that A&M didn't score enough points to win, as the Aggies averaged 39.1 points in 2011, which ranked fourth in the Big 12 behind Oklahoma State, Baylor, and Oklahoma. The problem was that Sherman often went into "management mode" once the Aggies took a lead, instead of continuing to do the things that had enabled A&M to build an advantage in the first place. Whether he intended to or not, Sherman's game plan often went from attacking in the first half to a defensive posture in the second half.

During the 2011 season, national champion Alabama converted nine of thirteen fourth-down attempts, while other conference champions such as Oregon (thirty-one fourth-down attempts) and Oklahoma State (fifteen) took more chances than Sherman's Aggies, who converted only two of ten fourth-down tries in 2011. Even when Sherman risked it on fourth down, it was usually a conservative call. Sherman's offensive philosophy was often sound enough to build a lead, but his play-it-safe mentality typically allowed opponents to stage dramatic comebacks.

Sherman also seemed to give his players too much leeway, often treating his A&M players much like the men he coached in the NFL. While that may seem noble, the reality is that eighteen- and nineteen-year-old kids need to be held accountable, and they need to be pushed and prodded far more often than twenty-seven-year-old professionals. Under Mike Sherman and his strength and conditioning coach, Dave Kennedy, the A&M players typically conducted weight workouts at their own pace. "Under Coach Kennedy], you just kind of worked at your own tempo and it was kind of the NFL mentality," said former A&M linebacker Jonathan Stewart, who played his first three seasons with the Aggies under Sherman before playing his senior season under new head coach Kevin Sumlin. "We definitely worked, but it was more leisurely. We'd get a set in, take a couple minutes off, and then get another set going. It wasn't until Coach Sumlin was hired and he brought in Larry Jackson [as his strength and conditioning coach] that we realized what a difference a high-intensity, fast-paced workout could make. Coach Jackson would kill us; I mean it would be pure torture in workouts, but it definitely made a big difference in how we played in the second halves of games. We wore teams out in 2012."

In 2011, too many times, Texas A&M itself looked worn out. As I pondered the future, I couldn't see how the Aggies would perform any better in the SEC, which promised to be an even more physically demanding conference. Besides, I wasn't convinced that Sherman even wanted to coach in the SEC. Back in 2010, he'd told me that he preferred to stay in the Big 12. Then after the 2011 decision was made to move to the SEC, Sherman responded like a soldier who had just been issued a command that he did not embrace. Sherman was a good soldier, mind you, and was never publicly at odds with me about the move to the SEC, but he was reluctant to even talk about it to the media. When he finally addressed the move at a press conference in mid-October 2011, Sherman seemed less than enthusiastic regarding A&M's future home: "I know it's hard to believe, but I haven't given [the SEC] a whole lot of thought, and that's the truth. As a coach you live from day to day and week to week. I really and truly have not thought about the long-term implications. I've thought primarily about this season. But I know our fans are excited about it, and the University is excited about that. I have a lot of respect for our Big 12 opponents, and getting ready for every ball game. In order to show that respect to them, I'll continue to focus on what we have to do here." When asked later in the press conference about recruiting in the SEC, Sherman said: "[Prospects have] been talked to about the [SEC]. They've also been talked to about it in a negative way from competitors. We talk to them in a positive way, why we need them. It's been addressed in recruiting, and it's obviously not something you can ignore when the question comes up."

Whether or not that was an accurate assessment, I believe Sherman revealed some of his true feelings about leaving the Big 12 for the SEC after what I viewed as the best moment of the 2011 season. On October 15, 2011, Baylor, ranked as high as twentieth nationally in one poll, came to College Station looking for its first win at Kyle Field since 1984. The Bears took an early lead in the game, and eventual Heisman Trophy–winning quarterback Robert Griffin III threw for a school-record 430 yards. But it wasn't nearly enough, as Tannehill threw for 415 yards and Ryan Swope caught four touchdowns to lead the Aggies to a 55-28 win over the Bears.

Considering all that Ken Starr and Baylor had said and done in an attempt to prevent Texas A&M from going to the SEC, the twenty-seven-point victory seemed particularly sweet to me. Even though Baylor was ranked and obviously had a golden opportunity to post its first win at Kyle Field in twenty-seven years, Starr didn't come to the game. Not many Baylor fans did, either. Baylor sold only 830 of the allotted 3,850 tickets. One of the highlights for me personally was that during a break in the game, the billboard referenced in chapter 9 that had once been located near Baylor's Floyd Casey Stadium made an appearance at Kyle Field. The vinyl covering that read, "Thou shalt not covet thy neighbor's conference deal" was unrolled and displayed momentarily by students on the front row of the second deck on the east side of the stadium. It was in plain view for the TV cameras, which was amusing to me. Apparently, some former students had sneaked the vinyl covering into Kyle Field the night before for Midnight Yell Practice and stashed it where the students would find it.

To his credit, Starr did email me to congratulate the Aggies on the victory, but I just couldn't resist throwing at least one barb in his direction, making a somewhat sarcastic comment. "Thanks for the note," I wrote to him. "I guess it's hard for your quarterback to handle such a big crowd." Up to that point in the season, Baylor had played four home games and one road contest at Kansas State, with the largest crowd being 49,399 at K-State. Despite an 11:00 a.m. start time, A&M packed a crowd of 87,361 into Kyle Field to see the Aggies whip Baylor. Admittedly, it was a catty thing for me to say, and I later regretted my response.

Apparently, Starr wasn't as offended by my comment as Mike Sherman was about something that happened during the late stages of the game. During the fourth quarter, as the Aggies began to run away from the Bears, Jeff Schmahl, Texas A&M's former senior associate athletic director for external operations, made the decision to run an SEC advertisement on the video board. The ad was received quite positively by the maroon-clad fans, who began chanting, "SEC, SEC, SEC." After the game, Sherman spoke to Griffin and praised him, saying: "If you're III, I don't want to meet I and II." Apparently, Sherman also spoke afterward to Baylor head coach Art Briles, who was livid about the score, the SEC chant, the ad on the video board, and probably many other burrs under his saddle. Inside the visiting locker room after the teams had cleared the field, Larry Bowen of the *Bryan-College Station Eagle* asked Griffin about what Sherman had said to him. Before the quarterback could answer, Briles jumped in defiantly and said: "Is that an A&M question? He doesn't have to answer that. Are you from A&M?"

Bowen replied: "Coach, I work for the *Bryan-College Station Eagle.*"

"Okay, he doesn't need to answer that," Briles said.

Perhaps Briles's anger is what prompted Sherman to call Jim Wilson the next day. Wilson was traveling for business on October 16, and when he arrived in Boston and turned on his phone, Sherman had left four messages for him. When Wilson called him back, Sherman was angry and said it was disrespectful to all Big 12 schools and to Baylor to run an SEC advertisement during the game. Wilson disagreed, but he was most perplexed about why Mike had chosen to call him to complain about the promo. "Because Bill Byrne told me it was y'all's decision," Wilson recalled Sherman saying. Wilson explained to Mike that the advertisement had been Jeff Schmahl's call on behalf of the athletic department, and that nobody associated with the Board of Regents or the University administration had been involved in the decision to run the promo. Sherman later apologized to Wilson for his displaced anger, but it was certainly clear to me at that time that Mike was uncomfortable even talking about the SEC, and he certainly wasn't interested in promoting the new league.

To me, that was a significant negative regarding Sherman's future at Texas A&M. Selling the SEC—to recruits, students, former students, donors, fans, and the media—was going to be a major part of the job, moving forward. We also needed to make an array of improvements to Kyle Field and other football facilities to compete for recruits in the SEC, and from a fundraising standpoint, the 12th Man Foundation needed our head football coach to be actively engaging prospective capital campaign donors.

That was never a job requirement that Sherman enjoyed or fully embraced. By nature, Sherman appeared to me to be an introverted person who never mastered the art of "working a room." I and others at the 12th Man Foundation failed miserably in attempts to encourage him to take a more active and aggressive role in any kind of fundraising efforts. He just wasn't interested in meeting, greeting, and mingling in a large group of people at receptions or dinners. He would do it, but if you placed Mike in a crowded room of donors and fans, he would gravitate toward a corner so that his interactions were limited. In one-on-one situations, Sherman could be quite engaging and entertaining, as Karin regularly reminded me. Mike Sherman is a deep thinker, and he is an honest, faithful, sincere man of high integrity. I have never spoken to a single offensive lineman who played for Sherman when he was a position coach who spoke negatively about the man. He is a masterful technician who truly understands the nuances and minute details of the game, especially in the trenches. But he is not a marketer, promoter, or salesman. Every time I looked at Mack Brown of Texas, Nick Saban at Alabama, Les Miles at LSU, Chip Kelly at Oregon, Urban Meyer at Florida and then Ohio State, and others, I saw visionary, tone-setting leaders who oversaw the program with a style much like the CEO of a company. But when I looked at Mike Sherman on the sidelines, carrying his huge, laminated card of plays that resembled a restaurant menu, I saw a coordinator or position coach. He was so involved in calling plays that he rarely interacted with players on the sideline. I know there are many coaching styles that work, but Mike Sherman as the head coach and offensive coordinator just was not working for Texas A&M.

Still, despite all these considerations, I was not absolutely certain that Sherman needed to be dismissed as head coach until after two different meetings following the loss to Texas on November 24, 2011. In fact, even though I sensed that a majority of our Board of Regents members were in favor of firing Sherman immediately after the Texas loss, I was still leaning toward keeping him. I tried making a case before the Board of Regents in support of him, thinking that it might be better to allow Mike to coach at least one more season, because Texas A&M was already looking at so many other changes once we officially began competing in the SEC in August 2012.

All that changed after first one meeting with Byrne and then another with Mike Sherman. Both of those meetings disturbed me enough to reverse my stance.

Members of the Board of Regents had been meeting in small, unofficial groups following the four-overtime loss to Kansas State on November 12, 2011, in Manhattan, and after the loss to Texas, Wilson contacted Byrne and encouraged him to develop a powerful and persuasive presentation regarding why he believed Sherman should be the head coach, moving forward. We all knew that Byrne was in favor of keeping Sherman; he'd made that clear. So Wilson made it clear to Byrne that for it to happen he really needed to devise a strong case on Sherman's behalf. A comment such as, "Because I'm the AD and I say so" would not be sufficient, Wilson told Byrne.

When Wilson met with Byrne in Byrne's office in Reed Arena, Byrne essentially ignored that advice. Wilson was underwhelmed by Byrne's presentation. He said that Sherman deserved another year, but he provided no compelling reasons and certainly didn't do Mike any favors in that meeting—not because he didn't want Sherman to stay, but rather because it seemed that he resented having to answer to non–football experts about this critical decision.

Several days later, on the morning of December 1, 2011, Wilson met with Sherman in his office at the Bright Complex, and I joined them via telephone from Washington, DC. This was Sherman's chance to make a case for himself, to give us something encouraging to possibly take to the rest of the Board. It was a tense meeting, and Mike seemed irritated that his job status was even in question. Nevertheless, he started off the meeting by taking full responsibility for the 6-6 season and the numerous blown leads. But as the meeting continued for roughly two hours, Sherman began raising some points that sounded more like excuses. He mentioned that recruiting was going really well, but he then said something that really struck me as odd: Sherman basically attributed the 6-6 season to a lack of senior leadership. That stuck in my craw like a chicken bone.

After four years on the job, he had not had enough time to develop senior leaders? Really? How long would it take—five, six, ten years? Along with all the other strikes against him, that comment put me over the top. After thinking about the meeting for an hour or more, I called Wilson, who was driving home to Houston from College Station. Dr. Richard Box, chairman of the Board of Regents, joined us in a three-way conversation. At that point, I made my recommendation to fire Mike Sherman. Box and Wilson concurred, and I was comfortable that a majority of the Regents would agree that it was time to move forward without Sherman.

At that point, I called Bill Byrne and instructed him to fire Mike Sherman. Predictably, Byrne was not happy, and he bristled in defense of Sherman. He was furious and hung up the phone without agreeing to inform Sherman that he had been fired. But Byrne then called me back and said, "I'll do it." Unfortunately, Byrne did not immediately call Sherman, and somehow, news of the decision we had made regarding Sherman was leaked to *Austin American-Statesman* columnist Kirk Bohls, which precipitated his ill-timed tweet. Consequently, Sherman's family, as well as thousands of others, learned about the firing before Byrne actually reached Sherman on his cell phone.

Later, Bohls said "I caught a lot of flak for breaking that story. I understand, because people are passionate and emotional about sports. But it is not my role or the media's place to decide when we release news. We are not trying to affect the news. When it happened—and obviously it was true—I was reporting what I was told, and I had every confidence that it was accurate. That doesn't mean I didn't feel badly for Mike Sherman, because he is a coach that I really like and respect. I think he is a good, sound football mind. I feel badly that I found out before Mike Sherman found out. That is not the way it is supposed to work, and I understand that. Unfortunately, in this day with social media and blogs and all of that, sometimes the news is broken before the due process takes place."

That was certainly the case in the firing of Mike Sherman. It happened in a terribly wrong way. But it wouldn't take long for practically everyone to realize that it had been the right move. Texas A&M needed a new coach to take the Aggies to a new league. Fortunately, we found the right man at the right time, and he then punched all the right buttons.

CHAPTER 11

"If You're Scared of That, Then Get a Dog"

By the time Johnny Manziel took the field for his Pro Day work-out/spectacle on March 27, 2014, the McFerrin Athletic Center on the Texas A&M campus was already filled with 223 credentialed media members, including live national television coverage by ESPN and the NFL Network. "I've covered a lot of Pro Days, but I've never seen as much media as there is today," tweeted veteran NFL reporter John McClain, who has more than thirty-five years' experience covering the NFL for the *Houston Chronicle*. "There are so many reporters, there might be fights, jockeying for Johnny."

Beyond the blockades that kept the media at arm's length, seventy-five scouts from thirty of the thirty-two NFL teams, including eight head coaches and eight general managers, lined the sides of the field to scrutinize and analyze every move that Manziel made. Johnny, who chose to wear a helmet and shoulder pads to better emulate game situations, performed to the rhythm of rap music as the throwing session began under the choreographed direction of California-based quarterback guru George Whitfield. "This is unlike any Pro Day that I have ever personally observed," said two-time NFL MVP and NFL Network host Kurt Warner, who was among the many expert observers in attendance.

It was, indeed, a remarkably unique setting for one of the most distinctive and compelling players in the history of college football—even before the moment, about ten minutes into the event, when the rollup door on the east end of the indoor practice facility opened to admit a golf cart occupied by former president George H. W. Bush, former first lady Barbara Bush, and the couple's two dogs. "This is the first [Pro Day] I have gone to with the president," joked Tampa Bay Buccaneers head coach Lovie Smith, as reported by Olin Buchanan of TexAgs.com. "Johnny has a little bit of flair to him. He's used to being on the big stage and performing."

There was no doubt about that. Manziel, who was eventually selected late in the first round of the 2014 NFL Draft by the Cleveland Browns, could command an audience and captivate a crowd unlike any other player in the history of Texas A&M University and perhaps even in the history of college football. Manziel possesses an "it" factor that cannot be measured or quantified by a stopwatch, a weight room maximum, scale, a statistical analysis, or even by the Wonderlic Cognitive Ability Test, which is given each year to players entering the NFL draft. Manziel only played two seasons at Texas A&M, but in a matter of months during the 2012 season—when he became the first freshman to win the Heisman Trophy—Manziel emerged as an iconic, captivating, polarizing, and fascinating national figure. In less than four months he became as recognizable in New York's Times Square as he was along Texas Avenue in College Station.

During the 2013 off-season—yes, the off-season—Manziel became practically larger than life. He made news everywhere he went, relaxing backstage with rap star Drake and behind the scenes with NBA megastar LeBron James. Manziel seemingly turned the entire sports world upside down when he overslept on a Saturday morning and subsequently made an early departure from the Manning Passing Academy in Louisiana. His whereabouts were not merely reported by ESPN or CNN, but also by the columnists at TMZ.com and The Hollywood Gossip. Prior to Johnny Manziel, only one Texas A&M football player had ever been featured on the cover of *Sports Illustrated*: Bubba Bean, in 1975. But during August and September of 2013, Manziel appeared on the cover of *Sports Illustrated* twice, as well as on the cover of *Time*, *ESPN–The Magazine*, and *Texas Monthly*.

"[Manziel]'s not famous in the way that other excellent college football players are famous," wrote Andy Staples of *Sports Illustrated*. "He's famous in the way that people who sing pop songs after quitting their Disney Channel shows are famous. . . . Manziel leaving the Manning camp early is news because everything he does is news. He fascinates us for reasons we can't even explain. Like Tim Tebow before him, Manziel moves the meter, even when he isn't doing much of anything. Manziel is ideal for today's twenty-four-hour news cycle. He likes meeting celebrities. He likes socializing at bars. Even though most of what he does wouldn't necessarily qualify as important news, he's just interesting enough. Tossed into the swirl of television, Internet media, social media, and sports talk radio, his adventures make their own gravy."

Obviously, not all the media attention regarding Manziel was positive or glowing. But in a span of less than two years, from when he started his first game at quarterback against Florida on September 8, 2012, until he was drafted into the National Football League on May 8, 2014, Manziel did more for Texas A&M's brand and national image than possibly any other person who has ever attended the University. Even on his Pro Day in March 2014, with Manziel in a black helmet and black jersey, the rock star quarterback's right arm and must-see magnetism delivered an invaluable amount of exposure to the University. As ESPN reporter Samantha Ponder tweeted shortly after the conclusion of Manziel's passing performance, "Everyone has an opinion on talent, but [it's] hard to argue that Texas A&M [isn't the big winner today] . . . A president, NFL GMs, and lots of free advertising."

The free advertising continued on Draft Day 2014 and beyond. Even though he slid all the way down to the twenty-second pick, Manziel was probably the biggest story of the draft. For example, the Browns used the eighth overall pick in the first round to take Oklahoma State cornerback Justin Gilbert. But on the day after the draft, the headline on the front page of the *Cleveland Plain Dealer* read, "HERE'S JOHNNY!" Less than twenty-four hours after the draft, the Browns announced they had sold 2,300 season tickets and noted that the team's sales staff struggled to answer all the phone calls the day after the draft.

From branding, marketing, and awareness viewpoints, Manziel's positive effect on Texas A&M University in two seasons in Aggieland was practically beyond calculation. It's difficult to even estimate the budget required to deliver as much positive publicity for Texas A&M through traditional advertising modes as Manziel did during his meteoric rise to fame from 2012 to 2014. But perhaps it's even more difficult to imagine Texas A&M's first two football seasons in the SEC without Johnny Manziel playing quarterback.

What would the "redeveloped Kyle Field" look like without Manziel's heroics and A&M's success in the first two years of the SEC? If he had never become the number 1 quarterback, could A&M have possibly finished number 5 in the final 2012 *Associated Press* rankings, the Aggies' highest finish since 1956? And would Texas A&M be perceived—as Fox Sports Southwest's Tully Corcoran wrote on National

Signing Day 2014—as the "coolest school in the state [of Texas]" without Manziel's contributions in 2012 and 2013?

My guess: no way. I am also absolutely, positively convinced that if Mike Sherman had been allowed to continue coaching at Texas A&M for a fifth year—the Aggies' first season in the SEC—Manziel would not have been the Aggies' quarterback. It's my sense that it must have taken some significant arm-twisting by former A&M quarterbacks coach Tom Rossley, along with former linebackers coach Dat Nguyen, to convince Sherman to offer Manziel, then a star quarterback out of Kerrville Tivy High School, a college scholarship. Nguyen and Rossley scouted the 2010 Kerrville Tivy-San Antonio Madison game after Manziel had committed to Oregon. Rossley was already completely sold on Manziel's multiple skills, and once Nguyen witnessed him in person, he also told Sherman that Manziel was such a sensational playmaker that the Aggies needed to do everything possible to persuade him not to leave the Lone Star State.

Problem was, Manziel wasn't the tall, prototypical pocket passer that I assumed Sherman coveted. He did way too much improvising for Sherman's taste, and he was much more of a risk taker than Sherman liked. On the other hand, "The guy was just a playmaker and a phenomenal football player," Nguyen recalled. "Coach Rossley was the lead guy on that recruiting trail, and I was just the guy tagging along with him and confirming everything Tom told Mike. Manziel may have been undersized as a quarterback in the estimation of some, but he clearly had a great presence on the field. He made things happen, and was absolutely the best player on the field." Somewhat hesitantly, Sherman agreed to offer Manziel a scholarship, and the youngster actually made an immediate impression on many of the assistant coaches during his redshirt season.

Fresno State head coach Tim DeRuyter, for example, recalls having an "aha!" moment in the fall of 2012 while watching an afternoon telecast of a Texas A&M game. DeRuyter's Bulldogs were playing at night on the West Coast, which allowed the first-year head coach to tune in to a few minutes of the Aggies' game. DeRuyter, A&M's defensive coordinator in 2010–11, was interested in seeing how some of the defenders he'd previously coached were adjusting to a different league and defensive scheme. But after watching a couple of minutes of the action, DeRuyter says he was taken back in time to the week leading up to the 2011 A&M-Baylor game at Kyle Field.

In preparation for that game, the A&M defensive coaching staff asked Manziel, then a true freshman, to run the scout team offense. Manziel's job was to do his best impersonation of Baylor's future Heisman Trophy–winning quarterback Robert Griffin III. DeRuyter realized it was practically impossible for anyone—especially a freshman who'd only been recruited by a couple of major college programs as a quarterback—to mimic the magnificence of the multitalented Griffin. But he hoped Manziel would at least be serviceable in simulating Griffin.

As the week progressed, DeRuyter says he grew increasingly frustrated with his entire defense for what he perceived as the players' half-hearted efforts. Manziel was making DeRuyter's defense look foolish in practice, and if an unheralded freshman could run circles around his defense, the coach wondered how badly Griffin would burn the Aggies. On October 15, 2011, however, A&M won the game, 55-28. Although Griffin passed for 430 yards, the Aggies held him to just fifteen net rushing yards on twelve carries. Too, A&M sacked Griffin five times, which came as a complete shock to DeRuyter, who had been anticipating the worst.

"It wasn't until after the game that my defensive guys told me Johnny was better and more difficult to tackle than RG III," DeRuyter recalled from his office in Fresno, California. "I was rolling my eyes, thinking those guys had just been lazy in practice or that they were messing with me. But then [in 2012], as I was watching a couple of A&M games, I was like, 'Well, I guess those guys were right and I was wrong.' He really is remarkable. I don't know how he learned it or inherited it, but even as a freshman scout-team guy, his attitude was, 'I'm the best guy on this entire field.' I've been coaching a long time, but I have never, ever had a guy running the scout team think he was the best player in the entire program. And yet, [Manziel] did. And he was."

While DeRuyter, Rossley, Nguyen, and other members of the coaching staff were sold on Manziel—secondary coach Charles McMillian was even petitioning Sherman to allow Manziel to move to safety if he wasn't going to play quarterback—Sherman was not completely convinced Manziel was the right man to be the Aggies' field general.

Sherman did not appreciate spontaneous quarterbacks who deviated from the norm . . . or the design of the play. Sherman actually reined in Ryan Tannehill's scrambling tendencies from 2010 to 2011. He wanted his quarterback to stand in the pocket as long as possible and then to throw the ball away if the play broke down: the opposite mentality from that which turned Johnny Manziel into "Johnny Football." At Texas A&M, Manziel rushed 345 times in his two years: more carries than 1985 Heisman Trophy–winning running back Bo Jackson had in his first two years at Auburn.

If Sherman had been the Aggies' coach in 2012, many people close to the program said that the strong-armed Jameill Showers would have likely won the starting quarterback job because he was a far more traditional player than Manziel. Several members of Sherman's former staff at A&M have said that he might have moved Manziel to wide receiver or permitted him to play defensive back to take advantage of his athleticism, rather than merely sitting him on the bench. But quarterback? Probably not. "I loved working for Coach Sherman and loved his professionalism, character, and knowledge of the game," Nguyen said. "But there's no way Johnny Manziel would have played quarterback for Coach Sherman. He wouldn't have tolerated Johnny's scrambling and throwing on the run. Mike was all about minimizing risks, while Johnny was all about extending plays and taking chances. The greatest thing that ever happened to Johnny Manziel at Texas A&M was the arrival of Kevin Sumlin. He provided the freedom and the offensive system to allow Johnny to do what Johnny does best."

Kevin Sumlin, along with Kliff Kingsbury, Sumlin's first offensive coordinator at A&M, was progressive and aggressive enough to allow Manziel to break some old-school quarterbacking rules and to become perhaps the most dazzling and mesmerizing quarterback in the history of college football. "The best way to describe him is that he is just different," former NFL head coach Jon Gruden said of Manziel on ESPN's *QB Camp 2014.* "The way he sees the field, the way he scrambles, the way he throws the ball off-balance sometimes is incredible. And in crunch-time situations . . . [his] improvisation skills are rare and just downright different. He also has tremendous confidence and competitive spirit on game day. He will not quit. I have never seen [the quarterback] position played like Manziel plays it."

If Sherman had not been removed—or if he had been replaced by a coach with an old-school offensive mentality—perhaps Gruden and the rest of the world would have never seen Manziel at quarterback. That would have been a shame.

While the fall semester of 2011 was extremely frustrating and disappointing because of our failures on the gridiron, it was filled with quite a few meaningful wins off the field. We sold the SEC to Texas A&M former students and fans and also sold Texas A&M to the SEC. Jason Cook had been a key member of our tight-knit inner circle in making the move to the SEC, and he was an invaluable marketing machine once the official invitation had been extended.

In August 2011, before Baylor played its tortious-interference, delay-of-game card, Cook had begun planting seeds for an ambitious marketing campaign. His strategy was to portray A&M to the league's passionate fans—from Louisiana to Florida—as a perfect cultural fit in the SEC. He also planned to show that A&M was entering the conference humbly, displaying due respect. The Aggies had not been a consistently powerful football program since R. C. Slocum was the head coach in the 1990s. Meanwhile, by that time the SEC had won five consecutive national championships, and Alabama was en route to winning a sixth straight title for the league at the end of the 2011 season.

Cook's plan was to buy advertising space during the SEC's premier game of the week, the 2:30 (central) p.m. time slot on CBS. He hired a media agency to produce spots that would clearly show that Texas A&M's traditions, passionate fans, game-day pageantry, Southern hospitality, and even its canine mascot (Georgia, Tennessee, and Mississippi State also have dog mascots) would make A&M the perfect addition to the league of champions. Unfortunately, by early August, CBS had already sold out its entire national inventory for the 2:30 time slot, something that had never been an issue with the Big 12's identical slot on ABC. Cook's plan B was to purchase regional spots during the 2:30 broadcasts when two SEC teams faced each other in the top seven markets within the SEC footprint. He also bought national spots for SEC games that were aired on the ESPN family of networks.

We couldn't actually pull the trigger on the marketing and advertising campaign until after the official SEC celebration was held on

September 26, 2011. Ironically, the first game in which A&M's SEC ads began airing pitted the Aggies against Arkansas. The response to those ads was overwhelmingly positive, and we made a big splash throughout the SEC domain. Cook also bought online advertising space through ESPN.com, CBSSportline.com, and SI.com, driving SEC fans to learn more about Texas A&M University. Many people across the SEC sphere of influence had no idea about Texas A&M's enrollment, its prestigious academic ranking, or its rich traditions. We combated the false impression that A&M was still an all-male, military institution, and we promoted Texas A&M's diversity and marketability. The theme of the ads, "Change the Game," effectively altered the false impressions that some may have had of Texas A&M. We continued to advertise throughout the 2011 football season and also bought airtime on bowl games involving SEC schools.

Each Saturday, when Cook monitored Twitter, Facebook, and Internet chat boards, he was delighted with the responses the ads were generating throughout the SEC fan base. Our message was beginning to resonate, and Texas A&M received an abundance of positive media coverage throughout the Southeast. For the most part, SEC fans began to embrace the Aggies as a perfect addition in their league.

At the same time, the A&M community went absolutely crazy with "SEC fever." From his previous experiences as a student at Mississippi State and a resident in the Southeast, Cook predicted that anything combining the A&M logo with the SEC's would sell so quickly that it would be difficult for College Station retail outlets to keep the merchandise in stock.

He was right. I was stunned by the allure and marketability of the SEC logo. A case in point was the dramatic sales generated by Aggieland Outfitters, once that retailer began placing the SEC logo on merchandise. "Moving to the SEC was an absolute game-changer for Aggieland Outfitters," said Dallas Shipp, the director of marketing and communications for the privately owned business. "Aggie fans bought hats that looked just like their old hats, simply because they now had the SEC logo on them. They demanded Polo [shirts] with the SEC mark on the sleeve to show off their new conference pride, and SEC-branded t-shirts flew off the shelves, too."

As SEC-related sales skyrocketed, Cook promoted A&M's new conference home to the Aggie family by appearing weekly on Tex-Ags.com's morning radio show with host Gabe Bock. He spoke to roughly twenty A&M clubs, not only around the state of Texas, but also, via Skype, around the country. Cook knew the colossal clout of the SEC brand far better than I . . . at least until I attended that year's BCS National Championship Game that matched second-ranked Alabama against number 1 LSU in New Orleans. The game wasn't particularly memorable, as the Tide rolled to a 21-0 win, but SEC pride practically oozed out of the Mercedes-Benz Superdome. At that game in that setting, I fully began to understand the uniqueness of the SEC, making me even more certain that we had made the right decision.

Meanwhile, on October 6, 2011, the Big 12 Conference took three significant steps toward gaining a modicum of stability. First, the league announced that it had invited TCU to replace Texas A&M as the Big 12's tenth member. Later in the day, it was announced that no institutional networks—not even the Longhorn Network—would be permitted to show high school games or highlights. And finally, the Big 12 Board of Directors agreed to a formal grant of television rights for a minimum of six years. The approval by the Board was unanimous . . . with an asterisk. The University of Missouri did not participate in the vote on the advice of legal counsel, presumably because two days earlier, Mizzou's governing board authorized Chancellor Brady Deaton "to take any and all actions necessary to fully explore options for conference affiliation."

This was the identical action Texas A&M's Board of Regents had taken before we made the move to the SEC. Deaton maintained that Missouri was "just beginning the process of exploration," but many sensed it was just a matter of time before the Tigers joined us in the SEC, becoming the fourteenth member of the league.

This was a potentially groundbreaking move for the SEC and highly significant, of course, for the Big 12. Obviously, the departure of Missouri would create more upheaval for the Big 12, as losing the Tigers would cost the conference one of its founding members (Missouri had been a 1907 charter member of the Missouri Valley Intercollegiate Athletic Association, which evolved into the Big Six, then the

Big Eight, and finally the Big 12). Mizzou also added stature to the Big 12 by its membership in the prestigious Association of American Universities. For the academicians keeping score, the SEC would now have four AAU institutions (Texas A&M, Missouri, Florida and Vanderbilt) compared to the Big 12's three (Kansas, Iowa State and Texas).

Just as at Texas A&M, many Mizzou fans also were concerned by the prospect of separating from traditional Big 12 rivals, especially the possible end of the Missouri-Kansas "Border War" game, which *Sports Illustrated* once described as the oldest rivalry west of the Mississippi River, going back to 1891. But the rivalry actually traces its roots to the 1850s, when the Kansas Territory was a bloody battleground involving anti- and pro-slavery sides.

"The mascots from each school are derived from antebellum fighting forces," wrote Robert Mays of Grantland.com. "'Jayhawkers' was the name given to pro-Union militias throughout Kansas, and the 'Tigers' were a group in Columbia, Missouri, who protected the town and university from Confederate forces. For all the ill feelings between the schools now, at their inception, the Jayhawks and Tigers were actually on the same side."

When the two schools began meeting in football games, less than three decades after William Quantrill's bloody border raid into Kansas and all the other violence of that era, Civil War veterans from both sides often joined the teams on the sidelines. The legacy of the former conflict was, quite literally, part of what made the Missouri-Kansas football Border War such an intense rivalry, right from the start.

From the University of Missouri's perspective, leaving the Big 12 for the SEC would jeopardize that rivalry as well as others, including Kansas State, Iowa State, Oklahoma, and Oklahoma State—some dating as far back as 1907. But, by early October 2011, a majority of Missouri fans seemed to be in the SEC camp. While some may not have considered Missouri to be the perfect geographical fit in the SEC, the addition of the Tigers did make sense to the SEC for many reasons.

After Texas A&M was officially accepted as the SEC's thirteenth member in September 2011, speculation immediately began as to which school would be the fourteenth. The primary reason for that was because a thirteen-school conference creates scheduling headaches. An odd number of members worked fine in the nine-school Southwest

Conference for decades and even in the eleven-school Big Ten after Penn State joined the league in 1990. But the eleven-team format worked because the Big Ten did not have a championship game or a two-division setup.

Once A&M was added to the SEC, Mike Slive and other league officials made it known that further expansion was not an absolute requirement. In other words, the SEC would not be pressed or pressured into adding just any other school for the sake of having an even number of members. On the other hand, if the right school could be found, it definitely made sense to have fourteen teams, as Mike Slive and other SEC officials knew from the experience of the Mid-American Conference.

In 2011, the MAC offered the sole example of a league that had made a thirteen-school configuration work from a football scheduling standpoint. In 2007, Temple University joined that league and pushed membership to thirteen, where it stayed until 2012, when the University of Massachusetts joined the conference. For the five years preceding that event, however, scheduling was often a nightmare in the MAC, with seven teams in the East Division and six in the West. For starters, the NCAA had to make a special exception for the MAC to even hold its championship game. The NCAA rule book states that in order to hold a championship game, a league must have two divisions of at least six schools each, and each school must play a round-robin divisional schedule. The NCAA allowed the MAC to essentially ignore that bylaw and hold its title game despite the fact that four teams in one seven-team division do not actually play a full round-robin schedule. Tiebreakers were also confusing and complex because not all MAC East Division teams played each other in a year.

Further, in examining a proposed thirteen-team SEC schedule, a number of troubling issues were instantaneously revealed. In the SEC, with a seven-school Western Division and a six-school Eastern Division, four teams in the West would not play all of the other six teams within their division each year. The four schools that did not complete a full round-robin schedule would play three games against Eastern Division schools. Meanwhile, three schools in the West would play all of the other six schools in their division and two conference games against Eastern Division schools.

Confused? It certainly wasn't easy to understand. But here's a hypothetical situation that may clarify the predicament: Depending on the luck of the draw, Texas A&M could have conceivably entered the Western Division in 2012 and avoided LSU—a fellow member of the Western Division—instead playing three games against Eastern schools (let's say Kentucky, Tennessee, and Vanderbilt, for the sake of example). If you look at how the actual standings played out in 2012, it's possible to imagine A&M going undefeated against that schedule. A&M would have avoided LSU, the only team it actually lost to within its division in 2012, as well as Florida, which tied for the Eastern Division title in 2012. Imagine the outrage from other schools in the Western Division if A&M had won the SEC West without facing LSU.

For many reasons, fourteen schools, with two seven-team divisions was a far more equitable and manageable number for scheduling purposes. And there was no shortage of candidates for that fourteenth slot. Practically every school in the Big 12, the ACC, and the old Big East was mentioned by one media outlet or another as a possible addition to the SEC. Many of the schools initially mentioned by the media—Florida State, Georgia Tech, Clemson, and Louisville, for example—likely would not have received the necessary votes from the presidents and chancellors of the existing SEC members. As we had discovered at A&M, the SEC brand is extremely powerful, prestigious, and lucrative. Texas A&M now has a recruiting and competitive advantage in the Lone Star State, precisely because the Aggies are the only school in Texas that belongs to the SEC. Quite frankly, I don't envision Texas A&M ever risking the loss of that distinction by supporting or promoting the future inclusion of Texas in the SEC.

Likewise, the University of Florida values and protects its status as the only SEC member in the Sunshine State. "Florida, Georgia, South Carolina, and Kentucky were all in agreement that all four would mutually block the inclusion of Florida State, Georgia Tech, Clemson, or Louisville," wrote Clay Travis of Fox College Sports' *Outkick the Coverage*. "The rationale was simple: none of those schools wanted to dilute their local brand value by bringing a second team into their market. Adding those schools also didn't make sense from an SEC Network perspective. New markets make a network more valuable; additional teams in the same market have no real value."

That's why a school like Missouri must have made sense to the SEC. Missouri brought new major television markets like St. Louis and Kansas City within reach. Further, the state of Missouri borders three SEC states (Tennessee, Kentucky, and Arkansas), and two of those states are members of the Eastern Division. On the other hand, the other ACC schools mentioned by the mass media as possible candidates to join the SEC—Virginia Tech, North Carolina, Maryland, and North Carolina State—were already part of a stable conference.

So, Mizzou was apparently interested in the SEC, and the SEC must have also been interested in the Tigers. Mizzou's decision was all about stability. "In an era of shrinking higher education budgets, [Missouri had] to pick the league that offers the most money and the most security for the longest time," wrote Andy Staples of *Sports Illustrated*. "There will come a day when taxpayers refuse to subsidize college athletics at public universities, and the schools in the conferences that make the most money will remain strong while the others fade away."

On October 28, 2011, the Big 12 Board of Directors voted unanimously to accept West Virginia as a full conference member, effective July 1, 2012. Roughly a week later, on November 6, 2011, the Southeastern Conference presidents and chancellors announced that the University of Missouri had been voted in unanimously as the fourteenth member of the SEC. With that hurdle cleared, the SEC then went back to work on scheduling, now with an even number of conference members.

Texas A&M and Missouri were both hoping for a marquee matchup at home in their first-ever SEC games. In fact, I had spoken with Mike Slive in the summer of 2011 about our need for a signature game at home to begin SEC play if Texas A&M did, indeed, join the conference. Mike promised me that he would keep that in mind when the time came, and he delivered on behalf of both Texas A&M and Missouri. In December 2011, the SEC released its schedule, and both the Aggies and Tigers were rewarded with big-time opponents for their respective conference openers on September 8, 2012. The Florida Gators were coming to College Station on that day, while the Georgia Bulldogs were headed to Columbia, Missouri, for the Tigers' SEC opener on the same day. Now, we just needed a head football coach who could prepare us to compete.

Since 1958, the National Football Foundation (NFF) and College Football Hall of Fame have held their annual awards dinner and Hall of Fame induction ceremonies at New York City's Waldorf-Astoria Grand Ballroom in early December. Over the years, the event has grown larger and larger, and nowadays, it isn't uncommon for more than 1,600 of college football's most prominent personalities and most ardent supporters to gather in the Big Apple for several days of celebration and recognition. The event also offers a great opportunity for administrators and coaches to network. I sent Bill Byrne to the fifty-fourth annual event, held December 6, 2011, with a firm mission in mind.

Mike Sherman had been fired on December 1 and held his press conference on December 2. While I lamented the way it had happened, it was now time to move forward and find the perfect man to lead Texas A&M into the SEC. I viewed this as a momentous, historic, and imperative decision in which we could absolutely not afford to make the wrong hire. From the 2002 season—R. C. Slocum's last as head coach—to the final game that Mike Sherman had coached on November 24, 2011, Texas A&M's combined record was just 63-60. That's practically the definition of mediocrity, as the Aggies had not produced a single season with as many as ten wins since the 1998 Big 12 championship season. But now Texas A&M had made its bold transition into the SEC, and we needed a remarkably vibrant, confident, and dynamic visionary to lead us into the new league.

Immediately after the news of the Sherman firing was tweeted out by Kirk Bohls, the media began speculating about Sherman's replacement. The name that was reported most often was Kevin Sumlin, who had just led the Houston Cougars to a perfect 12-0 regular season and was preparing his team to face Southern Mississippi on December 3 in the Conference USA championship game in Houston. That game was an interesting one from Texas A&M's perspective not only because of Sumlin, but also because Southern Miss was coached by College Station native Larry Fedora, who was completing his fourth season with the Golden Eagles after previously serving as an offensive coordinator at Florida and Oklahoma State. Southern Miss won the game, preventing the Cougars from earning a BCS invitation, but that certainly didn't diminish our perception of Sumlin.

Kevin Sumlin was born in 1964 in the lumber mill town of Brewton, Alabama, eighty miles northeast of Mobile—in the heart of SEC country—where his father, Bill Sumlin, coached football at Booker T. Washington High School. Roughly two years later, the Sumlins moved to Indiana, where Bill and his wife, Marion, went to graduate school and made careers as educators. Kevin Sumlin played football, basketball, and baseball at Brebeuf Jesuit Prep in Indianapolis before he walked on at Purdue, where he started at linebacker for four years. "He was a smart player, smart guy right from the get-go," Purdue coach Joe Tiller told Tully Corcoran of FOXSports.com. "He was athletic; he could run. Thought he could play in the NBA . . . Well, every football player does." After Sumlin's playing career was finished, he served as a graduate assistant at Washington State under Mike Price and then as a Tiller assistant at Wyoming and Purdue, with a brief stop at Minnesota in between. It was when Sumlin was an assistant at Purdue and was recruiting in Texas that R. C. Slocum first noticed him. "You'd see these lists in the newspapers of what schools the top recruits in Texas were considering each year, and it jumped out at me that there were quite a few kids listing Purdue," Slocum recalled. "I knew somebody was doing a good job of selling Purdue, and I asked guys on my staff who was recruiting the state of Texas for Purdue. I found out it was a guy named Kevin Sumlin, and I told the guys on my staff to introduce me to this guy at the next coaches' convention."

Sumlin served as assistant coach at Texas A&M during Slocum's final two seasons in Aggieland (2001–02), and Slocum later acknowledged that if he had originally made Sumlin the Aggies' offensive coordinator, he probably would have never lost his job.

Following Sherman's firing, Slocum spoke glowingly about Sumlin, as did the former A&M players who worked directly with Sumlin—receivers like Terrence Murphy, Bethel Johnson, and Jamaar Taylor. After leaving A&M following the 2002 season, Sumlin was hired at Oklahoma by Bob Stoops in 2003 as a special teams coordinator and tight ends coach. Sumlin was promoted to co-offensive coordinator in 2006, and a year later, Oklahoma ranked fifth in scoring (42.3 points) and nineteenth in total offense (448.9 yards per game) on its way to the Fiesta Bowl. Houston hired Sumlin in December 2007, and Sumlin vowed to use what he had learned from Tiller, Price, Slocum, and

Stoops to build up the Cougars' program. He didn't disappoint. Sumlin went 35-17 in four seasons with Houston, and the Cougars routinely ranked as one of the nation's highest scoring teams. Such success had hardly gone unnoticed. Prior to the 2011 Conference USA championship game, multiple media reports linked Sumlin to coaching vacancies at schools such as Mississippi, Illinois, Arizona State, and UCLA, in addition to Texas A&M. If he was the right man for the job at A&M—as many suspected—we needed to act swiftly.

While my relationship with Byrne had deteriorated dramatically over the course of 2011, I still had a great deal of trust and confidence in his ability to evaluate coaches. My instruction to Bill was to travel to New York, meet with as many qualified candidates as possible, and bring back his top recommendations. In the interest of confidentiality, I won't disclose the names of the coaches that Byrne talked to while in New York or after his return to College Station. But I know for a fact that he did his homework and spoke with numerous coaches or their agents about the possibility of coming to Texas A&M. When Byrne returned from New York, he recommended that we interview Sumlin.

I then spoke again to Coach Slocum, a tremendous asset and sounding board, who talked about his previous interview experiences and his fondness for Sumlin, advising me to include some of the engaged Board of Regents members in the official Sumlin interview. I then encouraged Bill Byrne to arrange for an interview with Kevin Sumlin as soon as possible. On Saturday, December 10, I met Bill Byrne at his house, and we drove to Houston together, where Bill had arranged for us to meet Sumlin at the Sugar Land Marriott Town Square. Regents Jim Wilson, Jim Schwertner, and Richard Box met us at the hotel, where we talked to Sumlin for a couple of hours before asking him to leave the room. Once Sumlin left the room, it only took a moment for us all to realize that we had the right man.

I had not met Sumlin previously, but I was particularly impressed with how he handled the interview. I knew he could coach; his record made that clear, as did Slocum and the players who had worked with him. But I was also quite impressed with his views on academics, his appreciation of Texas A&M, his enthusiasm regarding coaching in the SEC, and his confidence that Texas A&M could thrive in the nation's most respected conference. The Regents and Bill Byrne also asked a variety of questions, and Kevin made a strong and positive impression on us all. After a few minutes of internal discussion, I told Bill Byrne to make an offer.

By Monday, December 12—ten days after the awkward Mike Sherman exit press conference at the Bright Complex—we formally hosted the introductory press conference for Kevin Sumlin. So many things impressed me that day, beginning with the fact that many of the players from the 2001–02 A&M teams returned to welcome Sumlin back to Texas A&M. I also was impressed by how he publicly embraced the SEC and how he handled all of the reporters' queries, including the race-related questions. Sumlin is the first African American head football coach in Texas A&M history, and I was gratified by how he dealt with that issue at the press conference. "There are a lot of firsts that have happened for me as a coach," Sumlin said. "Hopefully in the next five years or so, [race] won't even be a discussion. Honestly, that's something that I really don't talk about. Every time it gets brought up, it's by media. Players don't talk about it in recruiting, parents don't talk about it in recruiting. It's never come up in the discussions that [Bill Byrne and I] have had. . . . I want to be known as a great coach at Texas A&M. Period."

Sumlin was great at the introductory press conference, but then again, most coaches are at peak performance in that setting. Perhaps the strongest early indication I had that Texas A&M had hired not only a great coach, but also one who was prepared to tackle the SEC challenge, came later in December. As the football team prepared to face Northwestern on New Year's Eve in Houston at the Meineke Car Care Bowl of Texas, Sumlin and his wife, Char, were gracious and poised in their interactions with Regents and others in our suite at the stadium. He was repeatedly asked about how he could possibly compete in the SEC West. Sumlin was not coaching the 2011 team in the bowl game, as Mike Sherman's defensive coordinator, Tim DeRuyter, had taken over as interim coach. But Sumlin was already becoming the face of the program: recruiting, representing A&M, hiring a staff, and answering reporters' questions.

After yet another loaded question regarding A&M's daunting task in the SEC, Sumlin delivered a rather memorable response. "I want to be around people who want to play at the highest level, who want to compete in the best conference in America in the best division in America," Sumlin said emphatically. "If you're scared of that, then get a dog. There's a bunch of guys in this state who want to be a part of [the SEC], and not only be a part of it, but have a chance to win there. As I've said before, I've been walking around for the last month with this SEC patch on [my sleeve], and it hasn't hurt me a bit."

At that point, I knew we had something special: someone bold enough to go head-to-head in the SEC. We had a head coach who wouldn't merely disappear into the imposing shadows cast by the likes of Nick Saban, Les Miles, and Steve Spurrier. Texas A&M had hired a progressive, innovative, confident coach with an edge: a coach who wouldn't be afraid to think outside the box or even to start a quarterback who didn't fit the stereotypical, old-school model. Times were, indeed, changing in Aggieland. And the best was yet to come.

CHAPTER 12

The Journey is Just Beginning

For almost a full year leading up to Election Day in 1948, printers who operated the linotype machines at the *Chicago Tribune* and other newspapers in the Windy City had been on strike in protest of the Taft-Hartley Act, a federal law restricting the activities and power of labor unions. As a result of that strike and the ensuing changes the *Tribune* made in its printing processes, the deadline to go to press was several hours earlier than other newspapers in the Central time zone and even earlier than many major dailies along the East Coast. The earlier deadlines had been inconvenient leading up to Election Day, but on November 2, 1948, the printers' strike would result in perhaps the most famously incorrect headline in the history of US newspapers. The polls and the pundits predicted early in the day that Gov. Thomas Dewey of New York would defeat President Harry S. Truman, and as the first-edition deadline approached, *Chicago Tribune* managing editor J. Loy Maloney made the headline call: "DEWEY DEFEATS TRUMAN."

Only 150,000 copies of the paper with that erroneous, all-caps announcement were printed before the *Tribune* changed the headline for the second edition. The incorrect headline may have been forgotten quickly except for a chance encounter two days later in St. Louis. Truman, traveling by rail to Washington, stepped to the rear platform of the train and was handed a copy of the *Tribune* early edition. The picture of President Truman holding up the newspaper forever cemented the headline as one of the most famous journalistic gaffes of all time. But to me, Truman's robust smile is what made the photograph so memorable. The *Tribune* had previously referred to Truman as a "nincompoop," and the paper's editorial staff—as well as many other newspapers—had been rather brash in its gloom-and-doom scenarios regarding Truman's reelection bid. Judging by the splendor of his smile, Truman's victory on November 2, 1948, was even sweeter because of all the negative commentary that had appeared in the press.

In that regard, I have a relatively good idea of how Harry S. Truman, the namesake for the University of Missouri's costumed mascot "Truman the Tiger," must have felt. The headlines entering the 2012 football season may not have been as bold and as glaring as "DEWEY DEFEATS TRUMAN," but the national and regional sports media were most certainly predicting dark, dangerous, and dismal times ahead for the Aggies. Cedric Golden of the *Austin American-Statesman* wrote that "the Aggies run the risk of getting their heads bashed in for the next few falls." The preseason media poll, released in mid-July 2012, picked Texas A&M to finish fifth in the SEC West, behind LSU, Alabama, Arkansas, and Auburn, and ahead of only Mississippi State and Ole Miss. Graham Watson of Yahoo! Sports' *Dr. Saturday*, wrote: "Make no mistake, this is going to be a learning year. There are going to be some tough moments and A&M is going to get blown out here and there. It's easy to look at the [2012] schedule and see the Aggies revert back to the team they were in Sherman's first year in 2008. A&M fans are going to have to be patient and give Sumlin a chance to put his mark on the program [as] it blazes its trail through the SEC. This season has the potential to be ugly at times."

Perhaps my personal favorite prediction came from Kevin Sherrington of the *Dallas Morning News* on June 30, 2012, the eve of our official entry into the SEC. Sherrington did much more than merely project struggles on the football field. "In a move as seismic as this one, it's nervy, at best, to take on so much at once," Sherrington wrote. "Maybe A&M football will flourish in the SEC. Maybe Eric Hyman will prove to be a better AD than Bill Byrne. Maybe Kevin Sumlin is a better head coach than Mike Sherman. Maybe Loftin can get Kyle Field remodeled before the place comes down around his ears. Maybe he goes four-for-four. Chances are pretty good he won't. In fact, I'd bet on it."

I'm not an expert when it comes to official scorekeeping or baseball vernacular. But looking back and assessing A&M's athletic developments from July 1, 2012—the Aggies' first official day in the SEC—to the conclusion of the 2013–14 school year/athletic calendar, I'd bet that most scorekeepers would say the Aggies (certainly not me individually) had gone four-for-four, with at least a couple of home runs.

With twenty wins in his first two seasons, Kevin Sumlin registered the most impressive two-year debut in the history of Texas A&M football. No other head coach at A&M had ever recorded more than eighteen wins in his first two seasons. And Sumlin's 11-2 record in 2012, his first year at A&M, is unprecedented in the Aggies' modern history. The last A&M head football coach with such an impressive debut was D. X. Bible, who in 1917 guided the Aggies to an 8-0 record while outscoring opponents, 270-0. Legendary A&M head coaches Homer Norton, Paul "Bear" Bryant, Gene Stallings, Emory Bellard, and Jackie Sherrill all endured losing seasons in their first year at A&M. So did Harry Stiteler, Jim Myers, Hank Foldberg, Dennis Franchione, and Mike Sherman. R. C. Slocum was previously the only coach in school history to take A&M to a bowl game in his first full season. The 1989 team was solid, going 8-4, earning a Sun Bowl bid, and finishing twentieth in the final AP poll. But that team couldn't compare to the 2012 Aggies. Sumlin's first team at A&M went undefeated on the road—including a stunning win at top-ranked Alabama—produced the first freshman Heisman Trophy winner in college football history, and finished in the top five of the final *AP* rankings.

Although it's difficult to put a dollar value on the amount of positive exposure Texas A&M received because of that success in 2012, we attempted to do just that. On January 18, 2013, Texas A&M officials announced that the historic end of the Aggies' 2012 football season—beginning on November 10, 2012, with the win over Alabama and concluding with the January 6, 2013, victory over Oklahoma in the Cotton Bowl—translated into $37 million in media exposure for the university. That figure was based on research conducted by Joyce Julius & Associates. One week later, an in-house study was released, revealing that the Texas A&M University System generated an estimated $4.3 billion for the Bryan-College Station community in 2012. That was a $540 million increase over 2011 and a $2.2 billion increase since 2002. University and city officials concluded that much of the increase in the contribution to the local economy was linked to A&M's move to the SEC, as attendance at athletic events increased by about 98,000 in 2012 from the previous year. In other words, Texas A&M's move to the SEC was a wise and quite profitable business decision, right from the start.

The success in 2012 also played a role in dramatically increasing the size and grandeur of the redevelopment of Kyle Field. Even before the start of the 2012 season, preliminary plans were being discussed to renovate the stadium: addressing safety issues, updating the suites on the west side of the stadium, modernizing the concourses and restrooms, and improving the appearance of the aging facility. Earlier I had insisted on addressing the east side of Kyle Field given its condition and the importance of our students who were the primary occupants of that side of the stadium. But the plan to upgrade Kyle Field was soon transformed into the largest redevelopment of a stadium in the history of college football. On May 1, 2013, the Texas A&M University System Board of Regents approved a $450 million renovation of Kyle Field that will increase the stadium's capacity to 102,500 by the 2015 season, making it the largest stadium in the SEC. Many factors contributed to the dramatic increase in the scope and comprehensive nature of the project, including the booming oil and gas industry in Texas, the individual leadership efforts of 12th Man Foundation board members like Sam Torn and Bob McClaren (co-chairs of the Kyle Field Redevelopment Committee), and more. But the Aggies' athletic success in 2012 certainly played a prominent role in the planning and especially the fundraising achievements for that and subsequent years.

"We know that we're not going to have one of our athletes win the Heisman Trophy every year," Torn told *12th Man Magazine* shortly after the official unveiling for the stadium's future. "We know that we may not win eleven or twelve games every year. But that's going to be our goal. One of our core values at Texas A&M is excellence. And to me, excellence means 'the best.' Our goal from day one has been to design the finest collegiate football facility in the country."

Shortly after Kevin Sumlin was hired to replace Mike Sherman as Texas A&M's head football coach, I called Bill Byrne to my office. He probably anticipated the purpose of the call. Bill and I had merely coexisted for quite some time, but after Sumlin was in place as the new leader of the Texas A&M football program, I believed it was an ideal time to begin seeking a new leader for the athletic department. Bill Byrne had accomplished many great things in the Aggies' final decade in the Big 12, but now that we were in the SEC I believed Texas A&M would benefit from a fresh outlook and new perspectives at the top.

When Bill arrived at my office, I was succinct. He had more than a full year left on his contract, which was scheduled to expire on August 31, 2013. I told him that I did not plan on renewing his contract when it expired, and I offered to buy out the final year, meaning that his last day as athletic director would be in May 2012. Byrne agreed to my offer, and we negotiated a lump sum payout of $690,000, or what he would have made in the final year of his agreement. Byrne announced his resignation at a press conference on May 8, 2012. One day later we announced that Texas A&M had engaged Atlanta-based firm Parker Executive Search and had named an eleven-member advisory committee to assist in the identification and selection of a new athletic director. Jim Wilson and Jason Cook served as co-chairs of the search advisory committee, and with fellow Board of Regents member Cliff Thomas, who played football at A&M in the late 1960s and early '70s, played a key role in actually interviewing AD candidates.

Under normal circumstances, I would have preferred to receive more input from the full search committee, which included prominent 12th Man Foundation donors such as Scott Taylor and Jack Little; professors Dr. Thomas Wehrly and Dr. Albert Broussard; softball head coach Jo Evans; athletics director of compliance David Batson; and former athletes Terrence Murphy and Adaora Elonu. In hindsight, though, it was a mistake on my part to form such a large committee, because I was absolutely committed to avoid any leaks regarding potential candidates. This was strongly reinforced by the search firm, which was clear in telling me that such a large committee would discourage many "sitting" Athletic Directors from even talking to us. For that reason, I confess I didn't really use most of the members of the committee until we had identified the person we wanted, which justifiably frustrated them. Yet anonymity was of vital importance to our candidate pool, as no sitting AD at another peer institution wanted to be perceived as having wandering eyes. Parker delivered to me an initial list of about twenty high-profile athletic directors across the country, and Wilson, Cook, Thomas, and I interviewed four of those candidates. Three of those prospective ADs were interviewed on a single day in mid-June 2012 in Atlanta, while the fourth candidate was unable to make it that day because his school, South Carolina, was participating in the College World Series in Omaha. His name was Eric Hyman.

The Gamecocks advanced to the championship series of the CWS on June 24–25, and we then arranged to interview Hyman in Dallas. We had all been impressed with the three candidates we met in Atlanta, but we had no consensus top candidate after the first three interviews. The fourth candidate, Hyman, possessed some qualities that we viewed to be particularly valuable. First, he'd been an AD in the SEC since taking over the leadership at South Carolina in July 2005. He was also quite familiar with the Lone Star State, having served as the TCU athletic director from 1998 to 2005. During his tenure in Fort Worth, the Horned Frogs recorded thirty-two conference titles, and the football program went to six bowl games in seven years. More than his experience, though, we were impressed with his genuineness. Hyman showed up at the airport with a piece of paper in hand that contained a list of his priorities and top objectives. He wasn't trying to find out what we wanted to hear; he merely defined his goals, his attributes, his views, his methodology, and his interest in Texas A&M. He impressed me with his candid responses and made it clear to all of us that he would never portray himself in a misleading manner. Hyman said he loved to watch games, but he did not play games. I thoroughly appreciated his authenticity and clarity. "I'd love the opportunity to lead Texas A&M into the SEC," he said, "but if I'm not a fit, I'm okay with that, too. What you see is what you get. This is who I really am."

By the end of the interview, we all viewed him as a fit for Texas A&M, and it was clear that Hyman recognized A&M as a golden opportunity. He knew about A&M's reputation and potential from his time at TCU; and he possessed a further appreciation of Texas A&M's traditions and culture, as his sister and son-in-law both attended A&M. As we discussed the passion of Texas A&M former students and fans and their excitement regarding the SEC, Hyman was further intrigued by the possibilities that Aggieland presented. He was stunned, for example, when we told him that on March 27, 2012, the Texas A&M athletic department and 12th Man Foundation had opened season ticket sales for the 2012 season...and sold out in the same day. It marked the earliest sellout of season tickets in school history.

A&M's passionate, SEC-crazed fans were also at their best later in the spring when the Aggie faithful, with the help of their SEC brethren, won ESPN's "Bring GameDay to Your Campus" online voting contest.

The fan base that earned the most votes during a ten-day period won the opportunity to host the GameDay crew—Chris Fowler, Kirk Herbstreit, Desmond Howard, Lee Corso, and Samantha Steele—on their campus in late July for the filming of a commercial that would run throughout the 2012 college football season. Jason Cook had challenged the A&M fans, saying: "Texas A&M obviously wants to show ESPN and our new SEC family the power of the Twelfth Man. Having a GameDay commercial shot on our campus would give Texas A&M tremendous exposure to a national audience, right in line with our move to the SEC this fall."

Texas A&M fans responded spectacularly as Aggies flocked to social media and online forums such as TexAgs.com to lead an aggressive voting campaign through the final hours of the contest. The 12th Man Foundation and The Association of Former Students challenged its donors and members to support the cause, as did high-profile former students such as Texas Governor Rick Perry and 2011 NFL Rookie of the Year Von Miller. The A&M fans helped to make it a two-school race in the final days, as Big Ten fans rallied to support Nebraska and narrow the A&M lead. But in one of the first examples of the power of the SEC family, fans from throughout the Southeast voted to push A&M over the top.

The forty-five second commercial, which also included Kevin Sumlin, Reveille, the yell leaders, and thousands of A&M fans and students participating in Midnight Yell Practice, was a nice feather in the Aggies' cap. But it was actually just one of many public relations victories in the spring and summer of 2012 that proved Texas A&M's fans were definitely ready for the SEC. The positive PR continued throughout the summer as the 12th Man Foundation supplied its donors with thousands upon thousands of maroon and white yard signs that announced, "This is SEC Country." Cook continued to build on the theme, complementing the literal grassroots yard sign movement with a statewide billboard campaign that blanketed Houston, Dallas, San Antonio, and even a billboard in Austin. Additional "This Is SEC Country" billboards greeted out-of-state guests from Oklahoma on I-35, from Arkansas on I-30, and from Louisiana on I-10 and I-20.

In the midst of all these branding, marketing, and online voting victories, Eric Hyman announced his resignation from South Carolina on June 29. The following day he was in College Station for his introductory press conference. Unfortunately, not all the Aggie sports news on June 29, 2012, was worth marketing or promoting. At 3:24 a.m. on June 29, a redshirt freshman quarterback by the name of Johnny Manziel was arrested on charges of possessing a fake driver's license, failure to identify himself, and fighting. He was jailed overnight, and his mug shot was particularly memorable, since Manziel was not wearing a shirt when he was photographed.

The arrest was made after College Station police saw then-19-year-old Manziel in a physical altercation with a 47-year-old man just after 2:00 a.m. in a street in the Northgate entertainment district, adjacent to campus. The fighting began after a friend of Manziel's pointed at the man and used a racial slur. A witness told police that Manziel stepped between the pair in an attempt to defuse the situation, but that a fight broke out after the man pushed Manziel. After stopping the fight, police asked Manziel for identification. Manziel gave officers a Louisiana driver's license showing a birthday in 1990; police then searched Manziel and found his real license with a birthday in 1992.

Following the arrest, Manziel was originally suspended for the entire 2012 season, leading the then-freshman to consider a transfer. But Manziel appealed the suspension, and Kevin Sumlin wrote a letter on his quarterback's behalf. Cooler heads prevailed, and Manziel was reinstated to the team. Honestly, since I didn't closely follow recruiting or high school football, the arrest was the first time I had ever paid any attention to the name Johnny Manziel. I heard his name again later in the summer when, on August 15, Sumlin announced that Manziel would be the Aggies' starting quarterback for the season opener, which was originally scheduled to be played against Louisiana Tech on August 30 in Shreveport, Louisiana. I was surprised by this, because I had read that coming out of spring practices, Jameill Showers had a slight edge in the race to replace Ryan Tannehill, who was by then a quarterback for the NFL's Miami Dolphins. "Johnny has performed the best at this stage, and we will proceed until the season opener with him getting the first-team reps," Sumlin said on August 15. "My policy is simple, really; the best player plays." Little did we know at that time that Manziel would not only be the best player at his position or on the roster, but by the end of the year, he'd also prove to be arguably the best player in all of college football.

Not long after the December 8, 2012 announcement that Johnny Manziel had become the first freshman, the second Aggie, and the seventy-eighth person to win the most revered individual award in American sports, a massive digital image of the quarterback appeared on one of the dazzling electronic billboards along the intersection of Seventh Avenue and Broadway in Midtown Manhattan. The eye-catching ad, conceived by Jason Cook and positioned strategically across from where the sharply dressed Manziel was captivating national media members on an unforgettable Saturday night at the Marriott Marquis, featured Manziel in a maroon jersey and suggested a new nickname for the burgeoning megastar: "Call him Johnny Heisman," it stated.

Winning the Heisman that night capped a two-city tour where Manziel picked up the Davey O'Brien Award in Orlando on his twentieth birthday (December 6) and then captivated audiences and media in New York, displaying poise and presence well beyond his years. In addition to seeing his likeness illuminated in America's brightest advertising lights following the Heisman ceremony, Manziel began making the rounds on the Big Apple's most famous television talk and news shows: *David Letterman*, *Fox & Friends*, and *Good Morning America*, to name a few.

At no point did Manziel appear to be overwhelmed by any of the madness or media frenzy that surrounded him. Just as Sumlin had described his quarterback throughout the 2012 season, no moment appeared to be too big for him. Manziel gracefully handled every appearance, reporter, and interview: appropriately mixing honesty, humility, and humor; paying tribute to a young boy with terminal cancer; honoring former teammate Joey Villavisencio, who died in a car wreck in 2011; selling Texas A&M's brand on an unprecedented level; and thanking God, his family, teammates, and coaches.

Perhaps the only way that December 2012 could have been any brighter, bigger, and better for Manziel and Texas A&M would have been if the Aggies had been in the hunt for the national title. And at the Heisman Trophy ceremony in 2012, A&M offensive coordinator Kliff Kingsbury admitted that if he had known as much about Manziel in the first game of the season as he did in December, the Aggies might have played Notre Dame and Heisman runner-up Manti Te'o in the BCS National Championship Game instead of Alabama. In hindsight, if everything else had played out as it did during the course of the 2012 season, the opening loss to Florida probably cost A&M a chance to play in the SEC title game against Georgia. Anything could have happened in that game, but at that point in the season, the Aggies were playing well enough to defeat any team in the country.

"[Not tackling him in practice] was a huge part of not knowing what we had," Kingsbury said in New York. "After the [20-17 loss to] Florida, I felt like we could have done a lot more with his legs with quarterback runs in that game. All spring, Coach Sumlin would blow the whistle when the defense would get close. Johnny would come over pissed off, spike the ball, and say, 'They wouldn't have gotten me.' I said (a little condescendingly), 'Sure, Johnny, they wouldn't have gotten you.' But come to find out, they wouldn't have gotten him."

While Kingsbury said he would have called the game differently if he could do it all over again, Texas A&M was still a big winner on September 8, 2012. Originally, the season-opener was scheduled for Thursday, August 30, in Shreveport against Louisiana Tech, but because of the threat of Hurricane Isaac, Louisiana Tech officials postponed the game until October 13. That meant that the first game of the season would also be Texas A&M's first SEC game in school history. I had initially hoped the A&M-Florida matchup would be a night game at Kyle Field and that ESPN's College GameDay crew would return to College Station to host the show in Aggieland, a little more than a month after shooting the commercial. Half my wish came true, as GameDay announced on September 1 that it would air the show from College Station. Unfortunately, kickoff time was 2:37 p.m., but the atmosphere inside Kyle Field was still spine-tingling and goose bump–inducing, especially as the Aggies built a 17-7 lead midway through the second quarter and carried a 17-10 lead into the locker room.

In the second half, Florida rallied for a 20-17 win, holding the Aggies scoreless in the final two quarters. But unlike the blown leads during the 2011 season under Sherman, the loss to Florida was not a case of A&M being out of shape. On the contrary, it was the Florida players who were pulling up with injuries—real or fake—that slowed down the pace of the game, and particularly slowed the A&M offense. The Aggies were obviously in superior shape, which was a credit to one of Sumlin's most important hires. Sumlin obviously assembled a great staff of position coaches and coordinators, but one of the major difference-makers in 2012 was Texas A&M Director of Football Sports Performance Larry Jackson, a standout linebacker and defensive end for the Aggies from 1991–94, who had worked as a strength coach at Oklahoma and Houston with Sumlin. Jackson said that his previous stops at other schools were business decisions, but when he accepted Sumlin's offer in January 2012 to oversee the strength and conditioning program at Texas A&M, it was much more than a calculated career move.

"This wasn't about business; this is personal," the perpetually vibrant and energetic Jackson told *12th Man Magazine* prior to the 2012 season. "This is home. I met my wife, Amy, here in the spring of 1994; we both graduated from here; I came back here after playing; and now I am thrilled to come back here and be in a role where I am in charge of the [strength and conditioning] program. I feel like I am getting to come back and train my brothers. They are my younger brothers, but they are my brothers. This is not just a job; this is my passion. I want these guys to get it right. It's time for this football team to fly around the field from start to finish. It's time to bring back the swagger and the winning ways."

That's exactly what Jackson helped to accomplish, as he set the tone for the entire program during the offseason. And as Kingsbury began to understand Manziel's full potential, the Aggies shifted gears, beginning the week after the loss to Florida on a road trip to SMU. In the second quarter at SMU, Manziel began making some of the jaw-dropping, head-shaking plays that carried him to the Heisman Trophy. Leading 7-0, Manziel scrambled forty-eight yards for a TD, faking an SMU defensive back out of his shoes. Two minutes later, he scrambled to his right and—on the dead run—threw a perfect strike across his body to Uzoma Nwachukwu for a twenty-six-yard score. Then with A&M facing third-and-nine from the SMU 42 early in the third quarter, Manziel was wrapped up for what appeared to be a sure sack. But he spun out of the tackle, drifted to his left and jumped awkwardly while hurling the ball over a leaping defender—delivering a strike to Kenric McNeal, who turned inside and raced 42 yards for the score.

Manziel and the Aggies then rolled past South Carolina State and Arkansas (the first SEC win in school history) and traveled to Ole Miss on October 6 in what many of the A&M players later referred to as the "turning point" of the season. In fact, the players pinpointed one series at Vaught-Hemingway Stadium in Oxford as the moment the Aggies truly began to believe that 2012 could be a magical run. With eight minutes and thirty-five seconds left in the game, A&M trailed the Rebels, 27-17, and began a key drive at the Aggies' own 12. On the first play of the drive, Ole Miss nose tackle Issac Gross broke free and wrapped up Manziel near the A&M goal line. Manziel's knee clearly hit on the goal line, but he managed to stretch the ball back across the stripe and into the green turf. Gross was livid that he missed recording a safety by a matter of inches, and Ole Miss challenged the call. But after further review, the call stood, and after a two-yard run by Ben Malena on second down, the Aggies faced third-and-nineteen from their own three.

From the shotgun, Manziel dropped about halfway back in the end zone and lofted a pass down the right sideline in the direction of 6-foot-5 freshman receiver Mike Evans, who was covered extremely well by the Rebels' Senquez Golson. But Evans, utilizing all seventy-seven inches of his long frame, leaped up and grabbed the ball over the 5-foot-9 Golson's head for a 32-yard gain. The "jump ball" was probably the pivotal play of the year, and Malena followed it with a thirty-six-yard run to the Ole Miss 29. And on the next play, Manziel raced twenty-nine yards to cut the lead to 27-23 and keep the Aggies in the game.

Then the A&M defense came up with another series to remember. With six minutes and twenty-four seconds left in the game, the Rebels had a golden opportunity to break their fifteen-game SEC losing streak by simply playing keep-away from A&M. Beginning a drive at its own 16, Ole Miss handed the ball to Jeff Scott on the first two plays of the drive, and he picked up fourteen yards and a first down at the UM 30. Scott also handled the ball the next three plays, picking up almost ten yards to set up a fourth-and-inch just shy of the Ole Miss 40 after Sean Porter made a great stop on third down. That's when Mississippi coach Hugh Freeze gambled by going for it on fourth down for a third time that night. The Rebels converted the first two tries, but the third time was not a charm. Running out of the shotgun, Ole Miss handed the ball to Scott for the sixth straight play. Jonathan Stewart beat Scott to the line of scrimmage and stopped him cold in his tracks for a slight loss. The Aggies took advantage of the short field, and on the fourth play of the ensuing drive, Manziel hooked up on a twenty-yard, over-the-shoulder pass to Ryan Swope for the game-winning TD.

A&M climbed into the rankings for the first time following the comeback win over Ole Miss and won another wild game, 59-57, over Louisiana Tech, the next weekend in Shreveport. On October 20, the Aggies built an early 12-0 lead over sixth-ranked LSU, but a couple of A&M turnovers just before halftime turned the game around and allowed the Tigers to escape with a 24-19 victory that left A&M at 5-2 for the season. Nobody could have possibly anticipated what happened next, as the Aggies prepared for a killer three-game road stretch to Auburn, Mississippi State, and Alabama. A&M rolled to shockingly easy wins at Auburn (63-21) and at seventeenth-ranked Mississippi State (38-13), setting up a showdown between the fifteenth-ranked Aggies and the top-ranked Crimson Tide on November 10 in Tuscaloosa.

Until that game, my favorite memory of attending an A&M football game was at the conclusion of the 1967 season, when A&M upset Alabama, 20-16, on New Year's Day in the Cotton Bowl. That game featured the teacher, Alabama head coach Paul "Bear" Bryant, against the pupil, Texas A&M coach Gene Stallings, a former "Junction Boy" and one of the captains of Bryant's 1956 Southwest Conference championship team at A&M. Stallings had also been an assistant coach at Alabama under Bryant from 1958–64, helping to lead the Tide to the '64 national title. Bryant loved Stallings practically like a son, and he was especially proud of his former player for leading the Aggies to the 1968 Cotton Bowl after beginning the year with an 0-4 start. When Stallings led the Aggies past his mentor in a monumental upset before a crowd of 73,800 in Dallas, Bryant walked to the middle of the field and grabbed Stallings in a gigantic "Bear" hug, carrying him around proudly for a few steps before placing him back on the ground.

Being able to see that game in person had to be my favorite memory of watching the Aggies...until November 10, 2012. No other regular-season game in the history of Texas A&M football ever did more for the Aggies' positive national perception than the tension-filled triumph in Tuscaloosa. It was the signature victory of the Aggies' sensational first season in the SEC. The national television broadcast on

CBS and the ensuing multimedia frenzy that followed the Aggies for weeks after the upset catapulted A&M into the national consciousness and served as Manziel's "Heisman moment." It also officially served notice to the skeptics who'd chastised the Aggies for leaving the presumably safer confines of the Big 12 for the SEC, proving that Texas A&M was not intimidated by any foe in college football's most dominant conference … not even big, bad Bama.

A&M took it to the Tide early, building a 20-0 lead at the end of the first quarter, and then the Aggies answered every Alabama challenge late in the game to register A&M's first road victory over a first-ranked team in 117 years of football. The victory vaulted A&M from fifteenth to ninth in the AP poll, and the national media raved about "Johnny and the Giant Killers." "This was Texas A&M, the new kid on the block with its new-fangled offense and its phenom freshman quarterback, beating the defending national champs and the SEC's reigning juggernaut on their own field," wrote *Sports Illustrated's* Stewart Mandel. "And in doing so…A&M raced to a 20-0 first-quarter lead against a defense that had not allowed twenty points in a game for nearly a year."

Alabama eventually closed the gap to 23-17, and with 101,821 fans howling inside Bryant-Denny Stadium, Manziel hooked up with Ryan Swope for a 42-yard pass between two Bama defenders. Swope paid a price for catching the pass, but one play later, Manziel connected with Malcome Kennedy for a 24-yard, over-the-shoulder TD pass that put the Aggies up, 29-17. The A&M defense did the rest. The Tide cut the lead to 29-24 with just over six minutes left in the game, and Bama looked to be in position to pull off a dramatic comeback victory when A. J. McCarron connected with Kenny Bell for a 54-yard pass to the A&M six-yard line late in the fourth quarter. One week earlier, McCarron had rallied Alabama to a 21-17 win over fifth-ranked LSU with a game-winning drive that covered seventy-two yards in five plays in just forty-nine seconds. But on first-and-goal from the A&M six, Kirby Ennis and Sean Porter stopped McCarron for no gain. Ennis, coming up big in the clutch, then stopped Lacy for a one-yard gain on second down. And Dustin Harris made a great solo stop at the A&M two when McCarron scrambled out of the pocket. On fourth-and-goal from the two, Alabama attempted to flood the right flat with receivers and run a pick play. But sophomore cornerback Deshazor Everett stepped in front of the receiver for the interception that helped seal the magical upset. It was the third turnover of the game forced by the Aggies. That, along with A&M's tremendous start, was the key to a victory that sent shockwaves across the country.

A&M then took care of business the next two weeks at home, coasting past Sam Houston State and Missouri before accepting an invitation to the 2013 AT&T Cotton Bowl against Oklahoma. Entering that game at Cowboys Stadium in Arlington, the big concern among many A&M fans was whether Manziel would be negatively affected by all the speaking engagements, trips, and television appearances that followed the Heisman Trophy presentation. He put those fears to rest on the first drive of the game, moving the Aggies seventy-five yards in eight plays to take an early lead they would never relinquish against "Big Game" Bob Stoops and his brother, defensive coordinator Mike Stoops.

Fittingly, Manziel produced yet another highlight moment to cap the drive. Facing third-and-nine from the OU 23, Manziel dropped back, turned his back to the defense, and scrambled to his left to avoid the pressure coming up the middle. He outraced four Oklahoma defenders to the edge and picked up a first down before apparently stepping out of bounds at around the eight. At least that's what FOX play-by-play announcer Gus Johnson and practically everyone else inside the stadium first thought. But Manziel managed to keep his feet in bounds the whole way, eluding a tackler inside the ten and finally skipping into the end zone like a little kid on the playground. By the end of the game—a 41-13 victory for the Aggies—Manziel, had produced a Cotton Bowl-record 516 total yards, including 229 rushing yards. As A&M celebrated the convincing win and the historic first season, the maroon-clad fans inside the stadium began the fittingly familiar chant, "S-E-C, S-E-C, S-E-C...."

My suspicion is that Aggies—and perhaps also Missouri Tigers, to a lesser degree—will be asking me for many years to come about my favorite individual memories and moments that occurred during the course of the 100-year decision that led Texas A&M University out of the Big 12 Conference and into the SEC. Those signature events did not end with the conclusion of the 2012 season and the 2013 Cotton Bowl.

For example, I will never forget the day in early May 2013, when the Southeastern Conference officially unveiled plans to launch the SEC Network in August 2014. Conference television network possibilities were at the root of all of the realignment talks in 2009, and the SEC Network promises to be the biggest and most profitable of them all. I was also delighted when Texas A&M was selected to play South Carolina in the first football game ever to be broadcast on the SEC Network.

While the second day of May 2013 was gratifying, the month also closed in unforgettable fashion. Entering one of the meeting rooms at the Sandestin Hilton in Destin, Florida, on the afternoon of May 30, 2013, I took my seat at the table along with other university presidents from the SEC schools and various members of the league's office. It was my second time to attend the SEC spring meetings, as I had also attended the 2012 event before Texas A&M University had actually competed as a member of the prestigious conference. But the 2013 meeting was far more memorable to me, because I truly felt like I was involved and affected by everything that was happening and every issue that was addressed. In 2012, Texas A&M was a welcomed guest at those meetings, but in 2013, A&M and Missouri were both truly part of the SEC family—and I do genuinely and sincerely emphasize the word "family" in describing this unique SEC affiliation.

That point was hammered home to me again once the meeting began and we were presented a packet of information containing financial numbers. As I removed the cover page and began studying the data, I found that the SEC would distribute approximately $289.4 million among the fourteen member institutions, representing the largest distribution in league history and the most revenue Texas A&M had ever received for being part of any conference.

That financial number, as impressive as it was to see in print for the first time, will grow considerably in years to come because of the economic impact of the SEC Network. The future is, indeed, remarkably bright for the SEC, but it was not the future potential that most captivated my attention at the 2013 meeting. What struck me as I studied the financial data was the equality of the SEC. Alabama, Florida, and LSU didn't receive more revenue distribution than every other school, even though they had accounted for the last seven national football championships and appeared on TV more often than Tennessee, Kentucky, and Mississippi State. Likewise, South Carolina and Arkansas didn't receive more money than A&M and Missouri despite having been longtime members of the league. Each school received the same amount—roughly $20.7 million. I couldn't help recalling prior experiences with the Big 12, where such equality was not the norm. The parity I was now seeing reconfirmed that Texas A&M—and Missouri as well—had made the right decision in moving to the SEC, both for the present and for the next 100 years.

Many other parts of the athletic landscape also worked out incredibly well for Texas A&M during the Aggies' first full year in the SEC. The women's soccer team won the SEC Western Division championship title in October 2012; Henry Lelei became A&M's first individual champion when he claimed the men's SEC cross country title; the Aggie volleyball squad claimed the Western Division title in November 2012; the Texas A&M men's and women's swimming and diving programs hosted the 2013 SEC Swimming and Diving Championships in late February 2013—the first-ever SEC championship held in Aggieland; A&M's women's basketball team stunned South Carolina, Tennessee, and Kentucky to win the SEC Women's Basketball Tournament in March; the women's tennis team won the regular-season SEC title in April and played in the national championship match in May; the women's track and field team won the outdoor SEC title in May; the men's track and field team won a national NCAA championship in June; and all those things—as well as many others—contributed to A&M finishing a school-best fifth place in the final 2012–13 Learfield Sports Directors' Cup. Not a bad start for our first year of SEC competition.

I will also never forget the buildup to the September 14, 2013, Alabama-Texas A&M game at Kyle Field, or the feeling inside the stadium when the Aggies jumped out to a 14-0 lead in the first quarter. Unfortunately, A&M didn't have enough defense in that game (or that season) to match or surpass the success the Aggies enjoyed in 2012. A&M lost the game to Alabama, 49-42, and lost three more games along the way to finish the regular season at 8-4 overall. It wasn't really a fitting end to Manziel's A&M career, but his last game—on New Year's Eve in Atlanta—and my last game as A&M's president, did feature an ending that could appropriately be described as "Manziel magic."

Duke scored touchdowns on its first five possessions of the 2013 Chick-fil-A Bowl en route to a commanding 38-17 lead at intermission. But then Manziel turned the second half into yet another personal highlight reel, dazzling teammates and fans, dumbfounding Duke defenders, and rallying the Aggies to the largest comeback victory in school history in a 52-48 thriller. Overall, Manziel tossed four touchdown passes, and the A&M defense, which had often appeared shocked and shaken in the first half, came up with a few big second-half stops and two key turnovers to secure the unforgettable victory.

Technically, that also happened to be the last football game played during my tenure as president of Texas A&M University. Karin and I moved out of the presidential home on the A&M campus in January 2014 and relocated to the University of Missouri, where I have begun a new chapter—perhaps the final one—in my professional life.

For Texas A&M, the fruits of our 100-year decision to move from the Big 12 to the SEC are just beginning to mature. SEC! SEC! SEC!

WORKS CITED

NEWSPAPERS

Wojciechowski, Gene. *Los Angeles Times*. August 2, 1990. Arkansas joins SEC; there may be more.

Staff reports. *The Deseret News*. August 11, 1990. Texas, Texas A&M may be looking to go to Pac-10.

Staff reports. *The Houston Post*. August 17, 1990. SEC may pursue Houston if Pac-10 gets Texas schools.

Mell, Randall. *Orlando Sun-Sentinel*. August 20, 1990. Miami talks 'informally' with SWC.

Associated Press. August 24, 1990. Texas and Texas A&M staying put.

Gold, Russell. *San Antonio Express-News*. Bullock called final play of the SWC. Lieutenant governor quarterbacked four Texas universities' entry into Big 12. May 25, 1997.

Wangrin, Mark. *San Antonio Express-News*. August 14, 2005. Power brokers: How tagalong Baylor, Tech crashed the revolt.

Associated Press. January 11, 2008. Sir Edmund Hillary, first to climb Mount Everest, dies at 88.

Jones, Tim. *Chicago Tribune*. November 20, 2008. Dewey defeats Truman: Well, everyone makes mistakes.

Thamel, Pete. *New York Times*. March 24, 2009. Chief of Tennis Tour Will Head the Pac-10.

Greenstein, Teddy. *Chicago Tribune*. March 1, 2010. Big Ten told it's safe to expand horizons.

Ringo, Kyle. *Boulder Daily Camera*. March 6, 2010. Conference conundrum: Pac-10 move expensive, but could be worth it for CU Buffs.

Ourand, John. *Sports Business Journal*. May 11, 2010. Pac-10 hires Hollywood agency CAA with star power in mind.

Associated Press. May 13, 2010. Missouri governor talks up Big Ten.

Carlton, Chuck. *Dallas Morning News*. May 31, 2010. Big Ten expansion on spring agenda at Big 12 meetings.

Tucker, Doug. *Associated Press*. June 1, 2010. Big 12's future remains cloudy as spring meetings open

Rabinowitz, Bill. *Columbus (Ohio) Dispatch.* June 4, 2010. Big Ten expansion: E-mails hint eyes are upon Texas.

Faraudo, Jeff. *San Jose Mercury News.* June 6, 2010. Pac-10 gives green light to pursue expansion.

Barfknecht, Lee. Omaha World-Herald. June 8, 2010. E-mails show presidents discussed issue in February.

Thamel, Pete. *New York Times.* June 9, 2010. Scramble to Save Big 12; Nebraska Said to Be Leaving.

Henderson, John. *Denver Post.* June 10, 2010. Westward ho! Colorado bolts to Pac-10 Conference.

Sherrington, Kevin. *Dallas Morning News.* June 10, 2010. Frank Broyles not surprised to see 'misfit' Big 12 die.

Thamel, Pete. *New York Times.* June 11, 2010. Nebraska Moves to Big Ten and Pushes Big 12 to Brink.

Haurwitz, Ralph and Bohls, Kirk. *Austin American-Statesman.* June 12, 2010. UT, Tech to join Pac-10. As Horns, Raiders head west, will Aggies go with them?

Zwerneman, Brent. *San Antonio Express News/Houston Chronicle.* June 13, 2010. A&M's board of regents expected to choose SEC. A&M on verge of making an SEC exchange. Despite likelihood that UT, other Big 12 brethren will pick Pac-10, Ags appear headed to football powerhouse.

Staff Reports. *The Topeka Capital-Journal.* June 13, 2010. Beebe makes pitch to save Big 12. Commissioner says conference compete with SEC's lucrative TV deal.

Thamel, Pete. *New York Times.* June 14, 2010. Despite flirtations, Texas agrees to stay in Big 12 and save it.

Wieberg, Steve. *USA Today.* June 15, 2010. Television deal allows Big 12 to survive; Pac-10 needs new plan

McCollough, Brady. *Kansas City Star.* June 16, 2010. 72 hours that saved the Big 12 from demise. From a hotel room, commissioner and his staff lobbied hard to keep 10 conference teams together.

Aron, Jamie. *Associated Press.* July 26, 2010. How Dan Beebe saved the Big 12.

Zwerneman, Brent. *San Antonio Express News/Houston Chronicle.* July 28, 2010. A&M expects $20 million annually from Big 12. A&M says

Big 12 must fulfill pledge. Legal action, another look at SEC possible if league doesn't pay $20 million.

Zwerneman, Brent. *San Antonio Express News/Houston Chronicle*. July 29, 2010. Aggies to Big 12: Honor your promise.

Hairopoulos, Kate. *Dallas Morning News*. November 26, 2010. Documents show inner dealings to keep Big 12 alive.

Maher, John. *Austin American-Statesman*. May 3, 2011. UT TV network: ESPN handles hiring, but UT, in some cases, can fire.

Gregorian, Vahe. *St. Louis Post-Dispatch*. May 29, 2011. A year later, Big 12 is back from the brink.

Barron, David. *Houston Chronicle*. July 15, 2011. NCAA wants to be sure plans to telecast UIL games don't give edge in recruiting.

Zwerneman, Brent. *San Antonio Express News/Houston Chronicle*. July 19, 2011. A&M to hold information session on UT network.

Carlton, Chuck. *Dallas Morning News*. July 20, 2011. Big 12 commissioner Dan Beebe: 'It's not going to happen until and unless the conference can make it happen with benefit to all and detriment to none.'

Zwerneman, Brent. *San Antonio Express News/Houston Chronicle*. July 21, 2011.Loftin: 'Uncertainty' in Big 12 because of Longhorn Network.

Zwerneman, Brent. *San Antonio Express News/Houston Chronicle*. July 26, 2011. Big 12 commish: Most Aggies don't want SEC.

Carlton, Chuck. *Dallas Morning News*. August 1, 2011. No high school games on Longhorn Network — for now

Finger, Mike. *San Antonio Express News*. August 2, 2011. Big 12 ADs: No high school games on Longhorn Network. Big 12 to restrict UT's network. High school games not allowed in coming season.

Beilue, Jon Mark. Amarillo News. August 8, 2011. Tech says no to Longhorn Network.

Carlton, Chuck. *Dallas Morning News*. August 10, 2011.What Rick Perry's quotes mean for A&M, Big 12's future.

Bohls, Kirk, and Golden, Cedric. *Austin American-Statesman*. August 11, 2011. Our take: The Texas A&M/SEC issue.

Riggs, Randy. *Austin American-Statesman* August 11, 2011. NCAA nixes Longhorn Network's hopes of airing prep games

Abouhalkah, Yael T. *Kansas City Star.* August 14, 2011. SEC rejects Texas A&M; good news for Missouri, Kansas.

Burch, Jimmy. *Fort Worth Star-Telegram.* August 17, 2011. Texas A&M warned of 'permanent mistake' by former governor.

Sherrington, Kevin. *Dallas Morning News.* September 14, 2011. Can Ken Starr save the Big 12? We're about to find out.

Zwerneman, Brent. *San Antonio Express News/Houston Chronicle.* October 1, 2011. Meltdowns now weekly affairs for baffling Aggies.

Zwerneman, Brent. *San Antonio Express News/Houston Chronicle.* October 3, 2011. Sherman won't address SEC even after official announcement.

Associated Press. October 6, 2011. Big 12 bans HS highlights from LHN.

Hairopoulos, Kate. *Dallas Morning News.* November 18, 2011. Newly obtained documents shed light on Aggies' decision to leave Big 12.

Bohls, Kirk and Halliburton, Suzanne. Austin American-Statesman. December 1, 2011. Aggies fire Mike Sherman; Houston's Sumlin, Louisville's Strong possible replacements.

Chatelain, Dick. *Omaha World-Herald.* December 31, 2011. Seat of power: How the SEC came to rule college football.

Zwerneman, Brent. *San Antonio Express News/Houston Chronicle.* April 25, 2012. For sake of job security, Loftin hands-on in athletics.

Sherrington, Kevin. *Dallas Morning News.* June 30, 2012. SEC could be right move, but Aggies doing it for wrong reasons.

Associated Press. June 30, 2012. Texas A&M officially joins SEC on Sunday, but move already paying off for Aggies.

Myerberg, Paul. *USA Today.* March 19, 2013. Texas AD on Texas A&M: 'We get to decide when we play again.'

MAGAZINES

Maisel, Ivan. *Athlon's Big Eight magazine. Summer 1995. So long SWC, hello Big 12.*

Cartwright, Gary. *Sports Illustrated.* October 30, 1995. 0:00. Time has run out on the Southwest Conference, but what a time it was.

Staples, Andy. *Sports Illustrated.* June 10, 2010. A&M to Pac-10? Not so fast.

Staples, Andy. *Sports Illustrated*. July 21, 2011. Texas' Longhorn Network sparking another Big 12 Missile Crisis.

Mandel, Stewart. *Sports Illustrated*. August 12, 2011.As rumor mill swirls, it's time to ask: What makes sense for SEC?

Cohen, Jason. *Texas Monthly*. September 2011. The Eyes of Texas Aren't On It.

Burka, Paul. *Texas Monthly*. November 2011. Farmers Flight!

Mandel, Stewart. *Sports Illustrated*. November 11, 2012. Texas A&M's upset win at Alabama could have far-reaching SEC impact.

WEBSITES

Brown, Chip. Orangebloods.com. June 3, 2010. Exclusive: Pac-10 set to invite six from Big 12.

Brown, Chip. Orangebloods.com. June 6, 2010. Pac 10 ready to make moves; Nebraska's decision is key.

Travis, Clay. AOLNews.com. June 9, 2010. A beautiful move: Texas A&M to SEC?

Brown, Chip. Orangebloods.com. June 10, 2010. A&M could throw off Big 12 six targeted by Pac-10.

Harris, Terrance. AOLNews.com. June 10, 2010. Surprise, surprise: Texas and Texas A&M not in agreement on Pac-10 move.

Brown, Chip. Orangebloods.com. June 14, 2010. Remaining schools in Big 12 close to saving league.

Barnhouse, Wendell. Big12Sports.com. June 14, 2010. Saved situation.

Katz, Andy. ESPN.com. June 15, 2010. Source: Influential group saved Big 12.

Dodd, Dennis. CBSSports.com. July 29, 2010. Pac-10's Scott blames Texas for his plan's demise.

Brown, Chip. Orangebloods.com. June 3, 2011. One Year Later: The Big 12 Missile Crisis revisited.

Barnhouse, Wendell. Big12Sports.com. July 7, 2011. Ten Days In June.

Sports by Brooks.com. July 19, 2011. College Football's First Nuke: Burnt-Orange Glow.

Ubben, David. ESPN.com. July 26, 2011. Big 12 Media Days: Best of Day 1.

Ubben, David. ESPN.com. July 27, 2011. Beebe: Aggies wanting SEC aren't majority.

Forde, Pat. ESPN.com. August 13, 2011. Realignment rumors again rampant.

O'Donnell, Wes. BleacherReport.com. August 14, 2011. SEC Expansion: Conference Made Smart Move by Rejecting Texas A&M.

Taylor, Jean-Jacques. ESPNDallas.com. August 15, 2011. Ego, envy will get Texas A&M nowhere; SEC will come calling eventually, but Aggies must get over Longhorns' success first.

Taglienti, Michael. BleacherReport.com. August 18, 2011. The Aggies' move to SEC not all about Longhorn Network.

Deitsch, Richard. SI.com. August 26, 2011. College Football TV Roundtable.

Travis, Clay. OutkickTheCoverage.com. August 29, 2011. Arkansas ignites Big 12, SEC Civil War?

Travis, Clay. OutkickTheCoverage.com. August 30, 2011. Big 12 bylaws on leaving are complicated, weak.

Staff Reports. CBSSports.com. September 3, 2011. Schools have called Pac-12; Big 12 days numbered?

Tramel, Berry. NewsOK.com. September 3, 2011. OU's sole focus now on joining Pac-12.

Travis, Clay. OutkickTheCoverage.com. September 7, 2011. Why Baylor's claims against the SEC have no merit.

Cartell, Sean. SECSports.com. September 25, 2011. Aggie roots: Texas A&M joins the SEC.

SanInocencio, Eric. SECSports.com. September 25, 2011. Texas A&M to the SEC: Barnhart's take.

Pennington, John. Mr.SEC.com September 27, 2011. A 13-Team SEC Schedule Is Not At All Ideal.

News services. ESPN.com. October 6, 2011. Report: Missouri hopes to join SEC.

Ubben, David. ESPN.com. October 15, 2011. A&M's big stop stuffs second-half failures.

Strickland, Carter. ESPN.com/HornsNation. October 15, 2011.Texas AD to A&M: Our schedule is full.

Staples, Andy. SI.com. November 6, 2011. Questioning Missouri's SEC jump? You'd have done the same thing.

Mays, Robert. Grantland.com. March 22, 2012. Kansas vs. Missouri: The End of the Border War. Looking back on one of sports' nastiest rivalries.

Hinnen, Jerry. CBSSportsline.com. April 24, 2012. The end for now? A Realignment Timeline.

Patterson, Chip. CBSSportsline.com. April 24, 2012. Conference Realignment Era: The Winners.

Watson, Graham. YAHOO!Sports.com. July 18, 2012. Underachievers: Texas A&M has to prove it belongs in the SEC.

Travis, Clay. April 10, 2013. Outkick The Coverage.com. Texas A&M's SEC Monopoly in Longhorn State.

Corcoran, Tully. FOXSports.com. December 31, 2013.Breaking right: The perfect timing of Kevin Sumlin's rise at Texas A&M .

Fowler, Jeremy. CBSSports.com March 8, 2014. Charlie Strong in favor of Texas resuming rivalry with Texas A&M.

Buchanan, Olin. TexAgs.com. March 27, 2014. Manziel breaks ground again in Pro Day workout.

BOOKS

Glier, Ray. *How the SEC became Goliath*. Howard Books. September 2012.

CPSIA information can be obtained at www.ICGtesting.com
Printed in the USA
LVOW05*0015300914

406460LV00001B/1/P